Praise for Rebirth

"This is the most comprehensive and scholarly study on rebirth and karma that I have seen and would, in my opinion, constitute an authoritative work on this subject for many years to come. I hope that Roger Jackson will encourage colleagues to work on Sinhala and Tamil translations of this book."

—GANANATH OBEYESEKERE, Emeritus Professor of Anthropology, Princeton University

"The fruit of a lifetime of deep engagement with the subject, Roger Jackson's *Rebirth* traces the history of Buddhist ideas about reincarnation across the Buddhist world from ancient times to the present. This is the definitive work on the topic. No other work matches it in terms of breadth and depth. Written in lively and accessible prose, and evincing Jackson's tremendous erudition on every page, *Rebirth* is a major contribution to the study of Buddhism and the history of religions."

—JOSÉ I. CABEZÓN, Dalai Lama Professor of Tibetan Buddhism and Cultural Studies, University of California, Santa Barbara

"*Rebirth* is the definitive study of Buddhist thought on this topic. Roger Jackson's scholarship is impeccable, attending to a vast literature with meticulous attention to both text and context; the narrative arc takes us from pre-Buddhist Indian thought through contemporary Western Buddhist attitudes, exploring arguments for the reality of rebirth, the metaphysics of rebirth, and the role that rebirth plays in the larger Buddhist project. This is an extraordinary contribution to Buddhist studies."

—JAY L. GARFIELD, Professor of Philosophy, University of Melbourne

"Erudite and eloquent, Roger Jackson takes the reader on a journey across the Buddhist world and across the centuries, from ancient India to contemporary America, setting forth both the mechanics and the poetics of rebirth along the way. For those who know little, you will learn much. For those who know much, you will learn more."

—Donald S. Lopez Jr., Arthur E. Link Professor of Buddhist and Tibetan Studies, University of Michigan

"While Buddhism has no dogma, it does rest on a unique 'view' that necessarily includes acceptance of the reality of karma and rebirth. This is a complex subject; it is not possible to understand this Buddhist view without both distinguishing ultimate from relative truth and at the same time recognizing the inseparability of these two truths. While Roger Jackson's new book on rebirth perhaps wisely avoids this complexity at a theoretical and philosophical level, it makes an important contribution to the discussion by approaching it at a very practical level. I found Dr. Jackson's dissection of the different ways Buddhists approach the subject of rebirth to be not only interesting and provocative but also a valuable contribution to the way the subject can be understood and presented in the modern world."

—Dzongsar Jamyang Khyentse, author of *What Makes You Not a Buddhist*

Rebirth

A Guide to Mind, Karma, and Cosmos in the Buddhist World

ROGER R. JACKSON

SHAMBHALA

Shambhala Publications, Inc.
2129 13th Street
Boulder, Colorado 80302
www.shambhala.com

Cover art: "Wheel of Life" © Chinch Gryniewicz / Bridgeman Images
Cover design: Sarkar Design Studio

9 8 7 6 5 4 3 2 1

First Edition
Printed in the United States of America

♾This edition is printed on acid-free paper that meets the American National Standards Institute z39.48 Standard.

♻Shambhala Publications makes every effort to print on recycled paper. For more information please visit www.shambhala.com.

Shambhala Publications is distributed worldwide by Penguin Random House, Inc., and its subsidiaries.

LIBRARY OF CONGRESS CATALOGING-IN-PUBLICATION DATA
Names: Jackson, Roger R. (Roger Reid), 1950- author.
Title: Rebirth: a guide to mind, karma, and cosmos in the Buddhist world / Roger R. Jackson.
Description: Boulder: Shambhala, 2022. | Includes bibliographical references and index.
Identifiers: LCCN 2021009072 | ISBN 9781611809022 (trade paperback)
Subjects: LCSH: Reincarnation—Buddhism.
Classification: LCC BQ4485 .J33 2022 | DDC 294.3/442—dc23
LC record available at https://lccn.loc.gov/2021009072

In memory of Frank Barone,
1947–2020
dear friend and Dharma brother

Now you know, or perhaps you don't—
and either way,
in the words of the nameless New York metaphysician,
"What it is is; it is what it is"

The wheel is turning and you can't slow down,
You can't let go and you can't hold on,
You can't go back and you can't stand still,
If the thunder don't get you then the lightning will.

Robert Hunter, "The Wheel"

Souls cross ages like clouds cross skies, an' tho' a cloud's shape nor hue nor size don't stay the same, it's still a cloud an' so is a soul. Who can say where the cloud's blowed from or who the soul'll be tomorrow? Only Sonmi the east an' the west an' the atlas, yay, only the atlas o' clouds.

David Mitchell, *Cloud Atlas*

Contents

Abbreviations

A	*Aṅguttara Nikāya*
AK	*Abhidharmakośa* (Vasubandhu)
AkBh	*Abhidharmakośabhāṣyam* (Vasubandhu)
AS	*Abhidhammathasaṅgaha* (Anuruddha)
ASm	*Abhidharmasamuccaya* (Asaṅga)
C.	Chinese
D	*Dīgha Nikāya*
GS	*Guhyasamāja Tantra*
HT	*Hevajra Tantra*
M	*Majjhima Nikāya*
MK	*Madhyamakakārikā* (Nāgārjuna)
MP	*Milindapañhā*
P.	Pāli
PV	*Pramāṇavārttika* (Dharmakīrti)
Skt.	Sanskrit
S	*Saṃyutta Nikāya*
SN	*Sutta Nipāta*
T.	Tibetan
VM	*Visuddhimagga* (Buddhaghosa)

Preface

In the early summer of 1974, just a few months after I had taken refuge and begun to study Tibetan Buddhism seriously at Kopan monastery in Nepal, I found myself at the Library of Tibetan Works and Archives in Dharamsala, India, listening to a discourse on karma and rebirth by the lama assigned by the Dalai Lama to teach the Westerners who flocked there, Venerable Geshe Ngawang Dhargyey, an accomplished scholar from eastern Tibet. To illustrate the workings of karma and rebirth, Geshe Dhargyey—translated by a young, English-speaking reincarnate lama, or *tulku*—spun out a lengthy story about two brothers who had committed equally serious but slightly different offenses against others during their lives as humans, with the result that, in the next life, one was born as a red fish with a blue head, the other as a blue fish with a red head—and each had to suffer endlessly the fear and hunger that dominate a fish's short and miserable life. Afterward, during lunch at the library canteen, I spotted the translator, and asked him about the story. "I'm assuming," I said, "that Geshe-la meant that story to be taken symbolically and not literally, right?" "Oh, no," he quickly answered, "it's meant quite literally." I gulped, and returned to my lunch.

The common Buddhist claim that we all have undergone countless previous rebirths, and that we will continue to undergo rebirth as long as we do not overcome the delusions that bind us to the ongoing process of rebirth known as saṃsāra, is difficult for most modern people to accept. If they are nonreligious, and take the scientific worldview as authoritative for understanding our world, they may well assume that because the mind is dependent upon the brain, and the brain ceases functioning at death, there simply is no life beyond the grave. If they are conservative Christians or Muslims (or, in many cases, Jews), they will assume that there *is* life after death, in the form of an eternal sojourn in a heavenly or hellish state, but certainly no reincarnation into a human, or any other, body. Even for many modern Buddhists, shaped as they are by scientific sensibilities and skepticism, the tradition's assertion of rebirth in a "hard" and literal sense can prove to be a stumbling block. This certainly was the case for me, and when, after my time in Nepal and India, I entered the graduate program in Buddhist studies at the University of Wisconsin-Madison to work with Professor Geshe Lhundub Sopa, the doubts I had and the questions I asked eventually were channeled into the PhD dissertation I wrote on the Indian pandit Dharmakīrti's classic, seventh-century attempt to demonstrate rationally such central Buddhist claims as the reality of rebirth and the possibility of attaining enlightenment. A significant number of recent Buddhist teachers, especially in the Theravāda and Zen traditions, do not concern themselves much with such metaphysical questions, preferring a more pragmatic, worldly way of thinking about the Dharma. Tibetan teachers, on the other hand (while certainly practical), tend in general to take traditional metaphysics quite seriously, and so it is their teachings and writings that have echoed in my mind over the years, and, for better or worse, kept the question of rebirth alive for me over the course of almost five decades.

This small book will not resolve my, or anyone's, questions about the possibility of rebirth—nor is it intended to do so. It is simply a probably foolhardy attempt to broadly survey two thousand-plus years of Buddhist discourse on the subject. I place the greatest emphasis on Indian Buddhism, because most of the ideas and practices adopted or adapted by Buddhists elsewhere in Asia can be traced to the texts and traditions that developed in the subcontinent between roughly 400 B.C.E. and 1200 C.E., but I will also address trends in the parts of Buddhist Asia that lie outside India and consider briefly the place of rebirth in modern Buddhist thought, especially in the West. For the most part, I seek simply to describe the Buddhist ideas and practices and to make them as understandable as I can. Now and again, though, a normative comment seems necessary, and near the very end, for what it is worth, I will say something of my own approach to the "problem of rebirth"—if, indeed, it is a problem.

I will begin, in chapter 1, by discussing the place of rebirth in a number of world cultures, ranging from African, to Polynesian, and Amerindian, as well as in Greek to other Western traditions. Chapter 2 provides some background on the early South Asian ideas of rebirth that likely were current at the time of the Buddha. Chapter 3 discusses what, if anything, we can discern of the Buddha's own attitude toward rebirth, and considers some objections to the common view that he believed in past and future lives. Chapter 4 outlines the details of the early Buddhist concept of rebirth, in terms of where one might be born—the five or six realms of saṃsāra. Chapter 5 explores the causal processes, both mental and physical, through which we actually take rebirth in one of the realms described in chapter 4.

Chapter 6 analyzes both the basics and nuances of karma, the positive, negative, or mixed actions that explain *why* we take rebirth in this or that situation. Chapter 7 offers a brief aside on "popular" images, texts, and practices, including visual depictions of the "wheel of life," story-literature, and some points of tension between Indian Buddhist theory and Indian Buddhist practice. Chapter 8 is concerned with Indian Mahāyāna Buddhist approaches to rebirth, including those of the Pure Land sūtras and Mādhyamika and Yogācāra philosophers. Chapter 9 examines the views and practices of the Indian tantric branch of Mahāyāna, known as the Adamantine Vehicle (Vajrayāna) or Way of Mantra (Mantranaya). Chapter 10 considers premodern (especially Indian) Buddhist attempts to defend or prove the idea of rebirth, touching on empirical, ethical, analogical, and rational arguments, and also puzzling out the knotty problem of how Buddhists can assert rebirth while denying that there is a "self" to be reborn.

Chapter 11 surveys the spread of Buddhism outside India, and examines premodern Buddhist attitudes toward rebirth in the Theravāda world of South and Southeast Asia, taking Sri Lanka as an exemplary case. Chapter 12 examines premodern Buddhist takes on rebirth in the predominantly Mahāyāna world of East Asia, taking China as an exemplary case. Chapter 13 examines premodern Buddhist perspectives on rebirth in the predominantly Vajrayāna world of Inner Asia, taking Tibet as an exemplary case. Chapter 14 addresses the status of rebirth in modern (roughly post-1800) thought in general and modern Western Buddhism in particular, delving into the various ways in which the idea has been received and interpreted in both Asian and Western cultural settings. The fifteenth and final chapter summarizes some recent debates about rebirth and seeks to chart a way forward in thinking about the idea in the twenty-first century.

To steal a rhetorical trope from Gregory Schopen's wonderfully wry prefaces to his essay collections, the major blame (or credit) for the existence of this book goes to Casey Kemp, who, when I submitted a ridiculously lengthy article on rebirth for Richard Payne's collection, *Secularizing Buddhism*, which she was editing for Shambhala, suggested that I take the material irrelevant to the volume's theme and make it the basis for an introductory book on rebirth. The process, of course, wasn't as simple as throwing together the excised article material and padding it a bit here and there; indeed, I've rewritten that text almost entirely, and, in the end, also included here (in chapter 15) some of the material on modern perspectives that was kept in my essay in the secularism volume (Jackson 2021). I'm grateful to Casey for suggesting I write the book, and for seeing it through the editorial process with such a fine combination of enthusiasm and critical acumen. I'm also grateful to Nikko Odiseos of Shambhala and Kurtis Schaeffer of the University of Virginia for postponing my work on another book for Shambhala so I could write this, to Breanna Locke for help with the production of the book, and to LS Summer for preparing the index.

I want to acknowledge, with deep reverence and gratitude, the various Tibetan lamas with whom I have studied rebirth and related ideas, either in person or from their writings or online videos, including, most prominently, Lama Thubten Yeshe, Lama Thubten Zopa Rinpoche, Geshe Ngawang Dhargyey, Geshe Lhundub Sopa, Geshe Ngawang Wangchen, Chögyam Trungpa Rinpoche, Dzongsar Khyentse Rinpoche, Khenpo Sherab Sangpo, Mingyur Rinpoche, Ganden Tri Rinpoche Losang Tenzin, Yangsi Rinpoche, and Geshe Dorjee Damdul. Academic colleagues with whom I have fruitfully discussed rebirth over the years are too numerous to list fully, but I would single out José Cabezón, Paul Griffiths, Elvin Jones, John Makransky, Beth Newman, John Newman, Troy Omafray, David Patt, Asuka Sango, Michael Sweet, Robert Thurman, and Leonard Zwilling. I want also to acknowledge the tremendous stimulation provided by the writings of such thinkers as Stephen Batchelor, Owen Flanagan, Richard Hayes, Evan Thompson, and B. Alan Wallace. I am most grateful, too, to my students over the years at Carleton College, whose interest in South Asian religion and Buddhism inspired me to develop and refine many of the ideas presented here. As always, many of my most thought-provoking conversations have been with friends without formal academic training in Buddhist studies but deeply thoughtful about the Dharma, of whom I would mention especially Linda Atkins, Mike Atkins, Frank Barone, Morgan Groves, Cathy Kennedy, Will May, David Monroe, Sue Solomon, and my lifelong muse, best friend, and debate partner, Pam Percy.

Rebirth

CHAPTER 1

Introduction

Rebirth in World Cultures

In his Pulitzer Prize-winning book *The Denial of Death*, anthropologist, psychologist, and philosopher Ernest Becker (1924–1974) asserts that a central purpose of human culture is to provide us human beings with an "immortality project." Such a project—be it participation in a social or political group, creation of a work of art, bequeathal of a legacy for our descendants, or adherence to a philosophical or religious system—brings meaning to our finite lives by assuring us that although we will, inevitably, undergo physical death, some aspect of ourselves will live on after the body's demise.[1] In many cultural systems, especially in the modern era, our personhood is lost at death, so our "survival" is symbolic more than actual—or if it is actual, it is through our descendants. However, a human cultural system that profoundly shaped premodern societies—namely, religion—is unique in its near-unanimous insistence that our personhood is *not* utterly extinguished at death and that we will, in some very real sense, continue to exist afterward, perhaps even eternally. And, among the world's multiplicity of religions—old or new, global, local, or small-scale, in this cultural region or that—there are two basic models through which our continuation after death is imagined (two *eschatologies*): (1) one in which we reside forever in a transworldly realm from which we will never return to earth, or (2) one in which we return one or more times to the world, whether in human, animal, or some other form.

Model 1 is, broadly, that propounded within the worldviews, or cosmologies, of normative Judaism, Christianity, and Islam, as well as Zoroastrianism, some forms of Daoism, and a number of small-scale religions in various parts of the world. Model 2 is most obviously identified with the cosmologies of religions of South Asian origin, such as Hinduism, Buddhism, Jainism, and Sikhism, but also is found in some forms of Daoism, some schools of ancient Greek religion, occasionally within Judaism, Christianity, or Islam, and in other smaller-scale traditions scattered across the globe. The two models are far from mutually exclusive and admit of multiple, complex variations, but they do at least lay out the eschatological possibilities in a rough and ready way.

Our concern here is primarily with Model 2, which describes a process that has, in various contexts, been labeled *rebirth*, *reincarnation*, *transmigration*, *metempsychosis*, *palingenesis*, or *metacosmesis*. I will, for the most part, refer to it as *rebirth*, since that is the English word most commonly—and accurately—used to translate the Sanskrit term *punarjanma*, itself among the most common words used by Buddhists (and South Asians more generally) to denote a postmortem process in which we return to some version of embodied existence.[2] I also will use the most commonly employed English term, *reincarnation*, taking it as more or less synonymous with *rebirth*. Admittedly, Buddhists often object to the use of the term *reincarnation* for the rebirth process, on the grounds that "incarnation" subtly implies a soul (*ātman*), a concept they typically reject. I will address this problem in chapter 10, but will observe here that while Buddhists typically deny the existence of a permanent, unified, independent self, they seldom (before the modern era) have denied rebirth. Hence, there is an important sense in which *something* or *someone* is reborn. Therefore, whatever its nature, Buddhists may at least broadly be said to accept the existence of a "soul."[3]

Types of Rebirth Eschatologies

According to the Sri Lankan anthropologist Gananath Obeyesekere, who has surveyed the world's literature on rebirth more thoroughly and thoughtfully than any other scholar to date,[4] rebirth theories are broadly divisible into what he calls *rebirth eschatologies* and *karmic eschatologies*, and also into *ethicized* and *non-ethicized* explanations for the rebirth process.

Rebirth eschatologies[5] are typical of (but not exclusive to) the "small-scale societies" found most notably among "tribal" groups in Africa, the South Pacific, Amerindian North America, and elsewhere, as well as in ancient Greece. In small-scale societies, they usually involve the idea that when a person is born into the human world, they have arrived here from a realm of ancestors—to which they will return after death, only to return again, and so on, in an unending cycle. In larger-scale societies like ancient Greece, it is less common to assume that one will be reborn into one's previous kinship group. Rebirth eschatologies, whether in small-scale societies or in ancient Greece, are not, for the most part, ethicized in the full sense of the term. They do, of course, assume ethical norms, but they do not, in a detailed and systematic way, tie one's situation and experiences in this life to actions performed in a previous life or what happens in a future rebirth to the quality of one's actions during this life. Complicating questions that lead to variations in rebirth eschatologies include whether rebirth is a good or bad thing; whether cross-species rebirth (e.g., human to animal, or vice versa) is the norm; whether identification of a person's previous life is possible, either through personal recollection or the analysis, by others, of one's physical traits and mental dispositions; and, perhaps most crucially, whether the tradition's cosmology includes a *soteriology*, a theory according to which a permanent state of spiritual liberation may be attained—in this case through transcendence of the process of rebirth.

Karmic eschatologies,[6] which are most often found in "larger-scale" societies influenced by Indic traditions (especially by Hinduism and Buddhism), typically involve a high degree of ethicization, in that our present situation is explained on the basis of actions (*karman*) performed in a previous life, and our postmortem destiny is keyed very precisely to the quality of our actions during this life. Most karmic eschatologies take our repeated rebirth as a suboptimal situation, because every birth is shot through to some degree with dissatisfaction, or suffering (*duḥkha*), and they often assert the process to be without beginning—but not necessarily endless, because they posit a soteriology, holding out the prospect of our eventual attainment of a liberated state that brings the rebirth process to an end. Complicating questions that lead to variations in karmic eschatologies include whether past lives may be remembered, and if so, how, and how reliably; what sorts of "realms" we may take birth in (e.g., animal, ghostly, heavenly, etc.); what sorts of actions lead to which rebirths; and what the liberated state is like (e.g., detached, gnostic, blissful, loving, wise, or some combination of these). With Obeyesekere's categories in mind, in the remainder of this chapter we will briefly survey non-Indic theories of rebirth, then, in chapter 2, pre- and non-Buddhist theories in South Asia, and, in chapter 3, the theory of the Buddha himself, to the degree that it can be determined.

Theories of Rebirth in "Small-Scale" Societies

Outside of South Asia, rebirth theories developed in a variety of small-scale and larger-scale societies, both non-Western and Western. We cannot detail all of them here,[7] but will briefly survey some representative examples. Small-scale non-Western societies in which rebirth theories developed are found primarily in sub-Saharan Africa, the South Pacific, and among Amerindian tribes, though such theories also have been noted among Siberian shamanic groups and some Australian Aboriginals.

For the Igbo of southeastern Nigeria[8] (who are themselves divided into various subgroups), the cosmos is pervaded and controlled by a creator spirit or oversoul, called *chi*, a term that also refers to helper-deities and human souls possessed of that spirit. At birth, as part of a bargain with the creator, a human is permitted to draw on the reservoir of cosmic chi for the personal soul that will accompany them through life, and at death, that chi will be returned to its source, while the individual travels as a ghost in one or more intermediate realms until it is time to reenter the human world with a fresh infusion of chi. In the Igbo conception, "a reincarnated ancestor returns to known kinfolk, often but not always into the same patrilineal group,"[9] and usually will be clearly identified as the incarnation of that ancestor. The conception of the spiritual constitution of a reborn individual is complex, for they are believed to be, at one and the same time, a specific ancestor reborn *and* a unique individual, who derives parts of his or her identity from both the paternal side of the family and from the maternal side. Though most individuals will achieve rebirth, some may fail to do so; they are referred to as the "bad dead"—a clear indication that for the Igbo, rebirth is a good thing and that the prospect of ancestral return is essential to maintaining the cosmic and social order and providing the individual with a larger sense of meaning and purpose.

Among the Trobriand islanders of Melanesia studied in the early twentieth century by anthropologist Bronislaw Malinowski (1884-1942),[10] it is said that when a person dies, the spirit, or *baloma*, travels in an unseen canoe to an invisible island called Tuma, where they will reside, as an ever-revivified youth, for an indeterminate period of time, before taking birth again in the same village and clan in which they died. Unlike the Igbo "ghosts," who are inaccessible to the living until they take rebirth, Trobriand balomas make regular visits to their previous abode, where they may be celebrated on ritual occasions and encountered, in dreams or visions, by villagers, who take their advice and injunctions on tribal matters with great seriousness. Eventually, "a spirit becomes tired of constant rejuvenation, [and] may want to return to life on earth. To do so, the spirit 'leaps far back in age, and becomes a small, unborn infant,'"[11] who emerges within the same matrilineal clan as its predecessor. Unusually, however, the Trobriand islanders never attempt to identify the ancestor of whom the newborn is an incarnation, believing such knowledge impossible; nevertheless, they live with the recognition that those born into their society have been there before and have returned to where they naturally belong.

As noted by Obeyeskere, belief in rebirth was "prevalent to some degree among virtually all North American Indian groups,"[12] and a nearly universal feature of these societies' rebirth theories is acceptance of the concept of *species sentience*, whereby "all living creatures belong to a larger, interconnected spirit-pervaded order."[13] Such an order allows for at least two versions of rebirth: *parallel-species reincarnation*, in which animals are only ever reborn as animals and humans as humans, and *cross-species reincarnation*, in which animals may be reborn as humans, and vice versa. Species sentience is especially well documented among First Nations and Indigenous Peoples living in what is now Canada, including the Inuit, Tlingit, and Kwakiutl. The Kwakiutl,[14] who have resided for centuries along the shorelines of Vancouver Island and southern British Columbia, present a complex cosmology in which cross-species *and* parallel-species reincarnation both are possible. According to them, after death the soul (*bexwune*) "travels to the world of animals... before coming back to the human world."[15] The animal incarnations are not random: the souls of sea hunters become orcas, those of land hunters become wolves, those of common people become owls, and those of twins become salmon.[16] After some years, most souls will be reborn in the human world, usually as a grandchild of the previous human incarnation. However, "not all souls are reincarnated eventually as humans. A person who dies at sea has his or her soul relegated to the world of the sea otters that capture it," where it will remain forever.[17]

As with the other instances of small-scale-society rebirth eschatologies mentioned here, the rebirth taken by a given Kwakiutl individual is, in Obeyeskere's terms, non-ethicized—in the sense that specific postmortem events and experiences are *not* linked in any detail to proper or improper conduct during the person's lifetime, as they are in a karmic eschatology.[18] However widely scattered, these small-scale societies also are unanimous in their assumption that rebirth is a good thing—or, at the very least, is vital to the proper functioning of the cosmos, society, and the individual. Nor, therefore, do any of their rebirth schemes entail positing a state in which an individual may transcend the rebirth process, for the process of cycling from one incarnation to another is simply the way things are and the way things are supposed to be.

Theories of Rebirth in European and Mideastern Societies

When we look to the relatively larger-scale European and Mideastern societies whose seedbed is the eastern Mediterranean region, we find sporadic evidence of concepts of rebirth, but very few settings in which it was the mainstream eschatology. The Greek historian Herodotus (c. 484–425 B.C.E.) credits the Egyptians with the belief that

> when the body dies, the soul creeps into some other living thing then coming to birth, and when it has gone through all things, of land, sea, and air, it creeps again into a human body at its birth. The cycle for the soul is three thousand years.[19]

Although there is no consensus among scholars that rebirth was in fact central to ancient Egyptian religion—which may have been of the Model 1 type of eschatology, admitting of no return to earth in the soul's onward journey after death—the concept may have been accepted in certain circles.[20] In any case, Herodotus credits ancient Greek ideas of rebirth, which are well attested, to Egyptian sources, although influences from western Asia, or even India, cannot be ruled out. Many notable Greek thinkers entertained one or another idea of rebirth, and such ideas were prominent, too, in a number of mystery schools, especially the Orphic;[21] here, we will touch briefly on just two figures: Pythagoras and Plato.

Pythagoras (c. 570–495 B.C.E.),[22] who spent much of his life in a Greek colony in southern Italy, may have been the first figure to call himself a "lover of wisdom," a philosopher, but his life and teachings are hard to extract from the tangle of myth and legend that came to surround him in later times. He is credited with a range of innovative ideas, including the mathematical theorem that bears his name, a musical system that transmits the "harmony of the spheres," an ethical theory that places a premium on asceticism and vegetarianism, and a cosmology that includes rebirth and allows for the possibility of remembering past lives—an ability Pythagoras is said to have possessed. He also is reputed to have founded a school through which he imparted various ideas and practices to his followers, and indeed, Pythagoreanism was a significant cultural force in the Greco-Roman world for many centuries. Pythagoras's idea of rebirth, as best we can determine, involves the prospect of cross-species reincarnation, with rebirth occurring immediately after death. Unlike the theories we have examined in small-scale societies, however, it does not presume rebirth into one's previous social group or family, and it does imagine a termination of the rebirth process, at least for a small elite, through living a pure life in a community of like-minded practitioners and learning to attune oneself to the music of the spheres, both during life and after death. Although in this respect, Pythagorean cosmology involves a soteriology—a salvation theory—and ethical practices that may be conducive to salvation, it is not, Obeyesekere argues, a fully "ethicized" theory of rebirth (that is, a karmic eschatology), in that no direct line is drawn between actions one performs in one life and the experiences and events one undergoes in another life.

The Athenian philosopher Plato (c. 425–347 B.C.E.)—to whom, as Alfred North Whitehead famously remarked, all of Western philosophy is but a series of footnotes—articulated a belief in rebirth in many of his dialogues, although his thought on the matter seems to have evolved over time, and never reached a final, systematic form.[23] His most famous exploration of the idea is found in the "Myth of Er" narrative in the tenth and final book of the *Republic*, in which a slain warrior, Er, awakens on his funeral pyre twelve days after his death and recounts the experiences he underwent in the otherworld in the interim.[24] According to Er, after death the souls of the departed are judged for their just and unjust actions during life, and subjected to appropriate punishment or reward in one or another region of the afterlife. After they have received their just desserts, they are allowed to choose the earthly incarnation (human or animal) they will take—although the choice is typically governed by sense desires, hence less than fully free; they then drink of Lethe, the river of forgetfulness, and undergo rebirth. There is no soteriology articulated in the "Myth of Er," but in other dialogues, such as the *Phaedo*, Plato lays out a scheme in which, after three rebirths, an elite minority of true philosophers will

> achieve a mode of being that permits spiritual fellowship with the gods and contemplation of the transcendental vision of Reality. The philosopher ceases to be reborn in the world of becoming, whereas ordinary human beings continue in it until... the cycle of rebirths lasting ten thousand years ends and a new one begins.[25]

The fate of unliberated souls at that time is never spelled out clearly, so most people's ultimate destiny remains uncertain. (The *Phaedo* also lays out a knowledge-theory based on *anamnesis*, the idea that we do not "learn" new things, so much as we "unforget" things we have known before; implicitly, therefore, memories from past lives are possible.) In any case, the Platonic vision of rebirth involves elements of both "ethicization," in that there is a general idea of cosmic justice in play, and soteriology, in that "salvation" is available at least to the very best among us—but because each of these is limited, Platonism is an instance not of karmic eschatology but of rebirth eschatology, albeit a highly complex one. Still, Plato's concepts distantly echo those of the karmic eschatologies that arose in South Asia, to which we will turn in the next chapter. They also helped lay the groundwork for visions of the afterlife that would develop in the great Abrahamic religions that eventually dominated cultural life in Europe, the Middle East, and beyond: Christianity, Islam, and Judaism.[26]

Friedrich Nietzsche (whom we shall encounter in chapter 14) notoriously described Christianity as "Platonism for the people."[27]

While this is true insofar as Christianity postulates the immortality of the soul, a system of punishments and rewards in which our actions on earth affect our situation in the afterlife, and a soteriology in which salvation is open at least to some, it is misleading when we consider the centrality of rebirth to Platonic thought and its absence in normative Christianity. Indeed, it seems quite clear that Christian eschatology follows what I have called Model 1, for while Christians accept the existence of the soul and its survival of death, the soul's ultimate disposition does *not* involve a return to worldly life; rather, depending on the quality of one's actions during our one and only life (as well as God's disposition toward us), we will—at the Final Judgment, if not before—either be rewarded in heaven, where we will enjoy eternal proximity to God, or condemned to hell, where we will be subjected to the tortures of the damned, the worst of which is absolute distance from God. There has been much discussion among Christian theologians over whether God might predestine us to salvation or damnation, how vital faith and "works" are to our final eschatological assignment, and whether there is a state of purgatory in which we might reside prior to final judgment—but in any case, rebirth does not enter the discussion. The picture is similar in Islam, where orthodox theology declares that "indeed we belong to Allah, and indeed to Him we will return" (*Qur'ān* 2:156), and asserts that, come the Day of Decision at the end of time, each soul will be judged on its merits and dispatched for eternity to paradise or hell. Muslims, like Christians, wrestle with a range of theological problems—including free will and determinism, the proper qualifications for dispensing worldly justice, and the status of non-Muslim religious believers—but once again, rebirth is simply not part of the standard picture.

Historically, however, Christianity and Islam both were influenced by a wide range of ideas and cultural practices, rebirth among them, and there certainly have been, and continue to be, a minority of Christians and Muslims who posit an eschatology based upon it. In the case of Christianity, rebirth seems to have been accepted by certain early Gnostic sects, as well as by medieval "heretical" groups influenced by Gnosticism, such as the Cathars, Albigensians, and Bogomils, and by Renaissance movements inspired both by Gnosticism (or some other esoteric movement) and by the recent rediscovery of Platonism and other forms of Greek thought. Although often suppressed and their proponents sometimes persecuted, these counter-eschatologies within the Christian West have never been fully eliminated, and they had much to do with the rise of esoteric schools in the early modern period and beyond—schools that have helped contribute to an acceptance of rebirth in the modern West that is more widespread than might be expected.[28] Similarly, though to a lesser degree, Muslims occasionally have entertained ideas of rebirth. Such notions are most common among Shi'ite communities, which were the Islamic groups most influenced by Platonism, but the majority of Shi'ites, such as the "Twelvers" of Persia, maintain orthodoxy in their rejection of rebirth, and the idea is largely confined to Ishmā'īlī splinter groups like the Nuṣarīyah, Druze, and Alewi.[29] In South Asian cultures where rebirth is a central belief, some Muslims have integrated Islamic orthodoxy with a modified version of reincarnation theory.

The third great Abrahamic religion, Judaism, does not typically accept rebirth (Hebrew *gilgul*, "rolling"), either, but Jews always have entertained a wide gamut of eschatological ideas, from those who reject an afterlife altogether, to those who follow a messianic model not unlike that of Christianity and Islam (which are partially patterned upon it), to an influential minority who posit rebirth: the concept seems to have been accepted by the great first-century philosopher Philo of Alexandria (b. 25 B.C.E.), who was deeply influenced by Plato, and is prominent in the esoteric traditions of medieval Kabbalists, such as that of Isaac Luria (1534–1572), as well as in the more recent Kabbalah-inspired Hasidic movements, which themselves are highly influential in the Jewish world. And, like the ideas of Christian esotericists, those of Jewish Kabbalists have had a small but significant impact in the modern world outside their home communities, hence contributing to ongoing discussions of the nature of the afterlife.

CHAPTER 2

Pre-Buddhist Indian Rebirth Theories

As noted in chapter 1, Obeyesekere restricts the "karmic eschatology," with its high degree of ethicization and its transcendental soteriology, to South Asia and the other Asian areas influenced by Indic culture. The latter include Southeast Asia, which was permeated by Buddhist and Hindu ideas and practices (and, to a lesser degree, those of the Jains and Sikhs); East Asia, with its infusion of Mahāyāna, or Great Vehicle, Buddhism; and Inner Asia, whose cultures were profoundly shaped by the tantric form of Mahāyāna Buddhism known as Mantranaya (the Way of Mantra) or Vajrayāna (the Adamantine Vehicle). Rebirth is—with yoga, karma, nirvāṇa, the caste system, and dharma—one of a handful of basic concepts associated in the popular mind with the religions of South Asia. However, although sophisticated Indic civilizations can be traced back to around 3300 B.C.E., rebirth seems only to have emerged as a central part of Indic cosmologies shortly before or during the time of the Buddha—the middle of the first millennium B.C.E.—and the Buddha himself may have been the first thinker in the subcontinent to articulate the idea clearly and in detail. His account of rebirth did not, of course, arise in a vacuum, and before turning to the question of what the Buddha thought and taught about the topic, we will briefly trace the emergence of theories of rebirth in India, so as to get a better sense of the context in which he taught his own cosmology, eschatology, ethics, and soteriology.[30]

As a historical caveat, the reader should be aware that early Indic literature—the Vedas, the Buddhist Vinaya and Sūtra collections, and certain Jain texts—is very hard to date with precision: most of it was handed down in oral form long before it was committed to writing, and although much of it may have been transmitted faithfully, other portions of it clearly underwent redaction over the centuries, so that many questions remain as to the absolute dating and relative chronology of many of the texts and, more to the point, perhaps, we cannot be certain whether the accounts we read of religious life in a given place and time (to the degree that these are specified) were written contemporaneously or viewed backward through the lens of later tradition.

Eschatology in the Earliest South Asian Civilizations

The earliest major Indic civilization for which we have material remains is that of the Indus River Valley and adjacent areas, which seems to have flourished between roughly 3300 B.C.E. and 1300 B.C.E. Since the late nineteenth century, archaeologists have discovered the ruins of a number of major cities and smaller settlements over a wide area corresponding to present-day Pakistan, northeast Afghanistan, and northwestern India. The cities, in particular, show evidence of considerable planning and organization, on a scale comparable to that of contemporaneous civilizations in Egypt and Mesopotamia. The ruins of these cities have yielded a handful of bronze and stone statuettes of female figures, as well as thousands of clay seals, which depict various human and animal subjects. These finds have yielded much speculation as to the nature of Indus religion, for example, whether there was a mother-goddess cult, worship of animal-shaped deities, a proto-yogic tradition, or perhaps even a notion of rebirth. Unfortunately, however, the Indus script has yet to be deciphered, so all such speculations remain just that.

The reason scholars have "found" goddess worship, animal deities, yoga, or rebirth in the remains of the Indus civilization is that although such ideas and practices became prominent in later South Asian traditions, there is little to no evidence of them in the earliest Indic civilization for which we have legible records, that of the Indo-Aryans. The Indo-Aryan civilization was founded by Indo-European migrants from central Asia who settled in the Punjab region starting around 1200 B.C.E. Their way of life was pastoral and nomadic; their society was roughly divided into four occupation-related "castes" (*varṇa*, literally "color"): *brāḥmaṇas* (brahmins), or priests; *kṣatrityas*, or warriors; *vaiṣyas*, or common folk; and *śudras*, or servants. Although the system became highly ramified and hierarchical over the course of three thousand years, these categories still retain meaning in modern India.

Over the course of a millennium or more, the Indo-Aryans expanded to the southeast along the Ganges river basin, then southward through the Deccan plateau, eventually coming to exert power and influence over most of the subcontinent—though their imprint always was deepest in the north.[31] Unlike the denizens of the Indus civilization, the Indo-Aryans have left very few material traces of their early life in South Asia. They did, however, bequeath us an extensive literary tradition—originally oral and later written—in one or another form of the Sanskrit language. Known as the Vedas, this vast collection of texts can be arranged more or less chronologically on the basis of linguistic and geographical analysis. It was mostly composed between the late second and the mid-first millennium B.C.E., and reveals much about changes to the Indo-Aryans' social and religious life as their civilization shifted from pastoral and nomadic at the outset to urban and agricultural later on. Its primary components are (1) the Saṃhitas, which consist of the Ṛgveda and three other collections of religious and ritual verses: the Yajur, Sāma, and Atharva Vedas; (2) the Brāḥmaṇas, which comment on the Saṃhitas and are mostly preoccupied with ritual procedure; (3) the "forest treatises," or Āraṇyakas, which investigate the philosophical and psychological implications of ritual practice; and (4) the Upaniṣads, which delve deeply into the meaning of sacrifice, self, and the world, and are among the most significant texts in the world's religious literature. These four collections, which are related in complex and highly schematized ways, came to form the corpus of "revealed" (*śruti*) Hindu scriptures.[32]

The Ṛgveda,[33] which is an anthology of the song-prayers of brahmin visionaries (*ṛṣis*), is generally regarded as the oldest and most important of the Saṃhitas, most likely dating to the late second millennium B.C.E. Hence, it is our best source for understanding early Indo-Aryan religion. That religion can be broadly characterized as polytheistic ritualism: it presumed the existence of a variety of powerful deities (*devas*) in control of natural and human phenomena (e.g., Indra for storms, Sūrya for the sun, Agni for fire, Varuṇa for the moral order, Yama for death), and prescribed sacrificial rituals (*yajña*) in which a consecrated fire would carry various substances, as well as praises, prayers, and petitions to these deities, so as to procure their favor. Most of the prayers request "this-worldly" boons from the deities: that one beget many sons, that cattle be healthy, that rivers run seasonably within their banks, that one "live a hundred autumns"—in short, that the cosmos be orderly (*ṛta*). In its later books, the Ṛgveda does occasionally speculate on how the cosmos began, attributing it variously to the One (Eka), the Lord of Creatures (Prajāpati), the primordial Person (Puruṣa), the All-Maker (Viśvakarman), Speech (Vāc), or an unknown god. It also concerns itself to some degree with death and the afterlife, though its eschatology is not very detailed or systematic. There does seem to be a notion that those who perform the sacrificial ritual properly will be rewarded after death by eternal life in the "world of the fathers" (*pitṛloka*) or heaven (*svarga*), while those whose ritual action (*karman*) is improper may be consigned to a gloomy "house of clay." What is not evident in the Ṛgveda is any explicit suggestion of the possibility of rebirth—although there are several passages that could be read anachronistically to suggest the idea, such as the one that states, of a dead person, "let him reach his own descendants, dressing himself in a life-span...let him join with a body."[34] By the same token, later commentators could mine the Ṛgveda for evidence that it propounds a liberated state outside of the cosmic order or describes yogic and contemplative practices for attaining that state—but as with rebirth, the evidence is scant.

A New Cosmology: The Upaniṣads

As we trace the course of Indo-Aryan religion from the Ṛgveda, through the Brāḥmaṇas and Āraṇyakas, down to the early Upaniṣads, we traverse over half a millennium (roughly from 1200 to 600 B.C.E.), during which time the culture expanded its reach to the entire Gangetic plain, and striking changes occurred in nearly every aspect of life. Thus, a nomadic and pastoral economy gave way to a more settled pattern, with villages and cities supported by agricultural activity becoming the norm. The superiority of the brāḥmaṇa caste was increasingly challenged by urban princes and merchants, who enjoyed newfound power and wealth. At the same time, the polytheistic ritualism upheld by the brāḥmaṇas—while never entirely supplanted, even to this day—was overlaid by an increasingly sophisticated "new" cosmology, in which the notion of *ṛta*—the cosmic order—was transformed into that of *saṃsāra*, a beginningless, ever-changing, and ongoing series of more or less unfortunate rebirths, fueled by ignorance, desire, and karma, which eventually will be transcended by attainment of a changeless and blissful liberated state (*mokṣa*) gained not through sacrificial ritual—which only can get us to heaven—but through detachment from desire and by intellectual and contemplative knowledge (*jñāna*) of the deepest nature of things, most often referred to as *brahman*, the single, permanent spiritual reality undergirding the cosmos, or *ātman*, the single, permanent spiritual reality underlying the individual. Early on,[35] brahman and ātman came to be recognized as the same reality, viewed from two different perspectives, and realization of it, whether in this life or after death, to entail complete liberation from rebirth and eternal enjoyment of an unchanging state of reality, knowledge, and bliss (*sat-cit-ānanda*). This new view of the world—which, though admitting of many variations, would become normative in South Asian culture—is often referred to as the saṃsāra-karma-mokṣa cosmology.[36]

How Indic values underwent this dramatic shift—mythologist Joseph Campbell went so far as to call it a "great reversal"[37]—has been the subject of much discussion. Many scholars suggest it was a by-product of the development of iron technology, which allowed for improvements in forest clearing—which in turn provided ample wood for the construction of towns and cities—and agriculture—where a better plow made for better tilling and more bounteous crops, even perhaps surpluses that could be sold. The new economic arrangement led to the emergence of new castes (most notably commercial groups), while improvements in weaponmaking increased the scale and lethality of warfare. The eastern Gangetic region in the mid-first-millennium B.C.E. was dotted with warring city-states ruling over a "brave new world," and it is not surprising that the old social and religious arrangements—developed for the small-scale nomadic life of the early Indo-Aryans—no longer seemed adequate, at least to some. Dissatisfied with the old order, many people looked elsewhere for meaning, and they began to experiment with ideas and practices quite different from those on display in the Ṛgveda. There has been considerable debate over whether the sorts of theories and techniques that turn up in the Upaniṣads reflect the natural progression of a unified Vedic tradition or were imported from groups outside the Indo-Aryan fold, such as tribal or Dravidian peoples, or even the remnants of the Indus civilization. There is no consensus on these questions—all the proposed answers may contain some truth—but that a significant, if gradual, shift in Indic values did occur, and that the Upaniṣads offer the first clear evidence of that shift, is widely accepted.[38]

The shift *was* gradual, however: although not evident in the Ṛgveda, notions suggestive of rebirth are explicated in a few Vedic texts that likely predate the earliest Upaniṣads. Thus, the ritual "recipe book" known as the *Śatapatha Brāḥmaṇa*, probably composed somewhere between the eighth and sixth century B.C.E. (hence one of the latest of that class of texts), suggests the possibility that after we have died, our sojourn in whatever realm we have entered may not be eternal, and that we may undergo "re-death," returning to earthly existence.[39] The *Śatapatha* does not, however, spin this suggestion into a full-blown theory of rebirth.

The Upaniṣad generally considered the earliest, the *Bṛhadā-*

raṇyaka, is a continuation of the tenth chapter of the *Śatapatha Brāḥmaṇa*, and turns the idea of re-death into a theory of rebirth. For instance, in a discussion on the nature of death and the afterlife, the brāḥmaṇa sage Yajñavalkya tells King Janaka that, just as a caterpillar, when it reaches the tip of a blade of grass, stretches out and finds another foothold, so the unenlightened self (*ātman*), when it discards this body, will seek and find a new one.[40] Elsewhere in the *Bṛhadāraṇyaka*, a kṣatriya sage, Jaivali, details the rebirth process as he understands it, explaining that after the body's cremation, the unenlightened self becomes smoke, then passes into night, thence to the fortnight of the waning moon, the winter months, the world of the fathers, and the moon, where it becomes the food of the gods; having been eaten, it passes into space, air, rain, and the earth—from which it grows as grain that is consumed by a man, whose seed is planted in a woman—from which, at last, the being is reborn.[41] The *Bṛhadāraṇyaka* describes two postmortem paths beings may follow: the way of the gods and the way of the fathers. The way of the gods is that of the knower of brahman, who at death becomes brahman, and is reborn no more. The way of the fathers is that of the ritualist, which leads to heaven, but eventually to further rebirth. And within the compass of those still subject to rebirth, the key factor determining the sort of rebirth one will take is the quality of one's actions—one's karma. As Yajñavalkya tells his student Arthabhāga, "one becomes good by good action, bad by bad action."[42] Good and bad action, in turn, are determined by the degree to which one is dominated by ignorance and desire. The more we are under the sway of these forces, the more unfortunate our rebirth; the less we give in to them, the better the outcome.

Neither the *Bṛhadāraṇyaka* nor any other early Upaniṣad that propounds rebirth—including the *Chāndogya* or *Kauṣītaki*—goes into much more detail than this about the operations of the process,[43] nor do they explicate extensively the emergent saṃsāra-karma-mokṣa cosmology of which rebirth is so vital a part. Thus, it is unclear (at least at this stage) whether cross-species rebirth is possible, whether plants figure into the rebirth scheme, and whether there is anything resembling a hell realm into which we might be born. It is also important to note that taken as a whole, the early Upaniṣads—far from focusing entirely on knowledge—are still primarily concerned with understanding Vedic ritual, albeit in a deeper way than was suggested in the Saṃhitas and Brāḥmaṇas. Nevertheless, it is quite clear that at the time of the first Upaniṣads, what Obeyesekere calls a "karmic eschatology," with its strong degree of ethicization, had begun to take shape in the subcontinent—as had the broader saṃsāra-karma-mokṣa cosmology. The growing influence of this cosmology—with its marginalization of ritual and the gods, its countervailing emphasis on ethics and gnosis, and its promotion of an ascetic, yogic, and contemplative lifestyle for attaining the soteriological goal of eternal union with brahman—is evident in such middle-period (sixth to fifth century B.C.E.) Upaniṣads as the *Keṇa* and *Kaṭha*, and would carry through into the later, most likely post-Buddhist, Upaniṣads (which include the *Īśa*, *Śvetāśvatāra*, and *Muṇḍaka*). Although, as we know from the study of archeological and textual remains, Hindu traditions would change in countless ways in the succeeding centuries—through, for instance, the rise of new gods and goddesses; the development of devotional movements dedicated to them; and changes in ritual practices, contemplative techniques, and philosophical perspectives—the saṃsāra-karma-mokṣa cosmology first suggested in the *Bṛhadāraṇyaka* and *Chāndogya*, then solidified by subsequent Upaniṣads, would remain normative for Hindu tradition ever afterward, receiving greater definition through the epics and texts like the *Bhagavad Gītā* and various Purāṇas, and continuing to be accepted by countless Hindus to this day.

Śramaṇa Traditions

Although the Upaniṣads do contain evidence of the power and influence of the kṣatriyas, the military and administrative caste, they were, like the rest of Vedic literature, produced primarily by the priestly brāḥmaṇas, whose values they most closely reflect.

As elite members of the Indo-Aryan community, brāḥmaṇas did much to shape what we now call Hinduism—a term of far more recent vintage, coined by the British on the basis of the earlier Muslim designation of the non-Islamic inhabitants of the subcontinent as "Hindus," due to their habitation in the watershed of the Indus River. In the pre-B.C.E. context, as later, brāḥmaṇas could be identified by their reliance upon the Vedic corpus as revealed "scripture"; their assertion of the divine origin of caste hierarchy; their worship of a range of gods and goddesses, most but not all of whom had roots in Vedic tradition; their practice of rituals centered on notions of fire and food; and their general acceptance of the saṃsāra-karma-mokṣa cosmology, with knowledge of some version of an immortal and unchanging self as a key component of attaining liberation within that cosmology.

Brāḥmaṇas were not, however, the only religious group in mid-first-millennium B.C.E. South Asia. Buddhist texts datable to the last part of that millennium identify a second major type of practitioner: the *śramaṇa* (P. *samana*).[44] The term, which literally means "striver" or "exerter," occurs in Vedic literature, where it typically refers to ascetic renunciants known as *munis*, who sometimes were seen as marginal to the Brahmanical mainstream, but whose spiritual disciplines undoubtedly influenced the tradition in various ways; indeed, some see in them the forerunners of the *sannyāsins* and *sādhus* that have been an accepted, if occasionally problematic, part of Hindu tradition for millennia. Whether contemporaneously or after the fact, the term was appropriated by Buddhist and Jain authors to describe a range of non-Brahmanical philosophers that flourished in north India in the mid-first-millennium B.C.E. They differed widely among themselves in their beliefs and practices, but were generally characterized by their rejection of the authority of the Vedas, which they replaced with a canonical literature of their own devising; their organization into distinct communities of practitioners (*saṅghas*); their tendency to downplay caste hierarchy; their focus on ascetic and contemplative practices; and—with notable exceptions—their acceptance of the saṃsāra-karma-mokṣa cosmology. Early Buddhist texts, including those of the only complete Indic Buddhist canon from a single school, the Pāli canon of what is now called the Theravāda, identify six major śramaṇa teachers, contemporaneous with the Buddha, whose views run the gamut from the skeptical agnosticism of Sañjaya Belaṭṭhiputta, to the atomistic eternalism of Pakhuda Kaccāyana, the hedonistic materialism of Ajita Kesakambalī, the amoralism of Pūraṇa Kassapa, the fatalism (Skt. *niyativāda*) of the Ājīvika teacher Makkhali Gosāla, and the pluralistic asceticism of the Nigaṇṭha (Jain) sage Nātaputta.[45] Here, we will touch briefly only on the last four, as they are the ones with the most interesting perspectives on rebirth.

Ajita Kesakambalī is described by the *Samaññaphala Sutta* (*Discourse on the Fruits of the Śramaṇa Life*) as holding that

> there is no fruit or result of good or bad deeds, there is not this world or the next, . . . there are in the world no ascetics or brahmins who have attained, who have perfectly practiced, who proclaim this world and the next, having realized them by their own super-knowledge. The human being is composed of the four great elements, and when one dies [the elements revert to their origin]. . . . Fools and the wise [alike], at the breaking up of the body, are destroyed and perish, they do not exist after death.[46]

Although he is not here identified as such, Ajita is clearly an early representative of an important but underappreciated strand of Indian thought: materialism. Later referred to as Cārvāka or Lokāyata, this movement—from which we have very little surviving literature[47]—represented a small but stubborn source of resistance not just to the saṃsāra-karma-mokṣa cosmology but to the very idea of religion. As best we can tell, its metaphysics were thoroughly materialist, its epistemology skeptical of any knowledge claims not based on the senses, and its ethics epicurean—if not downright hedonistic. Unsurprisingly, it was caricatured and criticized by many Hindu, Buddhist, and Jain writers, the most important of which for our purposes was the Buddhist philosopher Dharmakīrti (seventh century), who uses a Lokāyata argument against survival after death and the mind's independence of the body as the take-off point for his own proof of the reality of past and future lives and the separability of the mental and physical aspects of our being. We will examine this argument in some detail in chapter 10.

Pūraṇa Kassapa, described by later commentators as a proponent of amoralism or inaction, seems to have adopted the unusual stance that while past and future lives and the various realms of rebirth are quite real, they are not the result of karma, because karma is fruitless: no matter what deeds we perform—whether the most virtuous acts or the most heinous of crimes—there is no actual result from any of it.[48] If Pūraṇa has a theory of liberation from rebirth, it is not evident; what is clear is that—like the materialist Ajita but for different reasons—he rejects the efficacy of the spiritual practices undertaken by both brāḥmaṇas and śramaṇas.

Pūraṇa's view is somewhat similar to that of Makkhali Gosāla, who is well attested in both Buddhist and Jain literature, and is usually identified as the main teacher, during the Buddha's time, of the Ājīvika tradition, a śramaṇic school that enjoyed considerable support in the subcontinent for a millennium or more, before fading away.[49] According to Buddhist sources, Makkhali preached a complex cosmology that allows for millions of different kinds of rebirths (including three thousand hells!), thousands of different occupational classes, hundreds of different kinds of karma, and a process of attaining liberation from rebirth that takes 8,400,000 eons. Like Pūraṇa, however, Makkhali disconnects liberation from any notion of karma; as a result, there is, at least in principle, nothing we can do to alter our spiritual destiny: "Just as a ball of string runs till it is all unraveled, so fools and wise run on and circle round till they make an end of suffering."[50] This makes it sound as if Makkhali, like Pūraṇa, promotes fatalism and non-activity, but it's hard to imagine a spiritual community in which nobody ever does anything, and Obeyesekere is probably correct to suggest[51] that Ājīvikas thought that liberation might be hastened, at least for an elite, by ascetic practices that could bring about the shedding of the multiple complex karmas we accumulate over the course of countless lives. In adopting this attitude (assuming they did), Ājīvikas showed themselves akin to the Jains, and it is perhaps telling that Jain texts identify Makkhali Gosāla as a one-time disciple of their twenty-fourth Tīrthaṅkara, Mahāvira, known to the Pāli Buddhist tradition as Nigaṇṭha Nātaputta, to whom we turn next.

The teaching of Nigaṇṭha Nātaputta is not described in great detail in the Pāli canon. The *Samaññaphala Sutta* simply reports that he was bound by a fourfold restraint, and through this fourfold restraint came to be "called self-perfected, self-controlled, self-established."[52] The most extensive account is found in the *Cūḷadukkhakkhandha Sutta* (*Shorter Discourse on the Mass of Suffering*), where the Buddha describes an encounter with Jains living near him in Rājagaha (Skt. Rājagṛha), who practiced "continuous standing... and were experiencing painful, racking, piercing feelings due to exertion."[53] Asked by the Buddha why they lived thus, the Jains explain that their "omniscient" teacher, Nigaṇṭha Nātaputta (i.e., Mahāvira), has informed them:

> Nigaṇṭhas, you have done evil actions in the past; exhaust them with the performance of piercing austerities. And when you are here and now restrained in body, speech, and mind, [you are] doing no evil actions for the future. So by annihilating with asceticism past actions and by doing no fresh actions, there will be no consequence in the future. With no consequence in the future, there is the destruction of action. With the destruction of action, there is the destruction of suffering.[54]

The Buddha then interviews the Jain practitioners, and quickly establishes that they actually have no knowledge of their past or future lives, nor of what sorts of actions or inactions affect our happiness or suffering. He also dismisses their assertion that "pleasure is to be gained through pain" by demonstrating the relativity of these terms and his own attainment of supreme pleasure by means that do not involve self-mortification.[55] Elsewhere, Nigaṇṭha

Nātaputta is criticized for his claim to omniscience, his speaking insultingly to the Buddha, his eschewal of action, his jealousy of the Buddha's success in converting his followers, and the contentiousness and confusion of his followers after his death.

Such passages make it clear that the Jain community—whose monastic tradition includes both men and women and may predate that of Buddhism—was considered a powerful rival to the Buddha's saṅgha, undoubtedly competing with it for patronage and influence in the "spiritual marketplace" of mid-first-millennium B.C.E. north India. Because Jainism flourished in South Asia, produced an immense and impressive literature, and remains a small but vital religious community there even today, we know far more about its views of karma, rebirth, and liberation than is indicated in the early Buddhist sources—even if the classical form of the tradition may differ somewhat from that reportedly expounded by Nigaṇṭha Nātaputta in the Buddha's time. In brief, Jain metaphysics is a form of panpsychism, maintaining that awareness (*upayoga*), or soul (*jīva*), is found throughout the universe. The cosmos comes into and out of existence at regular intervals, but souls have no beginning or end. Therefore, we have lived before, and will no doubt live again, and, depending on our karma, we are subject to rebirth in any form that possesses even minimal consciousness, including that of a plant or mineral, as well as human, animal, heavenly and hellish forms. Karma is regarded as a subtle form of matter that obscures the naturally luminous soul. Thus, escape from saṃsāra requires the cessation of action to the greatest degree possible, ideally (that is, for monastics) through the practice of radical nonharming (*ahiṃsā*), celibacy, nonpossession (which may include nakedness), and various forms of self-mortification (which may include fasting unto death)—although knowledge, devotion, and meditation also are extolled. When through these practices the subtlest trace of our obstructive karma has dissipated, then our souls rise to the top of the cosmos, to reside there eternally as perfected beings, or *siddhas*.[56]

This, then—keeping in mind the appropriate text-historical caveats—was the north Indian world of the sixth and fifth centuries

B.C.E., as revealed in the early Upaniṣads and the earliest Buddhist and Jain texts: one in which new social and economic formations were coming into being, helping to upset long-established norms; the saṃsāra-karma-mokṣa cosmology increasingly (though not uniformly or uncontested) was used to frame the human condition; and the cities and forests teemed with philosophers, ascetics, and yogis—brāḥmaṇas and śramaṇas alike—who sought to solve the riddle of existence and show suffering beings the way out of the vicious circle of rebirths, or at least to some semblance of happiness in this life. The eschatologies developed by these teachers ranged from the materialist denial of any afterlife, to Vedic traditionalist assertions of an afterlife without rebirth, to amoralist and fatalist theories that accepted rebirth but denied its connection to karma, to the more or less well developed karmic eschatologies of the Upaniṣads and Jainism. To promulgate their doctrines, these teachers founded communities, some of which still endure, and those communities, in turn, produced texts, which continue to shape the surviving communities and provide those of us on the outside with a window onto the strange, yet strangely familiar, South Asia of the mid-first-millennium B.C.E. It is to perhaps the greatest product of that place and time, the Buddha, then, that we turn at last.

CHAPTER 3

The Buddha on Rebirth

Truth be told, we cannot be certain what the Buddha thought or taught about rebirth, because "the historical Buddha"—known to tradition as Śākyamuni, the sage of the Śākya clan—eludes us, as does his actual teaching. Assuming there really was a Buddha (and some have argued he was a mythical figure), the date of his final nirvāṇa (*parinirvāṇa*), which marks the beginning of the "Buddhist era," has long been debated by scholars, both traditional and modern. Traditional scholars may date the parinirvāṇa as early as the ninth century B.C.E. Modern scholars, employing disparate Buddhist chronicles as well as archeological evidence, argue for dates ranging from 486 B.C.E. to 367 B.C.E., with most nowadays inclining toward around 400 B.C.E. Whatever the year of the Buddha's passing, the original Buddhist "texts" were probably transmitted orally for a century or more, and even after they began to take written form—perhaps in the third century B.C.E.—they were not collected and redacted until very late in the first millennium B.C.E. And when they were written down, it typically was in languages that were not that spoken by the Buddha: Pāli, Gandhārī, or one or another version of Sanskrit. The written texts we have, which were produced by various "Mainstream" Buddhist schools,[57] are divided into three "baskets," or collections (*piṭaka*): the Sūtra (P. *Sutta*) Piṭaka, consisting of five collections (*nikāyas*) of the Buddha's discourses; the Vinaya Piṭaka, consisting of rules for the monastic community, with an explanation of the circumstances that led to each rule; and the Abhidharma (P. *Abhidhamma*) Piṭaka, consisting of later, abstract analyses of the nature and function of the various constituents—*dharmas* (P. *dhammas*)—into which Buddhists analyzed reality. These texts undoubtedly reflect the outcome of a long process of redaction, so that even in the case of the Sūtra and Vinaya material, we cannot be confident that what appears in them is "what the Buddha taught," or that issues and concerns germane to later Buddhists have not been brought into their presentation of the Buddha's original teachings. Scholars have labored mightily over the past two centuries to analyze the language forms, terminology, and social and geographical references in collections such as the Pāli canon, but both their methods and their conclusions are far from unanimously accepted, and here, we will use that canon as a whole, and the mythicized Buddha it represents, as our main resource for determining Śākyamuni's view of rebirth—understanding full well that we cannot determine that view with finality.[58]

Unlike the Gospels of Christianity, the Sutta and Vinaya collections found in the Theravāda Pāli canon—and their rough equivalents in the Sanskritic Āgama and Vinaya collections drawn from other Mainstream Buddhist schools that, except for fragments, are extant only in Chinese translation—do not have a primarily biographical focus, let alone an autobiographical one. Indeed, the first connected biographies of the Buddha all were composed early in the first millennium C.E., well after the Mainstream canons had been more or less established; these include such Sanskrit texts as the *Buddhacārita* (*Deeds of the Buddha*) by the great poet Aśvaghoṣa, the anonymous quasi-canonical *Mahāvastu* (*Great Matter*) and *Lalitavistara* (*Extensive Play*), as well as the *Nidānakathā* (*Connected Stories*), which serves as an introduction to the Pāli *Jātaka*, the collection of the Buddha's "pre-birth" stories.[59] Nevertheless, the Buddha is the prime speaker throughout the Pāli suttas, and what we hear from his lips includes a great deal of doctrinal exposition and discussion but also reports of his own experience. Without assuming that the Buddha *really* experienced or reported what is attributed to him in the canon, we will consider first some passages about rebirth that are "autobiographical" or "first-person" reports, and then assess the importance of rebirth within the Buddha's cosmology.

Rebirth in the Buddha's "First-Person" Accounts

As we read through the *Dhammapada* (*Verses on Dharma*), the famous Pāli collection of poetic aphorisms attributed to the Buddha, two stanzas in the "Old Age" chapter stand out starkly from the surrounding sayings:

> Many a birth have I wandered
> in saṃsāra, vainly seeking
> the builder of this house.
> Sorrowful is repeated birth.
>
> Oh, housebuilder, you are seen!
> You shall not build this house again!
> All your rafters are broken
> and your ridgepole shattered!
> My mind has reached the uncompounded!
> I have attained the end of craving![60]

The great pandit Buddhaghosa—whose fifth-century C.E. commentary on the *Dhammapada* provides a biographical context for every single utterance—explains that this was Śākyamuni's "victory song," spontaneously uttered at the moment of his awakening under the Bodhi Tree in Bodh Gaya. It is important to note that the idea of rebirth, and its conquest, is central to the verses. Using the metaphor of a house and its builder, the Buddha describes the repeated, "sorrowful" (or suffering; *dukkha*) births he had to undergo in saṃsāra. The house whose builder (or architect; *gahakāraka*) he seeks is saṃsāra—either the process as a whole or the individual births that constitute it—and the builder, whom he has finally "seen," is the cause of suffering: craving (*taṅha*). Because he has seen the housebuilder, that is, understood and overcome craving, his mind has reached the uncompounded (*visaṅkāra*), or nirvāṇa (*nibbāna*), and the house will never be built again—he is done with rebirth, hence with saṃsāra.

Implicitly, this song evokes the central teaching given by the Buddha in the *Dhammacakkapavatthana Sutta* (*Discourse on Turning the Wheel of Dharma*), his so-called First Sermon, delivered at Sarnath some seven weeks after his awakening: that of the four noble truths. There, Śākyamuni asserts (1) the reality of suffering (P. *dukkha*, Skt. *duḥkha*); (2) suffering's source (*samudaya*), which is craving; (3) suffering's cessation (*nirodha*), which is the uncompounded or unconditioned state of nirvāṇa; and (4) the path (P. *magga*, Skt. *mārga*) leading to nirvāṇa; detailed as the eightfold noble path that leads to the elimination of craving: right view, intention, speech, action, livelihood, effort, mindfulness, and concentration. At the conclusion of his discourse, the Buddha states: "Unshakable is the liberation of my mind. This is my last rebirth. Now there is no more renewed existence."[61] As with the *Dhammapada* verses, we cannot understand the *Dhammcakkapavatthana* or the four noble truths without recourse to the saṃsāra-karma-mokṣa cosmology. First, the "sentient condition" is suffering, which occurs over the course of multiple lives, and the reality of which presupposes the separability of mind and body. Second, because all things within saṃsāra originate from specifiable causes and conditions on the basis of the law of dependent origination (P. *paṭicca-samuppāda,* Skt. *pratītya-samutpāda*), suffering has an identifiable source, craving. (Karma is not mentioned here as a cause, but it is implicitly understood to be the unskillful actions, the opposites of the members of the eightfold path, that result from craving and lead directly to rebirth.) Third, the cessation of suffering and the purification and perfection of the mind in a state of uncompounded nirvāṇa is a real possibility. Fourth and finally, that perfected state is attainable through the elimination of craving and the negative actions that stem from it, through practice of the eightfold path. In short, from the standpoint of the *Dhammcakkapavatthana,* rebirth is the basic problem we all face and the elimination of the craving that engenders rebirth is the solution.

The Buddha's certainty about his own liberation from rebirth was rooted in the experiences he underwent under the Bodhi Tree on the night of his awakening. Although later biographical sources would describe these experiences in great detail, he does not recount them exhaustively in the Pāli suttas. There are, however, several discourses in the canon that contain autobiographical accounts of interest. In the *Mahāsīhanāda Sutta* (*Greater Discourse on the Lion's Roar*), Śākyamuni describes the range of extreme austerities he practiced during the years between his departure from home and his attainment of awakening, which, he observes, did not lead to liberation.[62] He further notes—contrary to the claims of those (perhaps Ājīvikas) who assert that "purification" comes about through enduring one's rebirths until the bitter end, or those who claim that some single rebirth will lead to purification—that there is not a single rebirth he has not endured, yet neither an individual rebirth nor the sum of them led to his liberation.[63] In the *Ariyapariyesanā Sutta* (*Discourse on the Noble Search*), he gives an account of the meditation teachers with whom he studied after entering the homeless life, the contemplative states they taught (the two formless states of nothing-whatsoever and neither-perception-nor-non-perception, respectively), his rejection of these states as not conducive to liberation, his travel to Bodh Gaya, and his attainment there of the "supreme security of nibbāna," in which one is no longer subject to aging, sickness, death, sorrow, and defilement. With his attainment of nibbāna, "knowledge and vision" arose in him to the effect that his liberation was unshakable and this was his final birth.[64] He goes on to describe his decision to teach, his journey to Sarnath, and his instructions to his first five disciples, which open the door for them to reach "that supreme goal of the holy life for the sake of which clansmen rightly go forth from the home life into homelessness"[65] In the "Parable of the Ancient City" found in the *Saṃyutta Nikāya*, Śākyamuni describes how as an aspiring buddha he set out to understand how it is that beings in this world have "fallen into trouble," and are born, age, die, and take rebirth, and how one might escape that trouble. Likening himself to an explorer who discovers a ruined city in the jungle, he describes how he gained liberation through first understanding the cause-and-effect sequence that leads to rebirth and then proceeding to eliminate the main causal factors, ignorance and craving. With their elimination, "the whole mass of suffering" ceased, and, he reports, "there arose in me vision, knowledge, wisdom, true knowledge, and light."[66]

Of even greater interest as a "first-person" account is that of the *Bhayabherava Sutta* (*Discourse on Fear and Dread*), where the Buddha describes how, living deep in the forest, he overcame his fear and dread of "awe-inspiring, horrifying abodes," concentrated his mind, and ascended through four contemplative absorptions (P. *jhāna*, Skt. *dhyāna*), in which, focused on a particular object, the mind successively sheds applied thought, sustained thought, rapture, and pleasure, until all that remains is "neither pain-nor-pleasure and purity of mindfulness due to equanimity." Then, he says,

> "When my concentrated mind was thus purified... and attained to imperturbability, I directed it to knowledge of the recollection of past lives.... that is, one birth, two births, three births... a hundred thousand births, many aeons of world-expansion, many aeons of world-contraction and expansion: 'There I was so named, of such a clan, with such an appearance, such was my nutriment, such my experience, such my experience of pleasure and pain, such was my life-term; and passing away from there, I appeared elsewhere;... and passing away from there, I reappeared here.' Thus with their aspects and particulars I recollected my manifold past lives."[67]

This, the Buddha tells his audience, was the first of three "true knowledges" he gained on the night of his awakening. The second, immediately following, was the "divine eye," through which

> "I saw beings passing away and reappearing, inferior and superior, fair and ugly, fortunate and unfortunate. I understood how beings pass on according to their actions thus: 'These worthy

> beings who were ill-conducted in body, speech, and mind... on the dissolution of the body, after death, have reappeared in a state of deprivation, in a bad destination, in perdition, even in hell; but these worthy beings who were well-conducted in body, speech, and mind...on the dissolution of the body, after death, have reappeared in a good destination, even in a heavenly world.'"[68]

Having thus directly known his own rebirths and those of others, the Buddha turns his attention to the four noble truths, which he thoroughly comprehends, and at that point, he says,

> "My mind was liberated from the taint (*āsava*, Skt. *āsrava*) of sensual desire, from the taint of being, and the taint of ignorance. When it was liberated, there came the knowledge: 'It is liberated.' I directly knew: 'Birth is destroyed, the holy life has been lived, what had to be done has been done, there is no coming to any state of being.'"[69]

This, then, is the third and decisive true knowledge gained by Śākyamuni on the night of his awakening.

The account in the *Bhayabherava* provides a wonderfully clear outline of what Obeyeskere calls a "karmic eschatology," in which (a) one's postmortem destiny is shaped by one's actions during life and (b) the overall aim of the religious system of which rebirth is a part is to escape rebirth altogether. This the Buddha vouchsafes simply because he has experienced it: he knows this cosmology to be true not merely by description but by acquaintance, firsthand. It is still an outline, though, and at least some of the details of the system would be supplied by the Buddha in other "experiential" reports found in the Pāli canon.

In terms of his own previous lives, the Buddha occasionally relates a past-life story in the course of a sutta, as when, in the *Mahāsudassana Sutta* (*Discourse on the Great Splendor*), he explains why the insignificant town, "right in the jungle in the back of beyond" where he has chosen to pass away, Kusinārā (Skt. Kuśināgara), is not insignificant at all: he himself had lived and died there seven times when it was the great city of Kusāvatī; in the last of these rebirths he was a wheel-turning king named Mahāsudassana, who embraced the Dharma, renounced the world, and passed away, thereby laying the foundation for his own parinirvāṇa there in his final life.[70] In the *Mahāgovinda Sutta* (*Discourse on the Great Steward*), the Buddha recounts a past life as a court steward who heard the Buddha's teaching in an encounter with a deity and took up the ascetic life, perfecting thereby the divine practices (*brahmācāriya*) of love, compassion, sympathetic joy, and equanimity.[71] Śākyamuni's most extensive recollections of his past lives occur in the *Jātaka* stories, which drew liberally on a fund of South Asian fables and circulated in oral form for several centuries before being committed to writing and, in some cases, given canonical status.[72] In each of these tales (which number 547 in the Pāli collection), the Buddha tells of a past life in this or that body and circumstance. He might have been human, animal, or divine, living in wealth or poverty, but in each case his actions illustrate the effort to practice, and exemplify, one or another moral virtue, whether generosity, patience, wisdom, or some other quality. In each case, he explains at the end who the various characters in the story are in the present, thereby linking present circumstances with past deeds, and providing an illustration of the first knowledge he gained on the night of his awakening.

The second knowledge Śākyamuni attained that night, we may recall, was of the passing away and rebirth of other beings in various realms, according to their karma. This, too, is further illustrated in the canon, in passages where the Buddha reports on the postmortem destinies of a number of people. Occasionally, he is informed of these events by deities, but most often he sees them with his own divine eye. Thus, in the *Janavasabha Sutta* (*Discourse about Janavasabha*), on being asked by the inhabitants of towns up and down the Gangetic plain what has become of deceased relatives who were his followers, the Buddha specifies that at least five hundred have become stream-enterers (*sotāpanna*, Skt. *śrotāpanna*), facing a maximum of seven more rebirths, at least ninety have become once-returners (*sakadāgāmin*, Skt. *sakṛdāgamin*), and at least fifty have become non-returners (*anāgāmin*), who after death and a brief sojourn in the Pure Abodes, would become *arhats* (P. *arahant*), who have no more defilements remaining and will never again be reborn.[73] In the *Mahāsīhanāda Sutta*, which describes the various supernatural abilities of a thus-gone one—a tathāgata such as he—the Buddha reports that by encompassing mind with mind through his supernal vision, he knows that there are five realms into which beings may be reborn, those of gods, humans, animals, hungry ghosts, and hell beings; and he adds that, with respect to each, he understands the nature of the realm, the way leading to it, how rebirth in the realm occurs, and what it is like to live in that realm, whether pleasurable, painful, or mixed.[74]

All these realms are described in greater or lesser detail throughout the Pāli canon, sometimes on the basis of the Buddha's claim to direct experience, sometimes more generally—although even in more general accounts, the weight of the Buddha's superknowledges (P. *abhiññā*, Skt. *abhijñā*) is felt. The heavens, which are multiple, are detailed in various suttas and in a late text known as the *Vimānavatthu* (*Mansion Stories*);[75] they are marked by intense experiences of pleasure and power, and by the great longevity of their denizens. The human realm, of course, with its mixture of pleasure and pain, wisdom and foolishness, is the main locus of the Buddha's teaching; it is divisible by such categories as the four castes, various types of religious teachers, monastic and lay practitioners, men and women, and so forth. The animal realm is detailed in all its variety in a few suttas, as well as numerous Jātaka tales; the texts tend to emphasize the hunger, thirst, fear, and sudden death to which most animals are prone. The hungry ghost realm, and the karma leading to it, is explored in another late canonical text, the *Petavatthu* (*Ghost Stories*);[76] it is marked by extremes of thirst, hunger, and physical and mental distress. The hells, like the heavens, are manifold—and are described nearly as often as their polar opposite. To cite just one example, in the *Devadūta Sutta* (*Discourse on the Divine Messengers*), after outlining the general connection between karma and rebirth, Śākyamuni describes the postmortem interrogation to which evildoers are subjected by Yama, lord of death and the afterlife, who asks them whether they did not recognize the various "divine messengers" sent to them during life: an infant, old people, sick people, lawbreakers subject to execution, and decaying corpses. He then reports in excruciating detail on the tortures of the various hells, such as the Great Hell, the Hell of Excrement, and the Hell of Hot Embers, adding pointedly at the end, "I tell you this not as something I heard from another recluse of brahmin. I tell you this as something I have actually known, seen, and discovered by myself"[77]—implicitly through the divine eye he gained as the second knowledge on the night of his awakening.

The Significance of Rebirth in the Buddha's Cosmology

When we combine the Buddha's many first-person reports of his experiences of the way things are in the cosmos with his even more numerous "third-person" assertions about the structures and processes that govern sentient life, it is hard to escape the conclusion that the entirety of his teaching in the suttas is explicitly or implicitly undergirded by the saṃsāra-karma-mokṣa cosmology. Thus, there are two, and only two, possibilities for living beings: continual suffering—whether in coarse or subtle ways—in one of the realms of saṃsāra on the basis of defilements (P. *kilesa*, Skt. *kleśa*)—or taints or contaminants (P. *āsava*, Skt. *āsrava*)—and defiled action (*karma*); or transcendence of saṃsāra through following the path of Dharma to a liberated state beyond defilement, action, and suffering, namely, nirvāṇa. The saṃsāric cosmos is complex, consisting most broadly of three "spheres" (*dhātu*)—those of desire, form, and formlessness—which may be mapped onto five or six general realms or "destinations" (*gati*). In earlier traditions,[78] these are, in descending order of purity and pleasure, the realms of gods, humans, hungry ghosts, animals, and hell beings. Later traditions[79] often add the realm of *asuras* (antigods) as a sixth, though its precise location in the hierarchy of realms (as just below or just above the human realm) is ambiguous. Six-realm schemes also sometimes demote hungry ghosts below animals within the hierarchy. Each of these realms, in turn, is subdivided in various ways.

The population distribution of the cosmos is such that the most beings are found in the hells and the other lower and more miserable realms, and the fewest in the higher and more pleasurable god realms.[80] This stands to reason, because the particular rebirths sentient beings undergo all result from their actions, their karma, and negative actions—as specified in such lists as the "ten nonvirtues," namely, killing, stealing, sexual misconduct, lying, slander, harsh speech, frivolous talk, covetousness, malice, and wrong view—are far easier to perform than virtuous ones. Karma, in turn, is driven by the various defilements to which beings are prone, such as craving, hostility, ignorance, pride, and jealousy. Of these, either craving or ignorance is most often identified as the "root" defilement, and in any case, these "afflictive mind-states" serve to reinforce one another, keeping the current of saṃsāra flowing ever onward. Incidentally, the "sentient beings" who perform actions and undergo rebirth are understood not as permanent, unitary, or independent selves but as a mere constellation of the five ever-changing aggregates (P. *khanda*, Skt. *skandha*)—matter, sensation, conception, mental formations, and consciousness—onto which we impute personhood.[81]

The way out of saṃsāra is one or another version of the Buddhist path, whether the eightfold noble path articulated in the *Dhammacakkapavatthana* or the three trainings explained elsewhere: those in ethics (P. *sīla*, Skt. *śīla*), concentration (*samādhi*), and wisdom (P. *paññā*, Skt. *prajñā*). Each of these is complex, as well. Ethics at its most basic level involves avoidance of the ten nonvirtues just mentioned and at its more advanced level the undertaking of various temporary or lifelong precepts, which, in various enumerations, were prescribed for both laypeople and monastics. Concentration involves bringing the mind into focus through the four absorptions—with their progressive elimination of cognitive and affective factors until only single-pointed serenity (P. *samatha*, Skt. *śamatha*) remains, and superpowers may ensue—and, often, too, through the four formless attainments that lie beyond the absorptions: infinite space, infinite consciousness, nothing whatsoever, and neither-perception-nor-nonperception. None of these states of concentration, either individually or collectively, suffices for liberation, because they lack the third training, wisdom, which requires us to understand the way things really are (*yathābhūta*), whether in terms of the four noble truths, the causal law of dependent origination, or the crucial doctrine of no-self. We must reflect on these topics intellectually but also realize them in direct experience, through performing insight (P. *vipassanā*, Skt. *vipaśyanā*) meditation, in which we observe the rise and fall of physical and mental events and comprehend their true nature as impermanent, suffering, and without self. With a direct realization of the way things are—the attainment of "right view"—we begin the process of uprooting our defilements, successively attaining the states of stream-enterer, once-returner, non-returner, and arhat. Arhats, who are free from saṃsāra, are divided into those "liberated by insight," who have minimal experience of the absorptions and formless attainments and those "liberated both ways," who have partially or fully mastered multiple states of single-pointed concentration and also gained insight. A Buddha is an arhat liberated both ways who also has a particular role to fulfill as a re-founder of the Dharma at a particular point in a cosmic and historical cycle. Thus, arhats are relatively common, while buddhas are exceedingly rare. The point of this rehearsal of early Buddhist cosmology is that rebirth seems to be an absolutely central concern: subjection to it is the key problem faced by sentient beings, and liberation from it the only hope for lasting peace and security.

Further evidence of the centrality of rebirth to the Buddha of the Mainstream canons comes from a more detailed consideration of the meaning of "right view," the first member of the eightfold noble path, and a key to the attainment of nirvāṇa. Right view, in turn, cannot be understood without knowing what comprises wrong view—the last of the ten nonvirtues mentioned above. Actually, there are many candidates for wrong view in the early tradition; these include:

- sixty-two mistaken positions regarding the nature of the cosmos, modes of argumentation, the possibility of postmortem survival, and paths to nirvāṇa, which are outlined in the *Brahmajāla Sutta* (*Discourse on the Net of Brahmā*);[82]
- ten views the Buddha declared undecided (*avyakata*), to the effect that the cosmos is (1) eternal or (2) temporary; the cosmos is (3) infinite or (4) finite; the soul is (5) the same as the body or (6) different from it; the tathāgata after death (7) exists or (8) doesn't exist or (9) both exists and doesn't or (10) neither exists nor doesn't;[83]
- the belief that liberation is achieved through such rituals as extreme asceticism, fire sacrifices, or immersion in holy rivers;
- the "personality view" (*sakkāyadiṭṭhi*, Skt. *satkāyadṛṣṭi*) that maintains that a permanent self (P. *ātta*, Skt. *ātman*) may be found within our complex of mental and physical aggregates;[84]
- and the positions of the six śramaṇa teachers contemporaneous with the Buddha, to which we were introduced in chapter 2.

Put together, these critiques make it clear that the Buddhist notion of wrong view could, and often did, extend to virtually every other religious and philosophical school in mid-to-late-first-millennium B.C.E. North India: brāḥmaṇa or śramaṇa, Vedic or Upaniṣadic, Ājīvika or Jain, skeptical, atomist, amoralist, or materialist.

It does seem, however, that the wrong view considered most pernicious is that of materialists like Ajita Kesakambalī, as there are a number of places in the Pāli canon where the Buddha asks rhetorically, "What is wrong view?" and answers with the words attributed elsewhere to Ajita, to the effect that there is nothing given, offered, or sacrificed; no results of good or bad actions; no this world or world beyond; no mother or father; no spontaneously born beings;

and no brāḥmaṇas or śramaṇas who have understood and taught about this world and the world beyond.[85] Such a view, the Buddha explains elsewhere, "causes unwholesome states to increase and wholesome states to diminish,"[86] and as we know, it is a central tenet of Buddhism's "karmic eschatology" that unwholesome states lead to unfortunate rebirths. Furthermore, such a view is demonstrably wrong, or at the very least, unprovable. The *Pāyāsi Sutta* (*Discourse on Pāyāsi*) describes a debate between the Buddha's disciple Kumāra-Kassapa and an avowedly materialist king, in which the king argues for his view by noting that despite his entreaties, no deceased friend or relative has ever appeared to assure him of the existence of an afterlife. He also suggests a number of particularly cruel experiments he might conduct, mostly involving the execution of convicted felons, whereby one might demonstrate "empirically" that when someone dies, no mind or soul is observed to leave the body and that as a result there is no survival of death. Kassapa rejects these and other arguments by Pāyāsi through a series of parables illustrating how absence of evidence is not evidence of absence, and in the case at hand, he argues that the nonobservability or unmeasurability of the departure of consciousness at death cannot show that no such event occurs, because consciousness is immaterial, hence beyond ordinary empirical detection. It is, however, visible to the divine eye of an awakened being, so while there is no empirical evidence against rebirth, there *is* empirical evidence in its favor. In the end, Pāyāsi converts to Buddhism, and is reborn in a lesser heaven, where he fully repents of his previous view.[87] For those who do not abandon wrong view, the postmortem destiny is dire: in the *Lohicca Sutta* (*Discourse to Lohicca*), the Buddha remarks, "I declare that wrong view leads to one of two destinies—hell or an animal rebirth."[88]

If "wrong view" is defined variously by the Buddha, with materialist perspectives often in the forefront, its converse, right view, is also given various contours. The most detailed discussion of the idea is found in the *Sammādiṭṭhi Sutta* (*Discourse on Right View*), which specifies that right view includes understanding of: wholesome and unwholesome actions, physical and mental nutriment, the four noble truths, aging and death, birth, clinging, craving, contact, the six sense faculties, consciousness, formations, ignorance, and taints.[89] Implicit here, and at many places in the canon, is the identification of right view with the key doctrine of dependent origination—whereby the rising and cessation of various causal factors is described. Thus, in the *Mahāhatthipadopama Sutta* (*Discourse on the Simile of the Elephant's Footprint*), the Buddha states that "one who sees dependent origination sees the Dhamma; one who sees Dhamma sees dependent origination."[90] Dependent origination is linked directly to right view in the *Kaccānagotta Sutta* (*Discourse to Kaccāna*), which describes the twelve links of dependent origination (to be discussed in chapter 5) as marking a middle way between eternalism (the belief in a persisting self or substance) and nihilism (the view that there is no causal regularity, let alone rebirth), hence definitive of right view.[91] Elsewhere, right view is implicitly linked to the recognition that all saṃsāric phenomena are marked by the three characteristics of existents, namely, that they are impermanent (*anicca*, Skt. *anitya*), suffering, and without self (P. *anattā*, Skt. *anātman*).[92] In many traditions, both early and late, the third of these characteristics, no-self, would come to be seen as the single understanding most conducive to uprooting defilements and attaining liberation, hence implicitly definitive of right view.

As in the case of wrong view, however, so in the case of right view there are numerous passages where acceptance of the saṃsāra-karma-mokṣa cosmology is determinative. Thus, in the *Mahācattārīsaka Sutta* (*Discourse on the Great Forty*), the Buddha specifies that right view consists in understanding the opposite of the materialist view. Thus, what is given, offered, and sacrificed, the results of good and bad actions, this world and world beyond, mother and father, spontaneously born beings, and brāḥmaṇas or śramaṇas who have understood and taught about this world and the world beyond—all are quite real.[93] The *Sevitabbāsevitabba Sutta* (*Discourse on What Is to Be Cultivated and Not to Be Cultivated*) identifies right view with the opposite of materialism, and specifies that the latter view "causes unwholesome states to increase and wholesome states to diminish."[94] Thus, although rejection or acceptance of the Buddha's "karmic eschatology" is not exhaustive of early Buddhist understandings of wrong view and right view, respectively, it is a key component of such understandings, and provides further evidence that it is difficult to make sense of Śākyamuni's teaching without reference to the saṃsāra-karma-mokṣa cosmology.

Three Scholarly Counterarguments

The evidence in the Mainstream canons notwithstanding, not every scholar agrees that the Buddha promoted a karmic eschatology. Those who assert that rebirth was less important to him than we have been led to believe usually argue either that (1) the *earliest* Buddhist texts do not prominently feature rebirth, (2) those early suttas show the Buddha to be far less interested in "right" view than in overcoming all views, including those of metaphysicians and cosmologists, or (3) even if the Buddha did teach rebirth, it was merely as a sop to the conventions of his day.

The first two are what we might call *text-stratification arguments*, in that they focus on those sections of the Pāli canon—and the roughly equivalent Sanskritic Āgamas now found in Chinese translation—that for various linguistic, sociological, and doctrinal reasons often are considered older than the other sections. The most commonly discussed of these texts is the *Aṭṭhakavagga* (*Book of Eights*), a compilation of sixteen suttas, mostly in verse, brought together by an unknown editor and later made part of the collection of short discourses called the *Sutta Nipāta*, which itself eventually was included in the fifth part of the Sutta collection, the *Khuddaka Nikāya*.[95] According to Steven Collins, these texts represent "a stage of Buddhist literature before the scholastic 'list-making' tendency came to pervade the whole corpus of the canon."[96] Or, as H. Saddhatissa more forcefully puts it, "They are devoid of [the] pedantry, niggling rules and regulations, [and] repetitive or stereotyped stock formulae which appear elsewhere in later strata of the canonical texts."[97] The two text-stratification arguments may be roughly characterized as the *minimizing-rebirth argument* and the *transcending-views argument*.

The minimizing-rebirth argument does not actually assert that the idea of rebirth is entirely missing from the *Aṭṭhakavagga*, but it does highlight the relative paucity of references to it in the various suttas. In the view of Gil Fronsdal,

> [In the *Book of Eights*,] the common Buddhist concerns of rebirth and ending the cycles of rebirth are primarily discussed in terms of what non-Buddhists believe. The *Book of Eights*' emphasis is on overcoming any longing for any form of future rebirth. In contrast to later Buddhist teachings that are predicated on the belief in rebirth, the *Book of Eights* presents a path of practice—attainable in this lifetime—that appears free from concern with multiple lives.[98]

While it is true that rebirth does not seem as central a concern in the *Aṭṭhakavagga* as in suttas elsewhere in the Pāli canon, there are references in it to the sage's avoiding states of becoming (*bhava*) or their "never returning" from the farther shore, both of which, in a larger Buddhist context, tend to imply future births.[99] Fronsdal implicitly accepts this when he notes that the *Aṭṭhakavagga*'s emphasis is on "overcoming any longing for any form of future rebirth"—which is precisely the point of the Buddha's observation of "the trembling beings of the world given to desire for various states of becoming; they are wrecked who cringe at death, not being free from *craving for* repeated birth."[100] So, while the text may not be preoccupied with the details of a karmic eschatology, there seems little doubt that the prospect of rebirth is accepted as real. If that is so, can a "concern with multiples lives" be very far behind? Indeed, despite the *Aṭṭhakavagga*'s lack of detailed discussion of rebirth, how it occurs, or the way to escape it, the concept was undoubtedly operating in the background and implicitly understood by those who recited or read the text.

The transcending-views argument focuses on the *Aṭṭhakavagga*'s frequent insistence that, as the *Paramaṭṭhika Sutta* (*Discourse on the Ultimate*) notes, the Buddha "does not depend... on knowledge; he does not take sides in the midst of controversy; he has no dogmatic views."[101] Indeed, as he asserts in the *Māgandiya Sutta* (*Discourse for Māgandiya*),

> "I do not say that one attains 'purification' by view, tradition, knowledge, virtue, or ritual nor is it attained without [these]. It is only taking these factors as the means and not grasping at them as ends in themselves that one... attains [purification] and consequently does not crave for rebecoming."[102]

It is possible to read statements like these—along with the Buddha's rejection, in the other parts of the canon, of more detailed speculative theories, such as the sixty-two theories of the *Brahmajāla Sutta*, the views of the six śrāmaṇa teachers outlined in the *Samaññaphala Sutta*, and the ten undecided questions of the *Cūḷamālunkya Sutta* (*Shorter Discourse to Mālunkya*) and other texts—as suggesting that Śākyamuni originally, and most basically, thought of spiritual practice as a psychological, ethical, and empirical undertaking, and that he was in fact not very interested in metaphysics or cosmology for their own sake.[103] It is not much of a stretch to conclude from this that he considered "no view" superior to "right view," and that the vast array of cosmological and metaphysical teachings he promulgated was a mere expedient, famously likened to a "raft" that takes us across the river of saṃsāra to the far shore of nirvāṇa, which may be discarded once the goal has been reached.[104] An implication of this approach is that the saṃsāra-karma-mokṣa cosmology, including its rebirth eschatology, perhaps need not be taken too literally, for the Buddha himself urged the rejection of all views, whether "right" or "wrong."

Although the rhetoric of transcending views would be picked up by various Mahāyāna thinkers, such as Nāgārjuna,[105] its importance in the discourse of Mainstream Buddhism probably should not be overstated. For instance, in the passage from the *Māgandiya Sutta* cited above, note that the Buddha does not reject "right view" but simply "views"—and the Pāli term *diṭṭhi* (as in the *Brahmajāla*) is often shorthand for the *speculative*, hence mistaken, views that must be contrasted with the correct views propounded by the Buddha, which are based on personal reflection, understanding, and experience. Recall, too, that while he specifies in the *Māgandiya* that purification is not attained through views, traditions, knowledge, virtue, or ritual, he adds, "nor is it attained *without* [these]." Furthermore, if there *is* some sense in which even right view has its limitations, it is not because such a view does not correspond to the way things actually are in the cosmos but because—since grasping and attachment are basic to the perpetuation of our suffering—it is *grasping* at views, not the views themselves, that is pernicious. As the *Māgandiya* passage also states, we should see views as "the means and not [grasp] at them as ends in themselves." If this is so, then "right view" cannot be reduced to a set of philosophical propositions that simply counter "wrong views," because the "rightness" of right view lies less in any literal truth it may articulate (though it certainly may articulate such truths) than in the way it is adopted—without grasping, attachment, or self-righteousness. In this sense, "right view" and "no view" may coalesce, as Paul Fuller puts it, "in a different order of seeing."[106]

A final note on the *Aṭṭhakavagga*: If it is as old as claimed, and if it passes over rebirth or scorns "views" to the degree suggested by the minimizing-rebirth and transcending-views arguments, this would be interesting (if far from conclusive) evidence that the Buddha himself was not perhaps as concerned with the metaphysics of rebirth as later tradition claimed. However, as Fronsdal himself acknowledges, the antiquity of the *Aṭṭhakavagga* cannot, in fact, be conclusively established,[107] and the temptation to regard its outlook and concerns as radically different from those found elsewhere in the Pāli canon should probably be resisted.

Finally, the *rebirth-as-mere-convention* argument acknowledges that the Buddha, as reflected in the early canons, discussed rebirth a great deal and spoke of liberation at least partly in terms of avoidance of future rebirth—but that in using such imagery, he was merely adhering to the standard cosmological conventions of his time, without believing such notions to be essential to the practice of his Dharma, which was above all pragmatic, psychological, and ethical. In his 2015 study, *After Buddhism*, Stephen Batchelor asserts that, as a basic methodological principle, he will

> ... bracket off any [dogmatic statement] attributed to Gotama that could just as well have been said by another wanderer, Jain monk, or brahmin priest of this same period. When he says that a certain action will produce a good or bad result in a future heaven or hell, or when he speaks of bringing to an end the repetitive cycle of rebirth and death in order to attain a final nirvana, I take such utterances to be determined by the common outlook of that time rather than reflecting an intrinsic element of the dharma. I thus give central importance to those teachings in Gotama's dharma that *cannot* be derived from the worldview of fifth century B.C.E. India.[108]

The Buddha was no doubt an original thinker and teacher of the first order, but to deny that he really accepted any of the common cosmological or metaphysical beliefs of his time and place is to set him entirely outside history and culture—a practice that Batchelor himself condemns and seeks to correct, precisely by trying to understand the Buddha as a man very much of his time and place. It not only is unsurprising that the Buddha articulated his vision within the general framework provided by his culture and society; it would be surprising if he did not adhere to many of the assumptions undergirding that framework, including, most prominently, the saṃsāra-karma-mokṣa cosmology. As we have seen, at the time of the Buddha this cosmology was still nascent, and the Buddha himself made vital contributions to the process of thinking systematically, and in detail, about its operations.

In short, despite these arguments, we have no principled reason for asserting that the Buddha did not (a) believe in rebirth, and (b) place it near the center of his way of conceiving the world and what lies beyond it.

CHAPTER 4

Where Rebirth Happens

A Quick Tour of the Buddhist Cosmos

As noted already, the Pāli suttas on which we have been drawing thus far, as well as the more or less equivalent Sanskritic Āgamas found nowadays in Chinese translation, were compiled, collected, and finalized in the last century or two B.C.E. and the early centuries of the Common Era. It is remarkable how much of the basic Buddhist worldview is contained in them, but they were not the only texts being produced in that era. The various Vinaya collections, with their focus on the rules and regulations governing monks and nuns, is at least as old, if not older, and Abhidharma literature (some of it canonical, some of it not), with its focus on systematic metaphysics and psychology, became an increasingly important preoccupation of intellectual elites within the monastic community. All of these literary developments (including the formation of canons) occurred within the context of the rise, within the early Buddhist community, of numerous sects, of which the most important probably were the Mahāsaṅghika, Sthavīravāda (P. Theravāda), Sarvāstivāda, and Saṃmatīya. Each of these, in turn, is divisible into sub-schools, so that the number of Mainstream schools is often said to be eighteen—though if anything, this is an undercount.[109] Furthermore, Mahāyāna sūtras and treatises began to appear as early as the first century B.C.E. In the next three chapters, we will try to deepen our appreciation for early Buddhist ideas about the structure of the cosmos and how rebirth comes about, continuing to focus primarily on material from the Pāli canon, but drawing at times, too, from canonical and post-canonical Abhidharma literature, and occasionally from a Mahāyāna thinker, where it seems fruitful to do so.

As noted in the last chapter, the cosmology espoused by the Buddha was of the saṃsāra-karma-mokṣa variety, admitting of two basic possibilities for living beings: (1) continued rebirth in one or another more or less unsatisfactory realm of saṃsāra or (2) transcendence of suffering and rebirth through attainment of the unchanging peace of nirvāṇa. Since nirvāṇa lies outside the scope of rebirth, we will leave it aside for the moment. As to the cosmos in which rebirth occurs, it is, as we know, broadly divisible into three spheres—those of desire, form, and formlessness—which are further divisible into five or six realms. In the sixfold scheme that we will use here, the realms are those of gods, humans, asuras, hungry ghosts, animals, and hell beings. The god realm is subdivided into twenty-six "heavens," so the cosmos is often said to consist of thirty-one realms, but if we consider the subdivisions of other realms (especially hell), the number is far greater. Since the form and formless spheres are the abode only of that tiny minority who have mastered the four meditative absorptions or the four formless states, respectively, sentient beings, overwhelmingly, reside in the sphere of desire. The demography of the six realms may be imagined as a broad-based pyramid, with vast numbers of sentient beings living in the hells, a slightly smaller contingent in the realm of animals, somewhat fewer among the hungry ghosts, fewer still in the realm of asuras, and considerably fewer in the human world, with those inhabiting the god realms the least numerous of all.[110] This "bottom-heavy" population distribution is, of course, due to the fact that the quality of one's rebirth depends on the quality of one's karma, and most beings, defiled, deluded, and unskillful as they are, accumulate far more negative than positive karma. We will address some of the nuances of karma theory in chapter 6; here, we will briefly survey the six realms of saṃsāra from the lowest to the highest, describing the causes, nature, and duration of experience in each.

The Hells

The Pāli suttas and other early texts typically refer to hell in general terms, as if it were a single, gruesome, subterranean destination to which malefactors of every sort are consigned, but the Buddhist penchant for categorization shows up occasionally in accounts of hell in these sources, as well. The most notable, perhaps, is in the *Devadūta Sutta*, in which those who have ignored the "divine messengers" informing them of the nature of saṃsāra—an infant, old people, sick people, lawbreakers subject to execution, and decaying corpses—and failed to mend their evil ways are consigned to a series of hells whose names only begin to suggest the tortures they entail: Hell, the Great Hell, the Hell of Excrement, the Hell of Hot Embers, the Wood of Sword-Leaf Trees, and the River of Caustic Waters—with a return for further punishment in Hell and the Great Hell. In these hells, one is burned, cooked, flayed, impaled, devoured, and split, and as a result feels "painful, racking, piercing feelings"—yet one "does not die so long as that evil action has not exhausted its result."[111]

Other hells are mentioned singly or in groups elsewhere in the suttas, and in the classical tradition a standard list developed of eight hot hells and eight cold hells, each of which is lower, more miserable, and of longer duration than the one preceding it; the duration of life in the lowest hells is almost beyond calculation. The hot hells are called the Reviving Hell, the Black Thread Hell, the Crushing Hell, the Screaming Hell, the Great Screaming Hell, the Heating Hell, the Great Heating Hell, and worst of all, Avīci, the Uninterrupted Hell. The cold hells, which parallel the hot hells under the earth, are the Blister Hell, the Burst-Blister Hell, the Shivering Hell, the Lamentation Hell, the Chattering-Teeth Hell, the Blue Lotus Hell, the Lotus Hell, and the Great Lotus Hell.[112] Each of these evocatively named destinies is bounded by four directions, and in each direction are four or five sub-hells;[113] with the addition of "occasional" hells, the number of hells easily can run into the hundreds.

The road to hell is paved with any number of possible transgressions,[114] ranging from wrong view, to adultery, to the five "heinous crimes"—matricide, patricide, killing an arhat, wounding a tathāgata, and sowing discord in the saṅgha—but in later traditions, being born there came to be associated above all with expressions of anger and violence, especially killing. Because one's postmortem destiny is determined by the quality of one's actions—one's karma—and because experience in the hells is agonizing to one degree or another, opportunities for performing positive actions while residing there are nearly nonexistent, and at the end of one's tenure there, when the karma that produced the rebirth finally has been exhausted, one is likely to die in abject misery, hence extremely unlikely to generate the sort of positive mind-state conducive to a higher rebirth; indeed, it is far likelier that one will fall into another hell or, at best, into a slightly higher bad rebirth, as an animal or hungry ghost.[115] In short, hell is easy to reach and very hard to leave.

The Animal Realm

Although animals are often mentioned in passing in the Pāli suttas, the animal realm as such is not discussed there nearly as much as the hells (or, for that matter, the heavens). Still, it seems to have been recognized as a possible rebirth right from the beginning of Buddhist tradition, and it is, with the human realm, one of only two destinations that are empirically accessible to all people. Unlike the human realm, it is unequivocally considered an unfortunate rebirth, ranking just above the hells in some schemes and just below the human realm in others.

Although the Buddha remarks, "I do not see any other order of living beings so diversified as those of the animal realm,"[116] animals are often, as in many cultures, broadly divided into those of land, sea, and air, and, in the *Balapaṇḍita Sutta* (*Discourse on Fools and Wise Men*), analyzed in terms of the food they eat or where they are born and die: some (e.g., elephants, horses, cattle, etc.) feed on grass, others (fowl, pigs, dogs, etc.) feed on dung, others (moths, maggots, earthworms, etc.) are born and die in darkness, others (fish, turtles, crocodiles, etc.) are born and die in water, and unspecified others are born and die in filth.[117] As may already be evident from such analyses, most animals live a miserable existence. There are some, such as the serpentine nāgas, that may live long and even prosper, but they are exceptional; the vast majority of animals live lives that are, in Thomas Hobbes's phrase, "nasty, brutish, and short." Their existence is dominated by desire and fear: by the need to acquire food, mate, and find shelter, and by the constant anxiety that they will be killed, whether by other animals or by humans intent on eating or sacrificing them. Because animals are said to lack the intelligence of human beings, the cause for rebirth among them is often said to be wrong view, or ignorance more broadly. Their very ignorance, however, somewhat lessens their karmic burden, for they cannot be held morally responsible in the way that humans and other intelligent creatures can. Indeed, Vasubandhu goes so far as to assert that moral transgression only is possible among humans.[118] Still, like hell beings, animals typically live and die in misery, hence have very little chance of attaining a higher rebirth in their next life.[119]

A final note on animals: although little discussed in the Sutta and Vinaya collections, they do feature prominently in the Jātakas, where many of the Buddha's previous births are said to have been in animal form. Most of these tales are actually meant to illustrate *human* virtues and vices, but they do give further insight into the way early Buddhists understood the nature of animal existence, including the occasional suggestion that some animals may actually be more moral than humans—or at least more moral than the worst of them.[120]

The Hungry Ghost Realm

In early Indic traditions, the Sanskrit term *preta* (P. *peta*) originally seems to have referred to "the departed," that is, the restless soul of anyone who had died and had to be nourished and placated so they might cease troubling the living and take their next rebirth—ideally in a heavenly realm. In Buddhist cosmology, *preta* still could refer to the not-yet-reborn departed, but it came increasingly to refer to a class of beings that might be described as "unhappy spirits" or "hungry ghosts." Although lacking a single physical location, hungry ghosts came to comprise a miserable "realm" of their own. Often dwelling in deserts, forests, bogs, cemeteries, or other inhospitable places, they generally remained out of sight to humans, but might be encountered by those with whom they had special karmic connections (such as family members) or those possessed of supernal vision, like arhats. The sufferings of hungry ghosts are not detailed much in the Mainstream suttas and Āgamas, but, as noted earlier, their miseries—and the misdeeds leading to them—are detailed at length in the late canonical *Petavatthu*, and are mentioned, as well, in another late text, the *Milindapañhā* (*Questions of King Milinda*). In the latter, hungry ghosts are described generally as having:

> body and limbs lean and rugged and dark, with head swollen, bloated, and full of holes, hungry and thirsty, odd and dreadful in colour and form, their ears all torn and their eyes ever winking, their limbs a mass of mortifying sores, their whole body the prey of maggots, their stomach all scorching and hot like a fiery furnace blazing in the breeze, yet with a mouth no larger than [the eye of] a needle so that their thirst can never cease; with no place of refuge to fly to, no protector to help them, groaning and weeping and crying out for mercy, [they wander] wailing o'er the earth.[121]

The *Milindapañhā* also identifies four subdivisions of hungry ghosts, which are detailed in the *Petavatthu*: the *vantāsikā*, who feed on vomit, the *khuppipāsino*, who are overcome by hunger and thirst, the *nijjhāmataṇhikā*, who may experience pleasure during the day and misery at night, and the *paradattūpajīvino*, who suffer greatly but are able to subsist on food offerings provided by humans—much as the *pretas* of early Indian traditions did.[122] Not surprisingly, the karma that leads to birth in the hungry ghost realm is quite negative. The *Aṭānāṭiyā Sutta* (*Discourse on Aṭānāṭā*) specifies that those destined to be hungry ghosts are "abusive speakers, slanderers, murderous and greedy folk, thieves and cunning tricksters all";[123] in later times, a hungry ghost rebirth is typically said to stem from the exercise of greed and miserliness—and the unquenchable hunger and thirst experienced by ghosts is a not-so-subtle reminder of the virtue of generosity—especially but not solely toward the Buddhist monastic community. As with the hells, the duration of a hungry-ghost-realm life is exceedingly long—by one calculation, on the order of 5,475,00 human years.[124]

The Asura Realm

The realm of asuras (literally, "non-gods" or "anti-gods") is perhaps the least fixed and stable part of the Buddhist cosmos. Indeed, as noted earlier, for most Mainstream Buddhist traditions, it does not constitute a distinct region of rebirth on a par with the hell, animal, hungry ghost, human, and god realms. As significant figures in Indic pantheons from the Vedic period onward, asuras were recognized and identified from the very beginning of Buddhist literature, but the way they were understood varied from source to source. This variability reflects the multiple connotations of the term *asura* in the broader Indic setting, which boil down to two different but partially overlapping concepts: (1) asuras as antigods, the "titans" of Hindu mythology who were overthrown by the Vedic gods, led by Indra, but continued to struggle with them for control of heaven and earth and possession of the nectar of immortality, and (2) asuras as demons, a class of miserable, malevolent entities who perpetually trouble beings of all sorts but especially gods and humans. Asuras-as-demons tend to have no fixed abode, though they are sometimes associated with hungry ghosts, and because of their status as "tormented spirits," they are quite clearly regarded as living in the lower realms of saṃsāra, above hell beings, animals, and hungry ghosts but below humans and gods.[125] Asuras-as-antigods, on the other hand, are typically found living in the ocean where Meru, the axial mountain of the traditional South Asian cosmos, slopes into the sea, having been relegated there after losing their war with the gods.[126] Thus located—and defined as much by their great power and longevity as their jealousy, dissatisfaction, fear, and aggressiveness—they constitute one of the higher realms of saṃsāra, above that of humans but below those of the various classes of gods.

It is asuras-as-antigods that are encountered most commonly in the Pāli canon and equivalent collections. They are, like beings in every realm, divisible into different classes; their chief is sometimes said to be Rāhu, the planetary deity that in Vedic astrology effects eclipses.[127] The nature of their experience is seldom discussed in detail in the early canonical literature, but we can discern from a host of references that they are (as in Hindu mythology) considered powerful, ambitious, war-like, and possessed of magical abilities, which they use repeatedly to try and wrest power from the gods—only to face inevitable defeat. Nor is the karma that leads to an asura rebirth often mentioned, though in the *Pāṭikaputta Sutta* (*Discourse on Pāṭikaputta*) the Buddha predicts that the "dog-man" Korakkhattia, whose ascetic practice consists of crawling on all fours and eating off the ground, "will die in seven days from indigestion and... will reappear among the Kalanañja asuras... the very lowest grade of asuras."[128] More generally, especially in later scholastic traditions, rebirth as an asura is said to be the result of such negative traits as envy, fear, arrogance, and haughtiness—mixed with certain positive qualities, which endow asuras with intelligence, wealth, and power. Unfortunately, their emotional afflictions tend to override their discernment, so they can neither enjoy their lives nor apprehend the truth.[129] And, like the inhabitants of other delusion-besotted realms, asuras have a hard time moving to higher realms in their next life.

The Human Realm

The human realm is, of course, the locale for most of the events depicted in the Mainstream Buddhist canons, and while the texts do not analyze it in quite the same way as the other realms, they have much to say about its nature, importance, and divisions. One point that is utterly clear throughout all of Buddhist literature is that the human world is counted as an upper realm, ranked beneath the god realms in terms of the pleasure, power, and longevity of its denizens but actually superior to the heavens in the opportunities it presents for understanding the nature of things, practicing Dharma, and attaining nirvāṇa—it is not, after all, for no reason that buddhas appear as human beings. Human existence is quite varied, but is broadly characterized by a mixture of physical and mental pleasure and pain and by the fundamental intelligence possessed by humans; indeed, the Sanskrit and Pāli word for "human" (*manuṣya* and *manussa*, respectively) is etymologically related to the verbal root for thinking (*man*). Unlike beings in the lower realms, humans are not so overwhelmed by suffering as to be incapable of intellectual discernment or wholesome action, and unlike the gods, they are not so caught up in pleasure and power as to ignore the very real suffering they endure—typically, these include birth, sickness, aging, death, separation from what is loved, encountering what is unpleasant, and not getting what one wants.

Like any rebirth in an upper realm, a human birth is difficult to attain: in an early and well-known simile, the odds of its occurrence are likened to the chances that a blind turtle that swims randomly beneath the great ocean and only pokes its head up for air once a century will, when it comes up, happen to put its head through the hole in a wooden yoke that is floating randomly on the surface of the same ocean.[130] Once it is attained, human life is short compared to that of beings in most other realms: the *Aṅguttara Nikāya* describes its brevity as like that of a dewdrop at sunrise, a bubble in a pool of rainwater, a swiftly rushing mountain stream, or a line drawn on water by a stick. Indeed, like a cow on its way to slaughter, we draw closer to death with every step we take.[131] Although in principle human life may last up to a hundred years, karmic circumstances make its exact duration difficult to discern; as a familiar saying goes, "it is hard to know which will come first:

tomorrow or the next life." Because death is certain and its timing is not, and because a human rebirth is such a rare and precious attainment, it is urgent that we use it well: to understand the four noble truths, undertake wholesome action, practice meditation, and attain liberation.[132]

The human realm is distributed among four "continents" (each flanked by two subcontinents) found in the four cardinal directions at the base of Mount Meru; of these, the southern continent, Jambudvīpa (Rose-Apple Island), is of greatest concern, for that is where buddhas appear and teach; the other three continents, though home to humans with longer life spans, are not thus blessed. Depending on the context, Mainstream canonical texts divide residents of Jambudvīpa into various social groups, for instance by sex (male, female, and neither), caste (brāḥmaṇa, kṣatriya, vaiśya, śūdra), religious practice (brāḥmanas and śramaṇas), wealth (rich and poor), appearance (beautiful and ugly), and so forth. The Buddhist community is broadly divided into laymen, laywomen, novice monks, novice nuns, fully ordained monks, and fully ordained nuns. Each of these may be subdivided: fully ordained monks, for instance, may be classified by their domicile (town or forest), their practice inclinations (toward either study or meditation), or their level of spiritual attainment (stream-enterer, once-returner, nonreturner, or arhat). Arhats may be further subdivided in numerous ways, by their level of meditative attainment, as described earlier, or by their involvement with community: those who attain liberation through hearing and applying Buddhist teachings, and live in community are *savakas* (Skt. *śrāvaka*, "hearers"), while those who attain liberation on their own and live "rhinoceros-like," far from any saṅgha, are *paccekabuddhas* (Skt. *pratyekabuddha*, "solitary buddhas"). Since the human realm is an upper realm, the karma that leads to birth in it must be primarily positive: typically, it involves the prior practice of three virtues: generosity (especially but not solely toward the monastic community), morality (as defined by the opposites of the ten nonvirtues), and meditation,[133] though the latter is not, perhaps, quite as crucial. The social, behavioral, and physical differences evident among people are explained by the

Buddha as due to the mixture of positive and negative karma that a given being brings to their human rebirth.[134]

An Excursus on Female Rebirth

One outcome of this mixture of positive and negative karma that requires some comment is in the realm of sex and gender, particularly as concerns females. To be born human is, of course, a good thing, but to be born as a human female seems an especially mixed lot. The Pāli canon shows marked ambivalence toward females, combining overtly misogynistic passages with those that expound women's virtues—not only the worldly but the spiritual, too. At the very least, it is evident that to be reborn female is not an especially happy destiny. The Buddha does acknowledge the various domestic and moral virtues displayed by women, repeatedly asserts their ability to be born in the higher realms, and even goes so far as to describe women as "the best of goods" and assert that "A woman . . . / May turn out better than a man."[135] However, he also specifies various disadvantages to being born female. Women cannot, for instance, typically participate in public life, because they are said to be anger prone, envious, miserly, and unwise.[136] In her domestic life, a woman is constantly beset by worries about the status of her birth-family, the status of the family into which she has married, whether she will have female rivals, whether she will bear sons, and how to exercise control over her husband.[137] Further, a woman is prone to five specifically "female troubles," suffering on account of separation from her birth-family after marriage, menstruation, pregnancy, giving birth, and service to men.[138] On a more cosmic scale, the Buddha asserts in the *Bahudhātuka Sutta* (*Discourse on the Many Kinds of Elements*) that a woman can never be a buddha, a wheel-turning monarch, or a powerful deity like Indra, Māra, or Brahmā—or, more properly, such beings never appear in female form.[139]

Arguably the most blatantly misogynistic passage in the canon is found in a verse attributed to the Buddha: "Women are the stain of the holy life: / Here menfolk are enmeshed."[140] He explains this attitude elsewhere, saying, "Bhikkhus, I do not see even one other form that is as tantalizing, sensuous, intoxicating, captivating, as much of an obstacle to achieving unsurpassed security from bondage as the form of a woman."[141] In the *Cātumā Sutta* (*The Discourse at Cātumā*), the Buddha likens women to sharks, preying upon the undisciplined monk who goes to a village, and there "sees... a woman lightly clothed, lightly dressed. When he sees such a woman, lust infects his mind... [and] he forsakes the training and reverts to the low life."[142] Although much blame for such situations is laid at the feet of women, who are said to be impossible to satisfy when it comes to either sex or childbearing[143] and often are directly or symbolically associated with worldly life, it is also clear that men bear some responsibility, too, for, as the Buddha suggests at one point to his cousin and attendant Ānanda, they must maintain discipline in the face of female temptation. Indeed, in the end the problem isn't so much women or men as it is sexual desire, which from the standpoint of monastic values can all-too-easily undermine the spiritual life of either men or women.[144] Because the Mainstream canons, and Buddhist texts generally, were for the most part composed by men for a male audience, it is unsurprising that women are disparaged there more often than men, for they are seen to pose a major moral and behavioral challenge to the texts' primary listeners or readers. The Buddha's most famous advice on such matters is found in the *Mahāparinibbāna Sutta* (*Great Discourse on the Final Nirvāṇa*), where in reply to Ānanda's inquiry about how to act toward women, he replies:

> "Do not see them, Ānanda."
> "But what if we see them, how should we behave, Lord?"
> "Do not speak to them, Ānanda."
> "But if they speak to us, Lord, how should we behave?"
> "Practice mindfulness, Ānanda."[145]

It is for such reasons that, based primarily on social considerations, the Buddha famously expressed reluctance to found a monastic order for women—a *bhikkhunī* (Skt. *bhikṣunī*) saṅgha. He was importuned to do so by the women of his native kingdom of Śākya, led by his stepmother Mahāprajāpatī, but he repeatedly refused the request, acceding only after the intervention of Ānanda—and then establishing for ordained nuns a set of eight "heavy rules" that clearly subordinated them to the male saṅgha.[146] From the Buddha's willingness to found a female order, it is quite clear that he regarded women as capable of seriously practicing the Buddhist path and seeing it through to completion by becoming arhats, fully liberated from saṃsāra. The suttas are replete with accounts of virtuous and accomplished bhikkhunīs, who receive full Buddhist teachings, give advice and counsel, "[teach]... the deathless state," accept offerings from laypeople, and attain not only higher rebirths but any and all of the four spiritual "fruits," becoming stream-enterers, once-returners, non-returners, or fully liberated arhats.[147] According to the *Mahāparinibbāna Sutta*, a buddha never passes away until his fourfold saṅgha—monks, nuns, laymen, and laywomen—are "accomplished, trained, skilled, learned, knowers of Dhamma... who will pass on what they have gained from their Teacher... and teach the Dhamma of wondrous effect."[148] Thus, because both male and female followers of the Buddha have become accomplished as befits their station, he is, as the saying goes, able to "die in peace"; if there were no accomplished female practitioners, he could not do so. Indeed, he affirms in the *Mahāvaccagotta Sutta* (*Greater Discourse to Vaccagotta*) that, let alone one,

> "there are not only one hundred... or five hundred, but far more bhikkhunīs... who by realizing by themselves with direct knowledge here and now enter upon and abide in the deliverance of mind and deliverance by wisdom that are taintless with the destruction of the taints."[149]

The two most significant early affirmations of the full spiritual capacity of females are found in two partially overlapping collections, the *Bhikkunīsaṃyutta* (*Connected Discourses on Bhikkhunīs*) in the *Saṃyutta Nikāya*, and the *Therīgāthā* (*Songs of the Female Elders*) in the *Khuddaka Nikāya*.[150] Each of these sources (along with their commentaries) presents the stories and songs of awakened female monastics, eleven in the case of the *Bhikkunīsaṃyutta*, 101 (seventy-three identifiable) in the case of the *Therīgāthā*. Those found in the *Bhikkunīsaṃyutta* are framed by stories, all of which involve the nuns' conversations with and triumphs over Māra. To cite just one example, the bhikkhuni Somā's attainment is challenged by Māra, who argues, "That state so hard to achieve / Which is to be attained by the seers, / Can't be attained by a woman / With her two-fingered wisdom." Refusing to fall into the trap, Somā replies,

"What does womanhood matter at all
When the mind is concentrated well,
When mind flows on steadily
As one sees correctly into Dhamma.

"One to whom it might occur,
'I'm a woman' or 'I'm a man'
Or 'I'm anything at all' -
Is fit for Māra to address."

"Then," adds the text, "Māra the Evil One, realizing, 'The bhikkhuni Somā knows me,' sad and disappointed, disappeared right there"[151]—just as he did when defeated on the night of the Buddha's awakening. Some of the most striking poems in the *Therīgāthā* are first-person celebrations of spiritual attainment, which echo, in their own way, the metaphorical "song of victory" attributed to the Buddha, with its imagery of the destruction of the house of saṃsāra. Here, just three examples must suffice. Dhammā sings, "Wandering about for alms, / but weak, leaning on a stick with limbs shaking, / I fell to the ground right there, / and seeing the danger in the body, my heart was freed."[152] Sihā dramatically recounts how:

Thin, pallid, and wan, I wandered for seven years.
I did not experience happiness by day or night,
intense suffering was what I had.

Taking a rope, I went to the forest, thinking
"It is better to hang than live this low life."

I made the noose strong and tied it to a branch,
but just as I looped it around my neck, my mind was set free.[153]

Finally, there is this, from Uttamā:

I enjoy whatever I want
that which is empty, without mark or measure,
I am a true daughter of the Buddha,
always delighting in nibbana.

The urge for all sensual pleasures is cut off,
whether they be heavenly or human,
the swirl of rebirth is completely finished,
now there is no more birth ahead.[154]

In short, a female rebirth in the human realm is far from ideal, but whatever social oppression women may have to suffer, if they become lay followers of the Buddha, they can gain higher rebirths, and if they take ordination, they can experience the full fruits of the spiritual life, becoming arhats just as surely as men can.

The Heavens

Like hell, heaven is often described in Mainstream Buddhist literature as a generalized "good destination" to reach after death, where life is long and the pleasure and power one enjoys there as a deity, or god (*deva*), are far greater than in the human realm.[155] In this sense, Buddhist conceptions of heaven are continuous with those of Vedic cosmology, with the corollary belief that heaven is a reward for proper action—good karma—performed during one's human lifetime. For instance, a male reborn in one of the lower heavens is said to be "accompanied by a retinue of celestial nymphs, [enjoying] himself supplied and endowed with the five cords of celestial pleasure."[156] Deities in the higher heavens partake of the sublime joys of meditation, which far outstrip those of mere sensual pleasure. Like many of the Upaniṣads, however, Buddhist texts make it clear that heaven is *not* the apex of possibility for sentient beings—a designation reserved solely for nirvāṇa. Furthermore, as suggested above, the mental and physical pleasure, the often-magical powers, and the great longevity typical of heavenly worlds can be a subtle trap, lulling the gods into complacency while obscuring from them the truth that even the highest heaven is still within the compass of saṃsāra. Indeed, as long and pleasant as a godly existence is, at least some deities, near the end of their karmically apportioned sojourn in heaven, experience signs of the impermanence of their status: their garlands begin to fade, their bodies begin to smell badly, and they have visions of the realm into which they next will be born—which may well be a considerably lower one.

As with the hells, Buddhists delighted in lavishly detailing the heavens. Located on or above the upper slopes of Mount Meru, they are divided into a multitude of specialized god realms, with the usual count being twenty-six.[157] Of these, six are contained within the highest reaches of the sphere of desire: the Heaven of the Four Great Kings, the Heaven of the Thirty-Three Gods, the Heaven of Yāma, the Heaven of Contented Deities (Tuṣita), the Heaven of Gods Delighting in Creation, and the Heaven of Gods Wielding Power over Others' Creations. Two are of special note. The Heaven of the Thirty-Three is a pleasurable abode presided over by great gods of the Vedic pantheon, of whom Indra, or Śakra, is the chief.[158] It is located on the summit of Mount Meru; thus, the deities in most every heaven above it dwell in aerial mansions (*vimāna*), which are described in detail in the late canonical *Vimānavatthu*. Tuṣita, the Heaven of Contented Deities, is where a bodhisattva, having completed all their rebirths but one, resides until it is time to descend to earth for the life in which they will become a buddha. Under the sway of one or another desire-sphere deity are a variety of minor deities who figure in human affairs, such as *gandharvas*, *yakṣas*, *kinnaras*, *mahoragas*, and others.

The sphere of form contains sixteen heavens, which are occupied typically, if not exclusively, by deities who have mastered one or more of the four levels of meditative absorption: three Brahmā heavens; three heavens marked by increasing levels of divine radiance; three heavens marked by increasing levels of divine glory; heavens occupied by, respectively, "very fruitful gods" and gods without cognitive faculties;[159] and five "pure abodes," which are limited to non-returners and arhats: the heavens of unfalling gods, untroubled gods, beautiful gods, and clear-sighted gods, as well as the Highest Heaven (Akaniṣṭha). The form-sphere deities often are referred to collectively as Brahmās, and certainly this name designates multiple deities for Buddhists. It may, for instance, refer to Brahmā Sahampati, who with Śakra requested the Buddha to turn the wheel of Dharma and is an earnest disciple of Buddhism, or it may refer to the Brahmā recognized as creator of the universe in many Hindu traditions—who, from a Buddhist perspective, merely *thinks* he is the creator but is not, since things come into being through multiple causes and conditions, not a single maker.[160] Finally, there are four heavens related to the sphere of formlessness, which are occupied by those who die in the midst of one of the four formless meditative absorptions: infinite space, infinite consciousness, nothing whatsoever, and neither-perception-nor-nonperception.

The karma said to result in a rebirth in one of the heavens is not unlike that prescribed for those who would attain the human realm: practice of the ten virtues that are the opposite of the three nonvirtues of body, four of speech, and three of mind;[161] proper observance of the five lay precepts; action on the basis of moral shame and moral dread; acceptance of the theory of karma; faith in the Buddha and his teachings; and performing acts of generosity, including making donations to the saṅgha and, if one has the means, undertaking public-works projects. As desirable as a heavenly rebirth may seem, however, and despite the pleasures that are promised to the virtuous, it is not the final destination on any sentient being's spiritual journey—which only can end in arhatship, the state in which saṃsāra has been completely transcended, hence rebirth is no longer a requirement. In that sense, even the most sublime of the god realms is still under the aegis of the truth of suffering—for any being that "appropriates" the aggregates that constitute a "person" is by definition subject to impermanence, hence to suffering, whether in the present or in the future.

Before turning in the next chapter to an account of *how* the process of rebirth is said to occur, we should note briefly a number of key points about the cosmology we have just described.

- First, however long lasting any particular rebirth may be, it is *never* eternal. Thus, both hellish and heavenly existences will expire when the karma that has produced them has been exhausted.
- Second, as intimated above, the process of rebirth is not "evolutionary," in that, depending on one's karma, a high rebirth may well be followed by a lower one.[162] In this sense, the rebirth process may be likened to the motion of a ferris wheel, where we may be at the top one moment and at the bottom the next.
- Third, all the realms of saṃsāra, however appealing they may seem, are by their very nature shot through with suffering, since they are impermanent, and impermanence always entails either immediate or eventual mental and physical pain.
- Fourth, in the Mainstream Buddhist tradition, and most traditions that developed later, sentience is restricted to beings with bodies, minds, and the capacity for independent locomotion, as well as the ability to suffer. As a result, unlike in Jain tradition, plants (not to mention minerals) do not possess consciousness, hence do not participate in the "drama of sentient existence."[163]
- Fifth, although it is commonly recognized in Buddhist literature that there is a sense in which humans may experience all the realms of saṃsāra within the scope of a single life—suffering physical agonies like those of hell beings, pleasures like those of the gods, and so forth—there is no suggestion in the texts that the realms are merely symbols for various human states

of mind and body. Indeed, it seems quite clear that the vast majority of Buddhists have believed in the actual existence of various postmortem realms, if not in every detail specified by one or another tradition.

CHAPTER 5

How Rebirth Happens

The Twelve Links, Dying, and Being Reborn

In the context of the Abrahamic religions (at least in their mainstream forms), our postmortem existence is determined by the omniscient, omnipotent God who created the universe. Our actions during our single human life may indicate the way we are likely to be judged, as may the degree to which we have developed faith in God, but in the end the decision is God's and God's alone, and by definition it cannot be gainsaid. Buddhists typically deny that the universe and the beings, environments, and events within it are brought into existence by a single creator, insisting instead that we and our worlds come to be through a multiplicity of identifiable causes and conditions, both physical and mental—though the mental causes are the most significant. As the first verse of the *Dhammapada* proclaims, in what is something like a charter for the Buddhist view of reality: "All things have mind as their forerunner; they are founded on mind, they are made up of mind, they are wrought by mind."[164] The causal process that leads to rebirth is typically laid out in the famous formula of the twelve links of dependent origination, the discovery, and undoing, of which the Buddha credits for his awakening in "The Parable of the Ancient City," cited in chapter 3.[165] The twelve-links scheme, in turn, is a spiritually significant instantiation of a more general causal law, also called dependent origination, that in many respects undergirds the Buddhist understanding of how the cosmos works. As the Buddha famously declares, "One who sees dependent origination sees the Dhamma; one who sees the Dhamma sees dependent origination."[166]

The Twelve Links

The Pāli canon contains two famous statements of dependent origination in its more general form. The *Mahāvagga* (*Great Chapter*) section of the Vinaya relates the story of the conversion of Sariputta (Skt. Śāriputra), who would become the disciple of the Buddha most renowned for his wisdom. Previously a disciple of the skeptic Sañjaya, he is brought into the fold not by the Buddha himself but by Assaji (Skt. Aśvajit), one of the Buddha's first five disciples, who, when quizzed by Sariputta on his teacher's doctrine, replies: "Of those dharmas that arise from causes the Tathāgata has declared the cause, and also their cessation; thus spoke the Great Śramaṇa." Because in saṃsāra everything arises from a cause, this is, essentially, a claim to the effect that the Buddha has accounted for everything, though the most obvious reference is to the causes of suffering and their cessation. Sariputta immediately attains arhatship, and when he shares the same teaching with his friend Mogallana (Skt. Maudgalyāyana), the latter also is awakened.[167] The formula uttered by Assaji would later come to be considered both a concise and magically potent statement of the gist of the Dharma, which was recited as a mantra, celebrated in a Mahāyāna sūtra, placed in stūpas as the "dharma body" of the Buddha, and inscribed on the base of countless statues of the late first millennium C.E. Another abstract formulation of dependent origination, encountered frequently in the suttas, runs thusly: "When this exists, that comes to be; with the arising of this, that arises. When this does not exist, that does not come to be; with the cessation of this, that ceases."[168] Put even more abstractly, the formula is: $x \rightarrow y$; $-x \rightarrow -y$. In short, causation operates at every level of the saṃsāric cosmos: the physical, the mental, the moral, and the spiritual. It is clear from the various passages in which this formula occurs, however, that it is usually meant to be understood not in the abstract but as applied to the twelve links of dependent origination, which explain how it is we suffer and are reborn, and whose members arise on the basis of the presence of certain factors, and cease upon the elimination of those factors.

The twelve links are enumerated repeatedly in the Mainstream Buddhist canons,[169] and while there are, of course, variations, there is great consistency overall among the presentations, of which the following, from the *Mahātaṇhasankhaya Sutta* (*Great Discourse on the Destruction of Craving*) is typical:

> "So, bhikkhus, with (1) ignorance as condition, (2) formations [come to be]; with formations as condition, (3) consciousness; with consciousness as condition, (4) mentality-materiality; with mentality-materiality as condition, (5) the sixfold base; with the sixfold base as condition, (6) contact; with contact as condition, (7) feeling; with feeling as condition, (8) craving; with craving as condition, (9) grasping; with grasping as condition, (10) becoming; with becoming as condition, (11) birth; with birth as condition, (12) aging and death, sorrow, lamentation, pain, grief, and despair come to be."[170]

The sutta next describes the links in reverse order, working from aging and death back to ignorance, then moves on to describe how, with the cessation of ignorance, formations cease; with the cessation of formations, consciousness ceases, and so forth, right up to the way in which the cessation of birth entails the cessation of aging and death, and hence sorrow, lamentation, pain, grief, and despair—"this whole mass of suffering"—also cease. To complete the presentation, the "unlinking" of the twelve factors is described in reverse order.[171]

Each of the twelve links, and their connection to the one that follows, requires some clarification. (1) Ignorance may refer to the misguided belief that we possess a permanent self or it may simply mean our ignorance of the four noble truths or the way karma and other vital worldly processes work. Either way, ignorance leads us to act in wholesome or unwholesome ways, and these actions leave in our mindstream (2) karmic formations, or imprints, that are the basis for the subsequent arising of a moment of (3) consciousness. Consciousness, in turn, is implicated with (4) mentality-materiality—more often translated as name-and-form—which is equivalent to the five aggregates that constitute a "person": form, or matter (materiality), and sensations (or feelings), conceptions, mental formations, and consciousness (mentality).[172] Mentality-materiality is the basis for the occurrence of (5) the sixfold base: the visual, auditory, olfactory, gustatory, bodily, and mental faculties that have the power to apprehend sights, sounds, smells, tastes, sensations, and mental objects, respectively. The encounter between sense-faculty and object is referred to as (6) contact, and contact, in turn engenders (7) feeling or sensation, which may be pleasurable, painful, or neutral. Quite naturally, we want to extend pleasurable (or sometimes neutral) feelings, and eliminate painful ones, and the wish to do so is (8) craving, a mental state that comes in three basic kinds: craving for pleasure, craving for particular rebirths, and craving for nonexistence—whether of specific pains or of existence more generally. The active form of craving is (9) grasping, or clinging, the act of holding on to some particular desired sensation or aspiration, which in turns leads to one's (10) becoming, or being, what it is one seeks. Becoming, in turn, leads inevitably to (11) birth, or arising, and (12) aging and death, or the decay and cessation, of whatever one has "become."

Although the twelve links may be understood as playing out within a single lifetime, or even in a single moment,[173] by far the most common interpretation is to see them as an account of how rebirth happens, hence stretching over two, three, or more lives. The three-life version is probably the most widespread. In this explanation, using myself as an example, (1) ignorance and (2) formations belong to Life 1, in which a particular ignorance-based action—anything from a murder to an act of generosity—planted in my mental continuum (specifically in my aggregate of mental formations) becomes the karmic seed for a particular future rebirth in the appropriate realm of saṃsāra—let's say hell or a god realm.[174] The karmic seed might encounter the conditions for that rebirth in the life immediately after the karma was performed, or it may have to remain dormant for many lifetimes before the right moment presents itself. Either way, however, the point where conditions are proper and (3) consciousness combines with biological fluids generated by the father and mother in the act of conception is the point where Life 2 begins. Consciousness combines with the body from conception to death, so (4) name and form, or mentality-materiality—a general way of describing the five aggregates—is woven into the very fabric of our existence. My aggregates are constantly in contact with the external world, with which I interact through (5) the six sense faculties, and that interaction entails (6) contact, followed by resultant (7) feelings, whether of pleasure, pain, or neutrality. Instinctively, I develop (8) craving for the perpetuation of pleasure and the elimination of pain. Proceeding through life thus buffeted by delusion and emotion, I arrive at the cusp of death, fearing annihilation and (9) grasping at the prospect of continued existence. Because I am not yet liberated, that is exactly what I get: the process of (10) becoming, or being, is perpetuated, leading me from Life 2 into Life 3, which begins at the moment of (11) birth—conception, actually—after which every other moment is already part of the process of (12) aging and death. And because I am ignorant of the nature of the whole process, which is codified in the four noble truths and the twelve links, it is certain that during Life 3 I will have many more opportunities to sow karmic seeds for still more rebirths.[175]

There are countless nuances to the operation of the twelve links, which Buddhist thinkers have explored right from the beginning. Probably the most important of these is the analysis of the links into causes and effects. Thus, regardless of how many lives are involved, the *causal* factors are typically said to be ignorance, craving, and grasping; the rest of the factors are resultant: formations, consciousness, name-and-form, the six sense faculties, contact, and feeling all stem from ignorance, while becoming, birth, and aging-and-death all result from grasping, which is based on craving. In that sense, ignorance and craving are the two crucial causal links, often referred to as the two roots, and it is strongly emphasized that it is the elimination of one or the other or both of these causes of suffering that sets in motion the unlinking of the other factors, release from rebirth, and the attainment of liberation. A related mode of analysis divides the links into three defilements (ignorance, craving, and grasping), two actions (formations and becoming), and eight results (consciousness, name-and-form, the six sense faculties, contact, feeling, becoming, birth, and aging-and-death).[176] Still another analysis describes ignorance, formations, and consciousness as projecting factors, name-and-form, the six sense faculties, contact, and feeling as projected factors, craving, grasping, and becoming as proactive factors, and birth and aging-and-death as produced factors.[177] Overall, as Bhikkhu Bodhi takes pains to point out,

> The sequence of factors should not be regarded as a linear causal process in which each factor gives rise to its successor through the simple exercise of efficient causality. The relationship among the factors is always one of complex conditionality rather than linear causation. The conditioning function can include such diverse relations as mutuality (when two factors mutually support each other), necessary antecedence (when one factor must be present for another to arise), [or] distal efficiency (as when a remotely past volitional formation generates consciousness in a new life). Moreover... at selected points in the series the links loop back in ways that reinforce the complexity of the process.[178]

Two final points about the twelve links are worth mentioning. First, the Buddha insists that one of the benefits of comprehending how it works is that by doing so we will be free from obsession with whether and how we existed in the past, whether and how we might exist in the future, and who, precisely, we are in the present—for a precise understanding of dependent origination puts all such questions to rest.[179] And second, as Vasubandhu notes, although dependent origination in general and the twelve links in particular are universally applicable "laws" that are "stable and eternal.... to say that there exists a certain eternal *dharma* called [dependent origination],... is inadmissible."[180] In this sense, neither dependent origination nor the twelve links exist "essentially" any more than other worldly entities or concepts do. Put another way, dependent origination is itself dependently originated.

Other Causes and Conditions

Central as they are, the twelve links are not the only categories through which rebirth is explained by Mainstream Buddhists. The *Paṭṭhāna* (*Conditional Relations*) of the Pāli Abhidhamma collection, for instance, describes twenty-four conditions (P. *paccaya*) through which, in various combinations, things, persons, and events, including rebirth, come to pass—or, more precisely, the eighty-two dhammas that constitute things, persons, and events come to pass. These are: the root, object, predominance, proximity, contiguity, conascence, mutuality, support, decisive support, prenascence, postnascence, repetition, kamma, result, nutriment, faculty, absorption, path, association, dissociation, presence, absence, disappearance, and non-disappearance.[181] Each of these conditions has multiple subsets, and if the *Paṭṭhāna* applied each of them to the eighty-two dhammas (and *their* multiple subsets) described in the Abhidhamma, it would, observes Bhikkhu Sujato, "probably be the largest book ever created, with many billions of combinations."[182] It is less important to describe in detail how these conditions might be used to explain rebirth than it is simply to marvel at the granularity of Buddhist attempts to describe the cosmos as the product of an infinite number of complex, transient mental and physical factors, but the *Abhidhammathasaṅgaha* does provide at least one instance that shows how the process might work, in terms of the factor of dissociation, that is, the factor whereby mental and material aspects of ourselves are kept apart, though related:

> The dissociation condition is threefold: (1) at the moment of rebirth-linking the heart-base is a condition for resultant (mental aggregates), and consciousness and mental factors for conascent matter, by way of conascence; (2) the postnascent consciousness and mental factors for this prenascent material body by way of postnascence; (3) the six bases, in the course of life, for the seven consciousness elements by way of prenascence.[183]

A simpler yet still quite complex notion of causation is expounded by the Sarvāstivāda school, as summarized in Vasubandhu's *Abhidharmakośa* (*Treasury of Abhidharma*). Here, conditioning factors are described in terms of six causes (*hetu*): the acting (*karaṇa*), coexistent (*sahabhu*), parallel (*saṃprayukta*), homogeneous (*sabhaga*), driving (*sarvatraga*), and retributive (*vipāka*) causes. Any of these causes could be analyzed in terms of rebirth processes, but retributive causes are particularly germane because they consist of "bad dharmas and impure good dharmas. . . . [whose] nature is to ripen,"[184] both in this life and future lives. Vasubandhu also describes four conditions (*pratyaya*): causal (*hetu*), immediately preceding (*samanantara*), objective (*alamabana*), and predominant (*adhipati*) conditions.[185] Vasubandhu's listings are generally accepted in the Buddhist logical tradition of Dignāga, Dharmakīrti, and their successors, but other causes and conditions are adduced there, as well. Thus, in his rational defense of the truth of past and future lives and other Buddhist metaphysical claims in his *Pramāṇavārttika* (*Exposition of Epistemic Authority*), Dharmakīrti speaks primarily in terms of substantial causes (*upadāna-hetu*), which are momentary events that must be homogeneous with—that is, of the same type as (*sabhaga*)—the moments preceding and following them; and cooperative conditions (*sahākāriya-pratyaya*), which may be broadly classified as either indispensable or merely assistant. In the particular case of how rebirth happens, Dharmakīrti asserts that the substantial cause is the moment of consciousness immediately preceding the first moment of a new life, while the cooperative conditions include ignorance, craving, karmic formations, and the body. Of these—as in analyses of the twelve links—ignorance and craving are the key conditions: ignorance is the background to our endless succession of deluded acts, while craving is the factor that directly "incites the continuum" of a subsequent rebirth.[186]

The Details of Death and Rebirth

Finally, there are a number of sources that focus on the actual mental and physical processes involved in the transition from one life to the next—on what happens during death and rebirth. Although it is just one fleeting event among many—an event we have experienced countless times before—the moment of death looms large in the Buddhist imagination, for it is the portal between one life and the next, fraught with both danger and possibility. In the *Saccavibhaṅga Sutta* (*Exposition of the Truths*), the Buddha defines death as "the passing of beings out of the various orders of beings, their passing away, dissolution, disappearance, dying, completion of time, dissolution of aggregates, laying down of the body."[187] In the Pāli Abhidhamma tradition, death is defined as "the cutting off of the life faculty (*jīvitindriya*) included within the limits of a single existence."[188] Death may be timely or untimely. Reasons for a timely death include expiration of the standard life span for a being in the realm in which they live, expiration of the karmic force that projected the particular rebirth in which the being finds themselves, and the sudden fruition of a destructive karmic imprint. Untimely death comes about through extrinsic conditions, as when a gust of wind blows out an oil lamp that otherwise would have continued burning.[189]

Because life is short, especially for a human, the opportunity to make spiritual progress may not last long, so the Buddha enjoins his disciples to maintain mindfulness of death, thinking, for instance, "May I live just a day...just [a single breath], so that I may attend to the Blessed One's teaching. I could then accomplish much!"[190] Although we all instinctively fear death, from the Buddha's standpoint, it is only those whose attitudes and actions have been unwholesome that need fear death, for theirs will be a lower rebirth; those who know they have acted well and are "devoid of lust, desire, affection, thirst, passion, and craving for sensual pleasures" are fearless, for they know they will be born into an upper realm.[191] Elsewhere, the Buddha assures his lay disciple Mahānāma that his death will be a good one, because "when a person's mind has been fortified over a long time by faith, virtue, learning, generosity, and wisdom...his body, consisting of form, built up of the four great elements, originating from mother and father, [will fail] but his mind...goes upwards, goes to distinction."[192] Later Indian writers, such as Vasubandhu, go into even greater detail about the moment of death, specifying, for instance, the number of faculties or powers (*indriya*)—physical, mental, and moral—that perish at the end of life of various beings in each of the three spheres of saṃsāra,[193] the part of the body through which consciousness departs at death—higher in the body if the next birth is in a higher realm, lower if the destination is a bad one[194]—and the way in which the physical elements that support the body are "split," or cease to function, just prior to death.[195] Vasubandhu adds a crucial observation: "Although...the state of death...is bodily and mentally 'weak'..., when a person has habitually practiced a certain defilement [or virtue], this defilement [or virtue], thus 'projected,' becomes active at the moment of death," and strongly influences the nature of the next rebirth.[196] Along slightly different lines, the Pāli Abhidhamma tradition recognizes the category of "death-proximate kamma," defined as

> a potent kamma remembered or done shortly before death.... If a person of bad character remembers a good deed [they have] has done, or performs a good deed just before dying, [they] may receive a fortunate rebirth, and conversely, if a good person dwells on an evil deed done earlier, or performs an evil deed just before dying, they may undergo an unhappy rebirth.[197]

Before discussing what happens immediately after death, we must pause for a moment to observe that early Buddhist thinkers were far from unanimous in their accounts of what, precisely, it is that "carries over" from one life to the next, or put more plainly, what it is that is reborn—with the understanding, of course, that what is reborn cannot be a metaphysical substance but, rather, is a succession of impermanent events. Some claim that name-and-form, or mentality-materiality—the five aggregates as a whole—carry over,[198] but this view is not common, because it is generally understood that the aggregate of matter (if not the potentiality for its reappearance) dissolves at death, so what must actually carry on is, in one sense or another, likely to be mental. Of the four mental aggregates—sensation, conception, mental formations, and consciousness—there is well-nigh universal agreement that, at a minimum, the aggregate of consciousness—our basic capacity for moment-to-moment awareness—moves from one life to the next. (Recall that the third of the twelve links of dependent origination, which connotes the moment of rebirth, is simply called "consciousness.") The "transitional" consciousness is sometimes qualified by such special terms as "rebirth-linking consciousness," or said to be aided by such additional factors as a "basis of existence" (*bhavaṅga*) or "obtainer" (*prāpti*) of a future birth.[199] Further, because not only consciousness itself but also various capacities, mental tendencies, and karmic seeds must "continue" in some way for the cosmos to make sense, other aggregates may also be said to continue; thus sensation and recognition are sometimes said to carry over, like consciousness, as a *capacity* required in the next life. The most important carry-over factors, however, are found in the aggregate of mental formations, for that is where memories, positive and negative mental tendencies, and karmic seeds all are "stored" until such time as the conditions are ripe for their fruition, whether in this life or in some future life. Minimally, then, nearly all Buddhists seem to agree that what is reborn is the consciousness aggregate and various factors within the aggregate of mental formations—all of which are immaterial, hence capable of unhindered movement across space and time.[200]

What happens immediately after the moment of death also is a topic of debate among different Buddhist traditions. Although the Pāli canon suggests once or twice that there may be an intermediate state one passes through when one "has laid down this body but has not yet been reborn in another body,"[201] the Theravāda scholastic tradition (like that of several of the Mainstream Sanskritic schools) insists that the moment of death in one life is followed immediately by "birth"—that is, conception—in the next life. The mechanism through which this occurs is called "rebirth-linking" (P. *patisandhi*, Skt. *pratisaṅdhi*), whereby the life continuum (*bhavaṅga*) of the previous life—a current of individuality that has carried us along from beginningless time[202]—links the death-time consciousness and its attendant formations to the first moment of the next life, without any pause.[203] Other Mainstream Buddhist schools, however, including the Sarvāstivāda, insist that we pass through an intermediate state (*anatarābhava*) between one life and the next. Vasubandhu states,

> Between death—that is, the five aggregates of the moment of death—and arising—that is, the five aggregates of the moment of rebirth—there is found an existence—a "body" of five aggregates—that goes to the place of rebirth.[204]

He further specifies that, "being projected by the same action that projects the [future existence], an intermediate being has the form of this being, that is, the being of the realm of rebirth to come after... conception."[205] The intermediate-state being is further described as being (at least in the desire-sphere) the size of a child of five or six, with all faculties fully developed, subsisting on odors—hence its designation as a gandharva (P. *gandhabba*), visible to "creatures of its class" and those with the divine eye, and possessed of supernatural powers.[206] There is no specific time limit to intermediate existence; according to Vasubandhu, the being's life "lasts as long as it does not encounter the coming together of the causes for its rebirth,"[207] though he cites various scholars who assert that it lasts seven days or seven weeks.[208]

"Birth," then, occurs the moment after a transfer has occurred, from either the last moment of a previous life or the last moment of an intermediate-state existence. Buddhist tradition recognizes four modes of birth: from a womb, from an egg, by moisture, and by apparition. The first two are self-evident. Moisture birth is attributed to maggots and other creatures that arise (their tiny eggs unseen) in such putrid environments as rotting corpses, cesspools, or sewers; while apparition is the instantaneous mode of birth for those in the heavens, hells, and certain other settings—including, at times, the human realm. Predictably, most descriptions in the canonical and commentarial literature focus on birth from a womb. The Buddha describes in the *Assalāyana Sutta* (*Discourse to Assalāyana*) how birth, or conception, requires three conditions: "There is a union of the mother and father, and it is the mother's season, and the being to be reborn (the *gandhabba*) is present."[209] According to Vasubandhu, the intermediate-state being intent on rebirth employs the divine eye to locate the karmically appropriate parents in the act of copulation. If he will be born male, he desires the female and feels hostility toward the male; the emotions are reversed for those to be born female, and in either case, craving intercourse with the copulator of the opposite sex, the being enters the womb and installs itself where the "semen and blood"—sperm and ovum—unite. At that point, "the aggregates harden, the intermediate being perishes, and birth arises that is called [rebirth-linking]."[210]

Vasubandhu and others go on to describe life within the womb, analyzing, for instance, how males or females are placed within the womb, how the "assigned" sex may change after conception, and how the embryo develops from month to month.[211] The most detailed early Buddhist account of conception and gestation is found in the *Garbhāvakrānti Sūtra* (*Discourse on Entry into the Womb*), a first- or second-century C.E. text not found in the Pāli canon, which describes the nature of an intermediate-state being, the physical and karmic conditions necessary for conception, the degrees of awareness with which the gandharva enters the womb, the nature of an embryo, the growth of the embryo over the thirty-eight weeks of gestation, and the various ills to which infants—and humans more generally—are prey. The inescapable conclusion is that birth and living both are marked by impermanence and suffering, and are best avoided altogether.[212]

CHAPTER 6

Why Rebirth Happens

The Mysterious Mechanics of Karma

As should already be evident, the "why" of rebirth is found above all in the notion of karma: actions of body, speech, and mind ("projecting karma") that may be either wholesome or unwholesome, and whose results ("ripening karma") are commensurate with the quality of the actions performed. Those results may be experienced either immediately or later in one's present life—as when somebody I have insulted either insults me back or retaliates against me later on—or in a future life—as when I am reborn in hell for committing murder, or heaven for performing acts of generosity. And just as actions I perform now will, when conditions are right, bear fruit in the near or distant future, so experiences I have now result from actions I have performed in the past, either in this life or a previous life.

Broadly speaking, karma is the Buddhist (and Indic) answer to the question whether the universe is "just" or not. The response is an unequivocal "yes," because in the amplitude of time, through our series of rebirths, everything of consequence we do will meet with a fitting reward or punishment, and everything I experience now is "deserved" in the sense that it is a result of actions performed by me at some point in the past.[213] From the Buddhist perspective, karma also is the response to assertions in Hindu and other theistic traditions that there is a single creator responsible for the diversity of the world; rather, asserts Vasubandhu, "the variety of the world arises from karma."[214] In other words, complex results must arise from complex causes, and indeed, for Buddhists the cosmos we inhabit is "created" primarily through the various actions of sentient beings, not by some single deity—whose existence Buddhists consistently take pains to refute.[215]

Karma also may be understood as the moral application of the universal law of dependent origination, in that it indexes a causal sequence in which, from a particular sort of ethically weighted cause (abstractly, "the arising of this"), comes a particular, appropriate experienced result (abstractly, "the arising of that"). Conversely, of course, as with the twelve links, the removal of the cause leads to the removal of the result—and the entire Buddhist path is a systematic effort to remove those causes that lead to suffering in this and future lives. Karma is a mechanism that provides the "energy" to bring about all sorts of experiences, but its fuel is the defilements or delusions that afflict all sentient beings. These may be overtly negative—as in mental states of desire, anger, jealousy, and so forth—or quite positive—as in mental states of love, compassion, generosity, patience, and so forth—but as long as they are governed by an underlying ignorance of "the way things are" (*yathābhūta*), the actions to which they lead will keep us—sometimes higher, sometimes lower—within the compass of rebirth. Thus, it is not sufficient to simply end karma by ceasing to act,[216] for as long as the underlying delusions persist, so will karma, and so will its results, for it is only when the fuel of ignorance and other defilements is exhausted that liberation is possible. Nevertheless, to observe and control karma is a crucial practice—indeed, the entirety of Vinaya literature, and much in the suttas, as well, is focused on proper behavior, or "ethics." And to act properly, we must understand what karma is and how it works, as expressed in both the Pāli canon and later commentarial literature.

Karma in the Pāli Canon

As with so many topics germane to rebirth, the basics of karma are clearly laid out in the canonical sources. In the Pāli canon, the definition of karma is quite simple: as the Buddha puts it, "It is volition, bhikkhus, that I call kamma. For having willed, one acts by body, speech, and mind."[217] Vasubandhu, writing in the Sanskritic tradition clarifies this slightly in his own definition: "[Karma] is volition and what is produced through volition."[218] And what is produced through volition is nearly everything: as the *Dhammapada* reminds us in the seminal passage already cited, "All things have mind as their forerunner; they are founded on mind, they are made up of mind, they are wrought by mind."[219] What is meant by mind, in this context, is one's intentional acts, along with the mental formations they produce—in other words, karma. But if the definition of karma is simple, and if the general relation between positive actions and pleasant results on the one hand, and negative actions and miserable results on the other, is easy to understand, the details of how karma actually operates in the cosmos are arcane to the point of inscrutability. Indeed, the complete mechanics of karma, especially of its fruition, can *never* be fully understood by the unenlightened. The Buddha makes it quite clear that the result of karma is—along with the domains of the buddhas and those in meditative absorption, as well as speculation about "the world," i.e., metaphysics—one of four "inconceivable matters." "One who tries to conceive them," he warns, "would reap either madness or frustration."[220] Along the same lines, a well-known Tibetan saying has it that understanding the depths of emptiness-theory is simple compared to comprehending the full workings of karma—for the latter requires an omniscient mind, or at least the sort of clairvoyant knowledge acquired by the Buddha on the night of his awakening. In this sense, karma is a "mystery" to most of us, but it *is* known by buddhas, and it *does* involve a precise mechanism, albeit an infinitely complex one.

Although we cannot understand karma in its full complexity, and the tradition shies away from attempting to describe it, there are a number of nuances of the concept that are specified in canonical and commentarial literature. For instance, in the *Saṅgīti Sutta* (*Discourse on Chanting Together*), the Buddha specifies that karma is fourfold: (1) good ("white" or "bright") karma, with good results;

(2) bad ("black" or "dark") karma, with bad results; (3) mixed good-and-bad karma, with mixed results; and (4) neither-good-nor-bad karma, which has neither good nor bad results.[221] The key here is the introduction of the notion of mixed karma, which opens the door to a recognition that most beings act with complex motives, which are not often solely good or only bad, and that the results commensurate with mixed actions may, especially in terms of rebirth, be correspondingly mixed.[222] As the Buddha explains elsewhere,

> Here, one performs bodily...verbal...and mental volitional activity that is both afflictive and nonafflictive. As a consequence [one] is reborn in a world that is both afflictive and nonafflictive. When [one] is reborn in such a world, contacts that are both afflictive and nonafflictive touch [one]...[and one] feels feelings that are...mingled pleasure and pain, as in the case of human beings and some devas and some beings in the lower worlds.[223]

Elsewhere, the Buddha adds even greater nuance to the picture, explaining how a single act with mixed motives can lead to complex results in future lives. He speaks, for instance, of a financier of Sāvatthi (Skt. Śrāvasti) who, in the distant past, donated generously to a solitary buddha (*paccekabuddha*), but immediately regretted the action, thinking the money might have been better spent elsewhere. As a result of his generosity, explains the Buddha, he was reborn seven times in heavenly worlds and seven times as a wealthy financier in the same city, but because of his ambivalence about the donation, he was unable to savor the pleasures available in those realms.[224]

Such stories can be, and are, multiplied manyfold. Thus, in the *Cūḷakammavibhanga Sutta* (*Shorter Discourse on the Exposition of Action*), the Buddha describes a variety of humans who either do or do not perform such nonvirtuous acts as killing or injuring living beings, begrudging others their status and happiness, withholding food and wealth from brāḥmaṇas and śramaṇas, disrespecting those worthy of honor, and not asking the wise about proper behavior. He goes on to describe the lower rebirths earned by the nonvirtuous acts and the higher rebirths earned by their virtuous counterparts, but adds the wrinkle that if previous karma dictates that such beings are born human, they will be, respectively, short-lived, ugly, uninfluential, poor, low-caste, or stupid.[225] In short, what we might call the "middle range" of saṃsāra (especially but not solely the human realm) is populated by sentient beings who experience a mixture of pleasure and pain due to their past performance of both good and bad actions. To be born human is definitely the result of positive karma, especially the practice of generosity and morality, yet, some humans are born into wealth and others into poverty; some are beautiful and others ugly; some are intelligent and others stupid; some will live long and others will die young—all as a result of positive or negative actions apart from those projecting the human rebirth itself, actions that determine the specific nature of the human life that is attained.

Karma in Abhidharma and Commentarial Literature

The picture of karma is complicated even further in the Abhidharma collections and the digests of their contents by the likes of Anuruddha, Vasubandhu, and Asaṅga. Indeed, they explore the topic in far greater detail than we can possibly cover here. We will, however, indicate some of the more important analyses found in the Pāli and Sanskritic sources, which provide further listings of types of karma, further explain the notion of intention, delve into the way particular karmas are "weighted," consider questions of individual and collective karma, describe the karma of intermediate-state and hell beings, and reflect on the all-pervasiveness and inescapability of karma.

While the Pāli canon (and its Sanskritic equivalents) focus primarily on the twofold description of karma and karmic results as good ("bright") or bad ("dark"), or the fourfold listing of good, bad, both-good-and-bad, and neither-good-nor-bad karma, the Theravāda Abhidhamma tradition generates further enumerations, such as analyses of karma in terms of (1) functioning, (2) order of ripening, (3) time of ripening, and (4) place of ripening, each of them fourfold.

In terms of (1) functioning, karma is divisible into (a) productive karma, which is "wholesome or unwholesome volition which produces resultant mental states and kamma-born materiality, both at the moment of rebirth-linking and during the course of existence"; (b) supportive karma, which "does not gain an opportunity to produce its own result," but can support and modify the experience of the results of productive karma; (c) obstructive karma, "which cannot produce its own result but nevertheless obstructs and frustrates some other kamma, countering its efficacy or shortening the duration of its pleasant or painful results"; and (d) destructive karma, which is "wholesome or unwholesome kamma [that] supplants other weaker kamma, prevents it from ripening, and instead produces its own result."[226]

In terms of (2) order of ripening, karma is divisible into (a) weighty karma—such as matricide, patricide, and other heinous crimes—which is "of such powerful moral weight that it cannot be replaced by any other kamma as the determinant of rebirth"; (b) death-proximate karma, mentioned earlier, which is "a potent kamma remembered or done shortly before death," potentially affecting the next rebirth; (c) habitual karma, which "is a deed one habitually performs...[which] in the absence of weighty kamma or death-proximate kamma,...generally assumes the rebirth-generative function"; and (d) reserve karma, which is "any other deed...potent enough to take on the role of governing rebirth" in the absence of the other three order-of-ripening-related karmas.[227]

In terms of (3) time of ripening, karma is divisible into (a) immediately effective karma, which "must yield its results in the same existence in which it is performed—otherwise...it becomes defunct"; (b) subsequently effective karma, which "must yield its results in the existence immediately following the one in which it is performed—otherwise...it becomes defunct"; (c) indefinitely effective karma, "which can ripen at any time from the second future existence onwards, whenever it gains an opportunity to produce results"; and (d) defunct karma, which is "kamma that was due to ripen in the present existence or the next existence but did not meet conditions conducive to its maturation." Defunct karma refers primarily to karma in the mindstream of an arhat at the moment of their final passing away.[228]

Finally, karma in terms of (4) place of ripening is divided into (a) unwholesome karma, which is understood chiefly through the traditional list of ten nonvirtues (three of body, four of speech, and three of mind); (b) wholesome karma pertaining to the sense sphere, which can be understood either through the ten virtues that oppose the ten nonvirtues, the three main causes of higher rebirth (giving, morality, and meditation), or ten good practices (the three just named, along with reverence, service, transfer of merit, rejoicing in others' merit, hearing the Dharma, teaching the Dharma, and rectifying one's views); (c) wholesome karma of the form-sphere, which is "purely mental action,... [consisting] in meditation that has reached absorption" in the first, second, third, or fourth meditative absorption; and (d) wholesome karma of the formless sphere, which also is purely mental action, and consists of meditation that has attained the absorptions of infinite space, infinite consciousness, nothing whatsoever, or neither-perception-nor-nonperception.[229]

The Sanskritic tradition also subdivides karma in various ways. Besides the classic fourfold division into good, bad, mixed, and neither,[230] authors like Vasubandhu and Asaṅga analyze karma into such categories as actions that are determinate (with their results definitely to be experienced) or indeterminate (with their results not necessarily to be experienced);[231] actions that are meritorious (tending to the human and some god realms), demeritorious (tending to the lower realms), or immovable (tending to the form and formless spheres);[232] actions bearing fruit in the present, the next, or some future life;[233] and actions related to perception (e.g., seeing), function (e.g., supporting), intention (willing—the very definition of karma), transformation (e.g., making something), or acquisition (direct understanding of the truth).[234]

Because, as we were just reminded, volition is intrinsic to the idea of karma itself, that notion, too, is analyzed in the Abhidharma digests. Thus, Asaṅga describes five types of volition, those that are either (1) occasioned by another's order; (2) occasioned by another's suggestion; (3) performed without knowing right or wrong; (4) performed under the influence of desire, anger, and ignorance; or (5) occasioned by distorted views. The results of the last two, adds Asaṅga, "will necessarily be experienced"; he implies that the results of the first three types of intention are less certain to arise, perhaps because of their moral ambiguity.[235] Vasubandhu, for his part, at one point counts twelve volitions, each of which relates to a specific point on the path to liberation, in particular in the process of detaching oneself from the sphere of desire.[236] Elsewhere, he describes the way in which wholesome or unwholesome volition may coexist with anywhere from one to ten courses of action, as, for instance, "when a person with an angry mind kills and steals at the same time."[237] In yet another passage, in dealing with the transition from one life to the next, he describes the way in which "mental volitional action, which is active, projects a new existence; this new existence, thus projected, is produced from the seed which is consciousness 'informed' through action."[238] It is in this way that karma—which is, at root, volition—leads to rebirth.

One of the most important contributions to karma theory made by later commentators is their articulation of the notion of the "gravity," "weightiness," or "heaviness" (*gaurava*) of karma. Thus, according to Vasubandhu, the moral gravity of a particular action only can be calculated when we take into account the nature of the volition ("to project the thought, 'I shall do this or that'"), the preparation ("bodily or vocal action with view to the [volition]"), the act itself (*adhisthāna*, literally, "the principal"), the field ("the person to whom one does good or evil"), and the "consecutive" (the consequences of action).[239] Asaṅga lays out a similar but even more complex scheme, whereby we must consider an action's domain (i.e., its general social context), its object (the nature of the person on whom one acts), its own-nature (the general moral quality of the act), its base (the moral quality of the actor), attention (the intentness with which the act is performed), intention (the nature of the aspiration involved), assistance (the degree to which one is abetted in the act), frequency (how often one performs the act), and its multiplicity (the action's effect on people other than the object).[240] Additional factors are sometimes adduced, as well, such as the fulfilment of the volition that incited the act and the actor's satisfaction at the act's completion.

Clearly, such fine calibrations go far beyond the "X is good, Y is bad" moral calculus most commonly presented in the suttas. Thus, to take two examples of a broadly negative action, killing, we could consider on the one hand, the actions of Lizzie Borden, who famously "took an axe / and gave her mother forty whacks, / and when she saw what she had done, / she gave her father forty-one." In all possible senses, this is an extremely grave action, from the malice of the volition, to the nature of the victims, to the viciousness and repetitiveness of the action, to the completion of the act, to the actor's satisfaction at the completion of the act. The consequence almost certainly will be rebirth in a hell realm in the next life. Indeed, Vasubandhu cites matricide and patricide as examples of "determinate" action, which is "accomplished through intense defilement," and brings definite results.[241] On the other hand, if I am lying in bed reading on a summer night, and am annoyed and then bitten by a mosquito, and attempt to brush her off but in the process kill her, and feel immediate regret, this remains an act of killing, but the volition is uncertain, the object is of a lesser order of being than one's parents, the manner of killing is not wholehearted, and regret ensues, so that its gravity is considerably less, and such results as it might entail may be mitigated in various ways, for instance through being experienced in a lesser way in this life rather than in a rebirth of which it is the principal cause.[242] In Vasubandhu's terms, my unwitting killing of the mosquito, performed with "weak defilement," might be classed as an "indeterminate" action, the precise retribution for which is uncertain—but which will definitely be milder than for deliberately killing one's parents.[243] Of course, positive actions may be calibrated in the same way: Asaṅga offers the example of giving, which will gain greater or lesser moral weight depending on one's motivation, the object of one's donation, the manner in which the gift is presented, the frequency with which one gives gifts, and so forth.[244] In short, the "gravity" of karma is a key concept for indexing just how complex a calculus is involved in passing moral judgments—complex enough that, in the end, only a buddha can understand it fully.

There are many other questions raised by karma theory that are addressed by the Abhidharma traditions.[245] Here, we can only touch on a few. One set of questions revolves around the sort of karma that may be accumulated by beings outside the morally significant human realm. It might seem that beings in the god realms are capable only of positive actions and beings in the lower realms capable only of negative actions, but Vasubandhu complicates this assumption by asserting that "in the three spheres of existence and in all the realms of rebirth the four types of good and bad action can be produced." He quickly adds, however, that there are some restrictions: outside the sphere of desire, no bad karma is produced, because form- and formless-sphere beings simply rest in their respective meditative absorptions until the karma projecting that existence runs out, while desire-sphere gods, despite their enjoyment of pleasure and power, may commit both good and bad acts. Of the lower realms, Vasubandhu comments only on the hells, asserting that one *can* perform good acts there, but because "there is no agreeable retribution in the hells," the result of one's good action cannot be experienced until a future life, or is indeterminate.[246] And, if positive action is possible at the lowest level of saṃsāra, it certainly can occur among animals and hungry ghosts—though given the suffering experienced in those realms, virtuous acts are probably few and far between. Vasubandhu also considers the karmic situation of intermediate-state beings—whose existence, we may recall, is denied by Theravāda and several other Mainstream Buddhist schools. He asserts that such beings *do* produce karma, but that "these actions bear their results [only] in the present existence"—that is, either in the intermediate state itself or in the rebirth to which the intermediate state is a prelude, since "all these states form, together with the intermediate state, only a single existence."[247]

Another, broader, set of questions concerns the "ownership" of karma. First, is karma solely individual or can it be collective, too? The basic stance of the tradition seems to be that karma is one's own. Thus, in the *Cūḷakammavibhanga Sutta*, the Buddha asserts, "beings are owners of their actions...heirs of their actions; they originate from their actions, are bound to their actions, have actions as their refuge."[248] Asaṅga elaborates on the Sanskrit equivalent of this passage, explaining that beings own and inherit their actions because "they experience the results of actions done by themselves," they originate from their actions because "they are not born without a cause or through an irregular cause," and have actions as a refuge because they are able to connect with "counteractive karmas" that oppose their negative actions.[249] At the same time, the suttas sometimes discuss what came to be known as "collective karma." As the Buddha describes it, "By way of elements...beings come together and unite. Those of wrong view come together and unite with those of wrong view....Those of right view come together and unite with those of right view."[250] In this sense, beings may form "karmic cohorts," but it is clear that collective karma is not some additional type of karma but simply a way of referring to the fact that beings with similar individual karmic tendencies form social groups, whether they be cabals, spiritual communities, castes, or nations. A related question is, can the merit accumulated through positive actions be transferred or shared? On the face of it, just as there is no collective karma above and beyond the karma of like-minded individuals because one's karma is one's own and no one else's, similarly, neither one's karma nor one's merit from positive deeds can actually be shared with another. However, the wish to do so is expressed in countless Buddhist prayers, rituals, and stories. It finds an early, "material" expression in the notion, mentioned in the late canonical *Milindapañhā*, that hungry ghosts may somehow partake of meritorious food offerings dedicated to them by humans, and is reflected in various post-canonical narratives, such as one in which the Buddha's patron, King Bimbisāra, feeds his deceased hungry ghost relatives by dedicating the merit of his food donations to the saṅgha; with this virtuous act, the offerings appear among his relatives to nourish them.[251] In any case, regardless of whether merit actually can be transferred, the intention to do so is itself considered a positive action, and at the very least of benefit to the one who aspires to do so.

A still more significant set of questions revolves around the "universality" of karma. One basic question is posed by Sivaka, who asks the Buddha to respond to the claim that "whatever a person experiences, whether it is pleasant or painful or neither-painful-nor-pleasant, all that is caused by what was done in the past." The Buddha replies unequivocally that such claims "overshoot what one knows by oneself and . . . what is known to be true in the world," for there are, in fact, eight different causes for one's experiences: disorders of bile, phlegm, and wind, and their imbalance, as well as change of climate, careless behavior, assault—and, lastly, karma.[252] Each of the first seven sources of our experiences seems, at least to some degree, to lack the crucial element of volition, since we are not really responsible for changes in our bodily humors or environment, nor for absentmindedness or a sudden assault. Although this is the stance of the early traditions, later thinkers tended to "maximize" karma, suggesting that the physical imbalances, climatic changes, inattentiveness, and assault we might suffer all may be traced to previous actions, such that there is no experience we undergo that lacks a karmic explanation—Vasubandhu, we may recall, asserted that "the variety of the world arises from action."[253] However, whether they assert that only some experiences are caused by previous karma or that all of them are, Buddhists agree that what happens to us results from identifiable causes and conditions.[254]

Conversely, we may ask whether all actions lead to karmic results. In other words, if we perform an action, must we necessarily experience the fruition of that action? The answer is unequivocally "no," since, given beginningless lives, each of us has, literally, an infinity of not-yet-fructified karmic seeds lurking in our mental continuum, so that no matter how many individual actions meet the conditions for their completion, there should always be more, and this would make liberation—Buddhism's central soteriological aim—impossible. While it is generally true that, as the Buddha states, "if a person does an action intentionally, then they will have to experience the results,"[255] the commentarial tradition makes it clear that the meaning of such claims is that one must experience the results of intentional actions "as long as saṃsāra continues"—which adds a crucial qualifier, and shows that, in the words of Bhikkhu Bodhi,

> The Buddha taught that the key to liberation was not the eradication of past kamma... but the elimination of the defilements. Arahants, by terminating the defilements, extinguish the potential for ripening of all their past kamma beyond the residue that might ripen in their final life.[256]

The "residue" a liberated or soon-to-be liberated being experiences in their final life is, above all, the body and the various experiences it undergoes; thus, even the Buddha, after his awakening, was still subject to headaches, illnesses, or accidents, all of which are explained as the outcome of previous negative karma.[257] More crucially, a liberated being, despite thinking, speaking, and performing bodily activities as ordinary beings do, does not "project" any karma that is bound to have results, for—as we saw in our discussion of the twelve links—the bases for the fruition of action are ignorance and craving, which an awakened being has entirely overcome.

CHAPTER 7

A Brief Note on "Popular" Traditions

In our discussion, over the past three chapters, of the realms of saṃsāra, the causal processes involved in life, death, and rebirth, and the complex operations of karma, we have drawn almost exclusively on canonical and post-canonical texts produced within the Mainstream Buddhist schools, especially Theravāda and Sarvāstivāda. Most of these texts were composed by scholarly monastics (overwhelmingly male) primarily for the edification of other scholarly monastics (mostly male), though some of them undoubtedly found their way to laypeople, too, first in oral form and eventually as written texts. The sūtras of the Mainstream canons vary in difficulty: most of them evince literary and philosophical qualities that make them reasonably accessible to an intelligent, though not necessarily literate, audience—whether monastic or lay—while a few are highly technical in their exposition and require a great deal of commentarial unpacking, hence are less "user-friendly." The Abhidharma literature and much of the commentarial tradition, on the other hand, tends toward abstraction, and typically presupposes advanced comprehension of the various concepts and categories into which Buddhist intellectuals divide reality. Even the ordinary educated monk or nun might be hard-pressed to understand these texts, and educated laypeople—let alone the illiterate (who were by far in the majority in ancient India)—would be left almost entirely in the dark.

In this regard, it is useful to remember that over the years—normative values and rhetoric notwithstanding—very few Buddhists, even monastics, have seriously aimed at the tradition's *summum bonum*, nirvāṇa, since the time, discipline, and social circumstances required for the contemplative life that leads to it were difficult to obtain, even in ancient India. Rather, before the modern era, most Buddhist monastics and almost all Buddhist laypeople preoccupied themselves primarily with practicing virtue so as to accumulate merit and gain a favorable rebirth in the next life, ideally in circumstances that would make the quest for awakening more manageable. And, to whatever degree monastics and laypeople attempted to live virtuously—not always an easy matter—they all faced such common sentient woes as illness, natural calamity, dissatisfaction, and death, and, being pragmatic, sought redress from those problems through any method available, including magic. These three "styles" of being Buddhist have been identified by a number of anthropologists, including Melford E. Spiro, who, on the basis of his research in Burma (now Myanmar), called them nibbanic, kammatic, and apotropaic Buddhism; and Geoffrey Samuel, who, working with Tibetan sources, described them as the bodhi, karma, and pragmatic orientations.[258] However termed, these three "ways of being Buddhist" are by no means mutually exclusive, but they do stake out the breadth of the territory that must be considered if we are to understand how Buddhists "on the ground," whether in ancient India or modern Asian societies, actually lived their lives.

Thus, early Indian Buddhists—understanding full well that most of their audience was (a) illiterate, (b) generally uniformed about Buddhist philosophy, and (c) more concerned with allaying worldly ills and/or gaining a good rebirth than attaining nirvāṇa, developed a variety of "popular" images, ideas, and practices that could serve to attract and edify both laypeople and monastics. In using the term "popular," I do not mean to resurrect long-discredited dualities between "elite" and "popular," or "big" and "little," or "universal" and "vernacular" religions; I merely want to signal that there are more and less technical ways of presenting religious ideas and ideals, and that the less technical presentations—which may include specimens of both visual art and literature, and which at their best are marked by aesthetic virtues such as richness of imagery, clarity of presentation, and depth of emotional resonance—may be of benefit to a range of audiences, from intellectual monastics, to ordinary monks and nuns, to wealthy and powerful laypeople, to farmers and other "common folk."

Buddhist Visual Art, the Wheel of Life, and "Karma Stories"

Although Buddhist visual art cannot be traced all the way back to the tradition's inception, it seems to have developed quite early, more or less contemporaneously with the texts, both oral and written, that lay out the contours of the Buddha's view of the world. The earliest Buddhist sites discovered by archeologists, which go back to the third century B.C.E., were monastic complexes of brick or stone that were generally oriented around a stūpa, a large monument, modeled on funeral mounds, that in its simplest versions consisted of a hemisphere, atop which sat a box, surmounted by a parasol. The stūpa was at its inception, and typically remains today, the most sacred part of any monastic complex, for it usually houses relics of the Buddha or one of his great disciples, which are believed in some sense to be "alive," hence worthy of veneration by the faithful. It is on the railings and gateways around stūpas such as those at Sañchi, Amarāvatī, and Bharhut that we find the earliest known Buddhist representational art, in the form of stone-carved reliefs depicting humans, animals, deities, and other beings engaged in various worldly and religious pursuits. We also find depictions of key events in the life of the Buddha, especially his conception, awakening, first teaching, and parinirvāṇa—though at this stage the Buddha is shown aniconically, his place in these events being represented, respectively, by an elephant, a Bodhi Tree, a wheel, and a stūpa. None of these early images provides a systematic guide to Buddhist rebirth cosmology, but it does give plastic form to the ways in which some early Buddhists imagined certain aspects of sentient life. The earliest images of the Buddha himself may have been produced in South Asia in the last century or so B.C.E., but the first securely datable images come from the first or second century of the Common Era, when they began to appear, more or less simultaneously, in Gandhāra in northwest India and Mathura in the north-central region. These images provided at last an iconic representation of the devotional focus of so many Buddhists, and at their best, they are "personally" moving and inspiring in ways that stūpas, for all their sublime proportions and lines, and despite their vivification by the Buddha's relics, never can be.

It is only, however, with the development of paintings of the so-called wheel of life (*bhāvacakra*) that Buddhist cosmology, including the realms of rebirth, comes to be depicted systematically. These images are best known from their ubiquity in Tibetan and other Inner Asian Buddhist settings, where they are typically found on a wall near the main door to a temple. They are not, however, a Tibetan invention, for they have discernible Indian roots. Both the *Mūlasarvāstivāda Vinaya* (*Discipline of the Mūlasarvāstivāda*) and the *Divyāvadāna* (*Divine Stories*), which are datable to the first centuries C.E., relate the tale of a king of the Buddha's time, Udrāyaṇa, who sends a gift of jeweled armor to Bimbisāra, the king of Magadha and one of Sākyamuni's earliest patrons. In reply, on the advice of his ministers, Bimbisāra sends Udrāyaṇa an image of the Buddha, painted on cloth, which includes in its lower portion teachings on refuge and morality, along with a visual depiction of the twelve links of dependent origination and the following verse:

> Take this up and give that up;
> Enter the Buddha's teaching;
> Like an elephant in the lotus pond
> Destroy the forces of Lord Death.
>
> One who mindfully engages
> In this way of discipline
> Will leave the wheel of birth behind
> And bring their suffering to an end.[259]

King Udrāyaṇa is delighted with this gift, comprehends the twelve links and their significance, becomes a follower of the Buddha, and invites Buddhist monks and nuns to his kingdom.[260] In his fifth-century *Visuddhimagga*, Buddhaghosa describes a "wheel of life" in which the hub is ignorance, the outer rim is aging and death, and the ten spokes in between are the links from formations through birth. He specifies that

> all this wheel's spokes (*ara*) were destroyed (*hata*) by [the Buddha] at the Place of Enlightenment...wielding with the hand of faith the axe of knowledge that destroys kamma—because the spokes are thus destroyed he is an arhat. [261]

Buddhaghosa does not specify that the wheel has been rendered artistically, but it is not hard to imagine how it could be. The earliest actual image of a wheel of life that is extant is a wall painting found at the Ajanta complex in western India, in the veranda of Cave 17, which has been dated to the late fifth or early sixth century C.E. Although it has been partly effaced, and we cannot see the hub, we can make out in the middle the panels depicting several of the five or six realms of rebirth, and symbolic images of at least some of the (probably) twelve links near the rim.[262] Whether this was the "original" form of the wheel of life or a stage in its development is unclear, but given the evidence of the *Mūlasarvāstivāda Vinaya*, *Divyāvadāna*, and *Visuddhimagga*, it is likely that actual images of the wheel of life, in one form or another, were part of the Buddhist landscape from a fairly early time.

It is said that the image of the wheel of life at Ajanta was copied in the seventh century by an artist-monk and taken to Tibet, where it became the prototype for Tibetan versions of the painting. It is that image that will be briefly described here. The wheel itself—which is held in the claws of a wrathful, flame-surrounded figure identified as either Māra, the lord of saṃsāra, or Yama, the lord of death—is divided into four concentric circles. Within a circle at the hub are three animals, each biting the tail of the one ahead of it: a pig, representing ignorance; a rooster, representing desire; and a snake, representing anger. These are the traditional "three poisons" that keep the wheel of rebirth turning. A second circle, just outside the hub, is divided into dark and light halves: in the dark half, a series of humanlike beings descend into ever more grotesque forms, while in the light half, beings ascend into ever greater beauty and ease. These represent the two basic types of karma we perform, wholesome (or "bright") and unwholesome (or "dark"). The third circle, which is typically the largest and most striking, is divided into five or six panels, each of which depicts in some detail one of the realms of rebirth. In cases where there are six realms, these are the abodes of gods, asuras, humans, animals, hungry ghosts, and hell beings; where there are five realms, the gods and asuras are found in the same panel, often depicted at war with one another. The upper realms are typically located in the upper part of the circle, the lower realms in the lower part. Sometimes, buddhas are depicted in each of the realms, as a reminder that even in the depths of saṃsāra the prospect of eventual liberation is available to all beings.

The fourth and final circle, in a narrow band at the wheel's outer edge, presents symbols of each of the twelve links of dependent origination. Although there are variations, the most common sequence (usually running clockwise from the top) begins with a blind man feeling his way with a cane (symbolizing ignorance), followed by a potter shaping a vessel (karmic formations), a monkey grasping the branch of a tree (rebirth-consciousness), an oarsman rowing a boat with four passengers (name-and-form, specifically the five aggregates), a house with many windows (the six sense faculties), a man and woman making love (contact), a man with an arrow sticking into his eye (feeling), a man and woman drinking liquor (craving), a woman picking fruit from a tree (grasping), a pregnant woman (becoming), a woman giving birth (birth), and a man carrying a white-shrouded corpse on his back (aging and death). The wheel, in short, is a graphic depiction of the first two noble truths, those of suffering and its origin. The area outside the wheel proper may be embellished in various ways, but often includes, in the upper right corner, a standing buddha who points to the upper left corner, where either another buddha, a Dharma-wheel, or a moon is depicted. The two verses prescribed by the Buddha for the painting sent to King Udrāyaṇa are sometimes written just below the buddha, wheel, or moon. This, of course, indicates the possibility of awakening and the way to gain it—the truths of cessation and path.

Quite apart from such visual depictions of the Buddhist cosmos, early Buddhists not inclined to the rigors of technical philosophy, or wishing to give flesh to the often dry bones of dharma theory, were able to draw on a wide range of story-traditions, most of which have been mentioned before. These are found scattered throughout the Sūtra and Vinaya collections of the Mainstream schools, but are especially prominent in such late-canonical or extra-canonical texts as the *Petavatthu*, with its cautionary tales of the miseries of the hungry ghost realm and the karma that leads to that suffering; the *Vimānavatthu*, with its descriptions of the delights of the heavens and the good deeds that bring them about; the *Jātakas*, with their inspiring stories of the Buddha's practice of virtue in previous lives; and the *Avadānas*, with their narratives (mostly set at the time of the Buddha) about the good and bad actions of a variety of people—famous or infamous, rich or poor, male or female—and their experience of the appropriate results of their actions in this and future lives.[263] Also in this category are early-first-millennium C.E. connected narratives of the Buddha's life, such as the *Buddhacārita*, *Mahāvastu*, *Lalitavistara*, and *Nidānakathā*.[264] Although written down and preserved by educated monks, many of these tales—which could serve either to inspire or terrify, or both—originated in oral traditions and have maintained a "popular" life of their own outside the written texts. Over the course of many centuries in many cultures, they have been recounted in sermons, enacted in rituals, and otherwise utilized to enliven the details of Buddhist cosmology and karma theory within a narrative framework colorful enough that the fear of perdition and the hope of heaven—or even full liberation—are deeply imprinted in the minds and emotions of their listeners or readers. And let us recall that those listeners and readers undoubtedly included both laypeople and monastics—for everyone enjoys a good story.

Scholarly Theories and Popular Practices

The images presented in the wheel of life and the wondrous tales told in the narrative literature did much to inform Buddhists in India and elsewhere about the tradition's normative "karmic eschatology," functioning, like religious art everywhere, to instruct their audiences by instilling in them feelings of pity, awe, terror, delight, and hope. Yet, like religious people everywhere, Indian Buddhists did not always think about life, or live their lives, within the bounds of traditional theory—in part because the human mind cannot always rest content within the straitjacket of conceptual constructs, in part because the theories themselves at times were in tension with elements of human psychology and culture. Two instances of the latter, which highlight the way in which "popular" religion may deviate from the ideal, are deserving of brief mention: the tension between (a) the theory of dependent origination and the appeal of miracles and (b) the theory of the six realms of rebirth and the ubiquity of "ancestor worship."

As noted earlier, dependent origination is, in its abstract formulations, a theory that asserts causal regularity throughout the cosmos and, in its instantiation in the twelve links, assures that the sequence of causes through which suffering arises can be comprehended, controlled, and, through proper practice of the Dharma, undone, thus assuring liberation. It is in part because of this profoundly "rational" core of his teaching that the Buddha, in the *Brahmajāla Sutta*, dismisses as unworthy of performance by his monks a whole slew of what we might call "magical" practices. These include reciting protective, manipulative, or destructive spells; engaging in divination or prophecy, whether through mirrors, young girls, gods, or the bodily signs of animals; employing unproven folk remedies (or even "standard" medicine) to cure illness; learning to control demons; and learning to speak with animals.[265] While the Buddha's rejection of such practices is based in part on the idea that they distract his followers from striving for the more serious but longer-term goal of liberation, his sense that they are—to use modern terms—"superstitious" or "unscientific" probably is in play, too. At the same time, however, in other canonical texts the Buddha offers protective and medicinal mantras for his followers' use, and certain suttas became popular early on for their protective properties. More broadly, as Sam van Schaik observes, "as far back as we can go in the Buddhist manuscript record, we find sources for magical literature," and indeed, the success of Buddhism, in India and elsewhere, seems as closely tied to monks' practice of magical rituals as to their exposition of the Buddha's sublime teaching.[266]

Furthermore, the Mainstream canons are full of tales of superhuman "miracles" performed by the Buddha and his followers, which mostly serve to convert nonbelievers. Granted, the Buddha discouraged the display of such powers by his monks,[267] but the stories remained in the canon, and accounts of superhuman feats became a standard—and very popular—element of Buddhist literature right up to the modern era. It can, of course, be argued that such powers are superhuman but not supernatural, in that they are a "natural" by-product of states of meditative absorption—but that makes them no less wondrous to those who hear or read about them, and leaves people no less likely to believe that, in some mysterious way, awakened beings can circumvent the causal and karmic laws to which we seem so inextricably bound, by aiding us in times of distress or perhaps even transferring their considerable merit to us.[268]

There are a number of ways in which Buddhism seems inimical to what nowadays are called "family values." On the social level, the Buddha and his successors encouraged men and women—both young and old—to abandon their biological families and take up the monastic life, which provided for them a new family, that of the Buddhist saṅgha. On the level of cosmology, the tradition asserted, virtually from the start, that after death, either immediately or within a short period of time, we take rebirth in another form, often in another realm—and that (unlike in many of the smaller scale societies described by anthropologists) the place where we take rebirth has no necessary connection to the family we belonged to in the previous life. In this sense, once we take a new rebirth we are "lost" to our surviving relatives, whose attempts to remain in contact with us, whether through prayers, rituals, or other means, will be almost entirely fruitless. This approach to the afterlife was at odds with that of the Brahmanical traditions of the Buddha's day, where the care and feeding of deceased ancestors was a central religious obligation—and remains so in Hindu traditions to this day. From the Buddhist standpoint, we ought to reconceive offerings to the dead as acts of generosity to those who are living. Yet, the sense of belonging to a particular biological lineage is deeply rooted in human beings, and in South Asia, despite the rise of the rebirth eschatologies of the Upaniṣads and various śramaṇa traditions, neither that sense of belonging nor the rituals attendant upon it ever was entirely eclipsed.[269] In theoretical terms, this meant that a place in the cosmology had to be found for the "ghosts" of relatives—hence the early introduction of the preta realm into the list of possible postmortem destinations. On a practical level, whatever their cosmological views, many Buddhists, both lay and monastic, continued to perform funeral and memorial rituals that would assure their continuing connection either to their departed relatives or to charismatic religious figures. Indeed, many laypeople continued to make food offerings to their ancestors, and many monastics sought to be buried after death in the vicinity of the relics of the Buddha or the tombs of great arhats.[270] These South Asian practices spread to other Buddhist cultures, and will be featured in our discussion of those settings in chapters 11 to 13.

One final caveat should be issued about the degree to which Buddhist theories were or were not actually practiced. Despite our modern tendency to assume that all premodern people devoutly accepted and practiced traditional religions, the evidence is clear from society after society—especially those deemed "large-scale" by Obeyesekere—that not everyone was a religious believer. As we noted in chapter 2, religious skepticism and metaphysical materialism have a long history in India, and we cannot doubt that at least a few of the Buddha's followers did not "buy into" the worldview that he promulgated; otherwise, we would not read so many strenuous rejections of wrong views, not only among brāḥmaṇas and śramaṇas outside the Buddhist fold but within the saṅgha itself. What's more, even if the vast majority of Buddhists implicitly or explicitly accepted their tradition's cosmological teachings, many of them did not actually behave in a way that showed they took the ideas seriously. Again, the evidence is more negative than positive: we simply have to consider both the sūtras' repeated accounts of bad behavior and its karmic consequences and the Vinaya's descriptions of the malfeasance of both monks and nuns, to realize that Indian Buddhists, like religious people everywhere and always, were far from perfect in their embodiment of the ideas and values of their tradition, which, as so often in religious life, promotes an "impossible ethical ideal" to be admired, perhaps even aspired to, but seldom, if ever, truly fulfilled.[271]

CHAPTER 8

Indian Mahāyāna Views of Rebirth

The Mainstream Buddhist literature on which we have mostly drawn so far probably contains the oldest stratum of texts we possess, for, as noted, there is evidence for the existence of certain Mainstream sūtras at least as far back as the reign of Aśoka in third-century B.C.E. India. To reiterate, however, these and other texts incorporated into the Pāli and other early canons reflect a long process of redaction, and we have no certainty that they contain verbatim "what the Buddha taught." The literature of what is regarded as the other major branch of Buddhism, the Mahāyāna, or Great Vehicle, goes back nearly as far, with some texts tentatively datable to the last century B.C.E. or the first century C.E.—around the same time as the Mainstream canons were being finalized and closed.

Origins of the Mahāyāna

The Mahāyāna looms large in the global discourse of Buddhism because it became prominent in both East Asia (China, Korea, Japan, Vietnam) and Inner Asia (Nepal, Tibet, Mongolia, Bhutan), and scholars and representatives of those cultures have translated and disseminated Mahāyāna literature, ideas, practices, and even institutions throughout the world, including the West, over the past two centuries. The canonical texts of the Mahāyāna—typically in the form of sūtras or tantras—claim as surely as do the Nikāyas or Āgamas of the Mainstream schools to be the word of the Buddha, promulgated during his teaching career in India. This view was roundly rejected by Mainstream traditions like the Theravāda, which regard Mahāyāna sūtras as completely spurious, written by monks who wished to legitimize their literary efforts by starting their texts with the usual formula, "Thus I have heard at one time," and going on from there to put words into the Buddha's mouth. The Mainstream canons became closed, and have remained so, for the better part of two millennia. Mahāyāna canons, on the other hand—like those compiled in Nepal, China, or Tibet—not only include much of the Mainstream canonical material, but a vast array of Mahāyāna sūtras and tantras, and in some cases they remain open to further revelations, hence are not completely closed. In any case, the influence of Mahāyāna literature throughout East and Inner Asia, and its appeal for those outside Asia, has been vast, so it is tempting to assume that the Mahāyāna was of great significance in India, such that within a few centuries of the Buddha's passing there were on the subcontinent two great, competing branches of Buddhism: the earlier, Mainstream schools such as the Theravāda/Sthaviravāda, Sarvāstivāda, Saṃmitīya, and so forth; and the upstart Mahāyāna, which had to claw for attention at first, but eventually overshadowed the Mainstream, monastery-based traditions because of the universality of its message and the accessibility of its practices.

There is a small grain of truth to this conception, in that Mahāyāna did gain increasing importance in India in the last centuries of the first millennium, but there is far more in it that is misleading. To begin with, Mahāyāna never was a unified "movement" or "tradition," with a fixed canon accepted by all its adherents and with institutions devoted solely to its propagation. In this sense, it is better to speak of Mahāyāna movements in the plural. Indeed, it seems clear that most of the authors responsible for writing down the Mahāyāna sūtras were themselves monks ensconced in monasteries governed by the monastic disciplinary code of one or the other of the Mainstream schools—whose Vinayas, not coincidentally, guide monastic life in the "Mahāyāna" territories of East and

Inner Asia to this day: the Dharmaguptaka in East Asia and the Mūlasarvāstivādin in Tibet and surrounding areas. Furthermore, both textual and epigraphic evidence makes it clear that Mahāyāna was but a minor blip on the radar of most Indian Buddhists until the middle of the first millennium C.E., or even later.[272] Granted, Mahāyāna writers produced vast quantities of texts, including, sūtras, commentaries, independent treatises, and, a bit later on, tantras and their attendant literature, but what impact these texts had on Indian Buddhists outside the circles that produced them is hard to determine. The Chinese traveler Yijing, who visited India in the late seventh century to collect texts and study monastic Buddhism there, observed that, living in the same monasteries, Mainstream and Mahāyāna practitioners

> adopt one and the same discipline (Vinaya), and they have in common the prohibitions of the five…"groups of offences"…and also the practice of the four noble truths….Those who worship the bodhisattvas and read the Mahāyāna Sūtras are called the Mahāyānists…, while those who do not perform these are called the Hīnayānists.[273]

In short, apart from the texts they read and certain ritual patterns they observed, Mainstream and Mahāyānist practitioners were difficult to distinguish, even a full half-millennium after the first Mahāyāna sūtras appeared on the subcontinent.

Granting that Mahāyāna texts did appear in various parts of India around the beginning of the first millennium C.E., the question still remains *why* the Great Vehicle movements arose, often in explicit contradistinction to the Mainstream traditions. Mahāyāna traditionalists generally acknowledge the belated appearance of their literature. They claim, however, that it *was* taught by Śākyamuni Buddha during his lifetime, but because the world was not ready for the advanced teachings of the Great Vehicle, they were hidden away until the karma of beings was such that they would be receptive to them. Skeptical of such claims, modern critical scholars have proposed their own raft of theories to explain the rise of Mahāyāna. These include speculations that Mahāyāna:

- arose out of the early Mahāsaṅghika schools as a philosophically adventurous response to the scholastic monasticism of the Mainstream schools, a sort of radicalization of basic Buddhist ideas about ontology, metaphysics, cosmology, and ethics;
- originated as a religiously accommodating movement (perhaps influenced by Hindu devotionalism) that was more accessible to common people than Mainstream traditions;
- grew up in connection with worship at stūpas;
- was at the outset simply a literary movement, concerned with the production of sūtras;
- began as a "cult of the book"—that is, with worship practices directed to the sūtras themselves, which were prized as much for their magical power as their content;
- was rooted primarily in a renewed emphasis on ascetic practices in the forests beyond the monastery walls;
- was inspired by new meditative experiments and experiences.[274]

There probably is some truth to many of these suggestions, and neither one entirely precludes the others. Most recent scholarship on early Mahāyāna has focused primarily on such notions as the production and worship of sūtras, forest asceticism, and meditative experimentation, but at this point there is little consensus beyond a broad agreement that for the first half of the first millennium C.E., the Indian Great Vehicle was immensely productive in literary terms but institutionally quite weak, generally being confined to small groups within (or outside) the Mainstream Buddhist monasteries that largely controlled both the discourses and the resources of the tradition on the subcontinent.

Distinctive Claims of the Mahāyāna

Yijing's observation that what distinguished Mahāyānists in the Indian monasteries he visited was their reading of Mahāyāna sūtras and their worship of bodhisattvas, and that otherwise they were hard to distinguish from their Mainstream brethren, is undoubtedly true, and we must not fall prey to the Mahāyāna rhetoric that insists on a vast gulf between the two traditions, for they shared a great deal in terms of social and institutional life, philosophical vocabulary, and religious practice. Nevertheless, when we consider the actual content of the Great Vehicle literature that appeared in the early centuries of the Common Era, we cannot but be struck by the radical nature of several important Mahāyāna claims:[275]

1. The basic categories used by the Mainstream schools to analyze reality—saṃsāra and nirvāṇa, awakened and ordinary beings, conditioned and unconditioned dharmas, the five aggregates, the six sense faculties, the twelve sense bases, the eighteen sense spheres, the four noble truths, the twelve links, and so forth—are, when analyzed with the "eye of wisdom," seen to have as their true nature emptiness (*śūnyatā*) of intrinsic existence (*svabhāva*), that is, as not existing permanently, independently, partlessly, self-sufficiently, or from their own side. They also are asserted at various points to be nondual (*advaya*); primordially peaceful and pure; of a single taste (*ekarasa*); synonymous with suchness (*tathatā*), sameness (*samatā*), and reality itself (*dharmatā*); and/or merely the product of mental elaboration (*prapañca*), mental construction (*vikalpa*), or mental representation (*vijñapti*).[276]
2. Buddhas are not, as generally maintained in Mainstream schools, few and far between. Rather, they are multiple and nearly ubiquitous, appearing not just periodically but in countless times and places, manifesting under various names and forms in specific "spheres of influence" called buddhafields (*buddhakṣetra*) or pure lands. The most significant of these are Akṣobhya Buddha's eastern realm of Abhirati, the land of "lapis lazuli radiance" (Vaiduryaprabhā) overseen by the medicine buddha Bhaiṣajyarāja, and, most important of all, Amitābha Buddha's western paradise of Sukhāvatī. Each of these domains was seen as an enormously blissful, Dharma-suffused postmor-

tem destination that might be attained by proper devotion, virtue, or meditation—and was seen, too, as superior to any god-realm by virtue of either lying entirely outside saṃsāra or in a liminal space between cyclic existence and full awakening. Our own "earthly" realm, presided over by Śākyamuni, came to be referred to as the Sahā world, which sometimes was regarded as being coextensive with saṃsāra, and at other times as a pure land that only appears defiled to those blinded by delusion. Buddhas are not confined to their own fields, and they can and do visit, and interact with, one another.[277] And, although buddhas may be differentiated from a worldly perspective, at the deepest level, they are one.

3. Each Buddha may be conventionally understood as consisting of several "bodies" (*kāya*), the most common number being three. First is the Dharma or Truth Body (*dharmakāya*), which is equivalent to a buddha's nondual and omniscient awakened mind, possessed of limitless wisdom, compassion, and power, and sometimes seen as coextensive with reality itself; it is at the level of the Dharma Body that buddhas are indistinguishable. There also are two form bodies (*rūpakāya*): an Enjoyment Body (*sambhogakāya*), which appears in a glorious form in Akaniṣṭha heaven to teach Mahāyāna ideas and practices to advanced bodhisattvas until saṃsāra ends; and an Emanation or Transformation Body (*nirmāṇakāya*), which takes multiple guises—and appears in all the realms of saṃsāra—so as to assist ordinary sentient beings in fulfilling both their mundane and spiritual aspirations. For beings of the present era, the most significant Emanation Body was the appearance, in our Sahā world, of Śākyamuni Buddha, who was in fact merely the projection of a long-awakened buddha, who enacted an earthly "career" as an example and inspiration to struggling humans.[278]
4. Not only are buddhas multiple and ubiquitous, but every single being—no matter how evil or low-born, no matter how deluded they may have been in the past or are at present—will someday become a fully awakened buddha, with their own pure land.

This is the distinctively Mahāyāna teaching that is sometimes referred to as the single-vehicle (*ekayāna*) doctrine, but better known as the teaching on buddhanature (*buddhadhātu*), or the tathāgata-matrix (*tathāgatagarbha*), which, in its developed form, insists that each of us—by virtue of our possession of a clear, luminous, and empty mind—has the potential to eliminate defilements and achieve full awakening. This is in stark contrast to the Mainstream view that while each of us is capable of becoming an arhat, only a tiny minority ever become buddhas. Furthermore, Mahāyāna literature often denigrates the "mere" nirvāṇa sought by most Mainstream Buddhist practitioners, regarding it as inferior to full buddhahood, a mere way station on the road to a buddha's full awakening.[279]

5. If all of us—even those who have become arhats in the Mainstream tradition—will eventually become buddhas, then each of us must, like Śākyamuni before his own awakening, first traverse the ten-stage path of the bodhisattva (a "being intent on awakening," or buddha-to-be), with its corresponding "perfections" of generosity, morality, patience, effort, meditation, wisdom, skillful means, aspiration, power, and gnosis. To be truly "perfect," each of these virtues must be practiced within the context of a recognition of the emptiness—the absence of intrinsic existence—of every subject and object of an action, as well as of the action itself. The Mainstream traditions recognized the role of the bodhisattva, too, but because buddhas are extremely rare from their point of view, bodhisattvas are equally rare, and because the buddha of our era was Śākyamuni, the bodhisattva practices that receive the most attention from Mainstream writers are those he undertook in the vast stretch of time between his formal vow to attain buddhahood and his attainment of that state in his final life.[280]
6. The bodhisattva is motivated not just (as, supposedly, are Mainstream practitioners) by the wish for personal liberation but by the awakening mind (*bodhicitta*), the loving and compassionate aspiration to become a fully awakened buddha so as to benefit

all sentient beings—even if it requires taking countless rebirths in the lower realms in order to do so. To reinforce their dedication to the welfare of beings, bodhisattvas often undertake their own set of vows, which supplement monastic vows if they are ordained and add to lay vows in the case of non-monastics. They deepen their commitment through meditations in which, for instance, they reflect on the sufferings of beings in various realms of saṃsāra, then consider that, in the amplitude of beginningless time, each being has been their loving mother, and should be aided just like one's own mother if she were suffering. They also practice meditations in which they perform mental exercises that involve equalizing themselves with others, exchanging themselves with others, and taking on the sufferings of others while sending to others their own virtues. Like the perfections, all this is undertaken out of "objectless compassion": the understanding that both oneself and the sentient beings whom one assists are empty. In terms of everyday conduct, a bodhisattva must undertake every action with the awakening mind as the motive, perform the action with a recognition of emptiness, and conclude the action by dedicating—turning over—to suffering sentient beings any merit that has accrued.[281]

7. Bodhisattvas typically are monks, or occasionally nuns, but Mahāyāna literature also at times extols laypeople—including laywomen who range from queens to courtesans—who are on the path to awakening. Gods and goddesses may also be bodhisattvas. High-level bodhisattvas possess not just deep compassion and profound wisdom but immense power, as well, such that even while absorbed in states of deep meditative concentration (*samādhi*), they may manifest in multiple realms so as to assist beings in various ways. Some of these advanced bodhisattvas became the focus of devotional cults in India and beyond, which celebrated them for their distinctive qualities and activities. Thus, Mañjuśrī came to be associated with wisdom, Samantabhadra with meditation and other vir-

tuous practices, Kṣitigarbha with his vow to empty the hells, the female bodhisattva Tārā with the removal of obstacles, Vajrapāṇi with the exercise of power, and the "down-looking lord" Avalokiteśvara with rescue from all sorts of worldly predicaments, whether those in distress found themselves in the heavenly, human, or infernal realms. Some bodhisattvas preside over their own domains: Mañjuśrī, for example, is associated with the Five-Peaked Mountain (Wutai Shan) in north-central China and Avalokiteśvara with Mount Potalaka, a mythical peak in south India. Such high-level bodhisattvas are said to have attained "nonabiding nirvāṇa," an awakened state in which they are no longer subject to the defilements and vicissitudes of saṃsāra but, unlike arhats, they have not escaped into a quiescent nirvāṇa.[282]

8. In assisting sentient beings, both buddhas and advanced bodhisattvas exercise a variety of skillful or expedient means (*upāya-kauśalya*), which broadly signify their ability to teach and interact with less-developed beings according to those beings' intellectual, emotional, and cultural circumstances. A pedagogical corollary of this is that the apparent contradictions found in Buddhist sūtras simply reflect the fact that the Buddha was tailoring his message to different audiences with differing needs. The specific application of this to scriptural traditions is the claim that the Mainstream sūtras were delivered as provisional teachings to those of lesser capacity, while the Mahāyāna sūtras were taught to those of greater capacity—with different ones being considered the Buddha's definitive and final word.[283]
9. The ritual corollary of the doctrine of skillful means is that a wide variety of religious practices may be fruitfully undertaken by monastics and laypeople alike, including, worship of teachers, buddha-images, or holy objects such as texts or stūpas—through such means as pilgrimage, circumambulation, prostration, making offerings, singing songs of praise, chanting mantras and spells (*dhāranīs*), appealing for assistance, confessing misdeeds and receiving absolution, and so forth. All these, along with

other virtuous activities, build up in the practitioners a "store of merit" (*puṇyasambhāra*) that will ensure a positive rebirth and, at the time of awakening, produce a buddha's form bodies.

10. The ethical corollary of the doctrine of skillful means is that buddhas and advanced bodhisattvas may, if the situation warrants, transgress ordinary morality, by engaging in apparent acts of stealing, lying, sexual misconduct, and even killing. Such acts are to be undertaken only by those spiritually developed enough to know precisely what the karmic consequences of both action and inaction will be—and as we may recall, the details of karma and its results are one of the great mysteries of Buddhist thought. In any case, as various sūtras make clear, any being advanced enough to engage in ethically transgressive skillful means is well past delusion and defilement, and will not suffer negative karmic consequences for their acts, for they are helping suffering beings—even the most malevolent—attain a better destiny.[284]

These distinctive and sometimes dramatic Mahāyāna claims have obvious implications for the Mainstream Buddhist "karmic eschatology" surveyed in earlier chapters, with its delineation of the five or six realms of rebirth, explanation of the rebirth process through the links of dependent origination and other causal factors, and description of the operation of a karmic system in which good is rewarded and evil is punished, in this and subsequent lives. Leaving aside for the moment the assertion of the emptiness of all concepts and entities, we may note that the notion of buddhafields or pure lands adds to Buddhist cosmology a new set of options for a postmortem destination that is not yet full awakening—yet by virtue of lying partially or wholly outside saṃsāra and being presided over by buddhas is definitely preferable to the traditional god realms. The idea that buddhas are ubiquitous—appearing even in the lower realms—may take just a little of the sting out of our natural fear and loathing of saṃsāra. Similarly, the guarantee that every sentient being, even the basest, someday will become a buddha clearly provides a perspective from which our present delusion and suffering seem less acute, our prospects less hopeless. The bodhisattva's willingness to enter into any number of unfortunate rebirths so as to assist sentient beings—to "march into hell for a heavenly cause"—partly subverts the Mainstream Buddhist view that rebirth is in every circumstance something to be avoided, showing that it can actually be a situation to which we might aspire. The ability of any practitioner to offer a confession of misdeeds to a visualized assembly of buddhas and bodhisattvas, who then purify the supplicant, seems to suggest that the law of karma is not nearly as ironclad as it seems, and that easy absolution is actually available to all. The bodhisattva's willingness to turn over the merit gained from compassionate acts seems to militate against the supposedly individualized nature of karma in Buddhist theory. And, discussions of the ethical application of skillful means by buddhas and bodhisattvas show that Mainstream analyses of good and bad actions and their consequences may not be sufficiently nuanced to fit all cases.

Nevertheless, these Mahāyāna claims do not come close to breaking basic Buddhist cosmology—they merely bend it. Rather than obviating the traditional realms of saṃsāra, the ideal of pure lands merely supplements it by providing one or another new "borderland" destination just outside, or on the edge of, the wheel of life. The fact that buddhas or bodhisattvas may appear even in the lowest realms does not turn those into pleasant destinations, but only indicates that there may be moments of relief in the course of a generally miserable existence. The promise that each of us some day will become a buddha does not come with a specific time frame, and if it does, it is a very long one indeed, making our present sorrows and exertions no less significant than if no such promise had been made. The bodhisattva's aspiration for rebirth does not mean that saṃsāra is not a vicious circle, only that highly motivated and spiritually advanced beings may "play" in it by taking rebirth for the benefit of others. The "easy absolution" apparent in rituals of confession is not really so easy, since true purification of negative karma only is achieved through our own realization of the nature of reality, not through any priestly remission or "buddha ex machina." The wish to transfer one's merit to other sentient beings is seldom, if ever, taken literally, for it does contravene karmic law—and, as we have seen, such a wish is a feature of Mainstream traditions, too. Finally, the apparent transcendence of karmic cause-and-effect by a buddha or bodhisattva employing transgressive skillful means is nothing of the sort, for such beings are by definition free from delusion and incapable of performing an evil action, let alone suffering unfortunate consequences. Indeed, while the Mahāyāna's approval of a spiritually advanced being's transgressive acts expands the boundaries of what might be considered "good," it still adheres to the traditional definition of karma as intention: the buddha or bodhisattva's deeds are motivated by the pure wish to benefit sentient beings to the utmost; hence, regardless of how they may appear to the literal minded, those acts must be considered "good."

Karma and Rebirth in Five Mahāyāna Wisdom Traditions

If Mahāyāna *does* pose a meaningful challenge to Mainstream Buddhist cosmology, it is likeliest to be found in the realm of ontology and metaphysics described in the first point above, which noted that a variety of Great Vehicle "wisdom traditions" subjected the very nature of reality—and the categories used by both Mainstream and Mahāyāna Buddhists to describe it—to withering analysis and critique, asserting them to be empty of intrinsic existence, nondual, mind only, and so forth. In this section, we will briefly discuss several of the best-known Mahāyāna wisdom perspectives—those of the Perfection of Wisdom literature, the Madhyamaka school of philosophy, the Yogācāra school of philosophy, the literature on buddhanature, and the tradition of the *Avataṃsaka Sūtra*—and then reflect on the implications of these perspectives for traditional Buddhist cosmology.

The *Aṣṭasāhasrikā-prajñāpāramitā* (*Perfection of Wisdom in*

Eight Thousand Lines), along with its verse summary, may date from as far back as the first century B.C.E., making it one of the oldest, if not *the* oldest, of all Mahāyāna texts. Like most of the forty or so Perfection of Wisdom texts that appeared in India in its wake—the longest covers a hundred thousand lines, the shortest consists of a single syllable (the primal Sanskrit vowel *a*)—the *Aṣṭasāhasrikā* explicitly or implicitly addresses a variety of Mahāyāna themes, including the nature of Buddhahood and awakening; the delights of pure lands; the path and practices of the bodhisattva; the importance of wisdom and skillful means; and the veneration and practice of perfect wisdom as a path superior to the worship of relics, the construction of stūpas, or even adoration of the Buddha.[285] It also suggests that the teaching of the Perfection of Wisdom represents a "second turning of the wheel of Dharma," which supersedes the teaching promulgated by the Mainstream schools in the wake of the Buddha's "first sermon" at Sarnath.[286] Incidentally, the Perfection of Wisdom—Prajñāpāramitā—is personified as a goddess, just as in certain Greek traditions wisdom is incarnate in the goddess Sophia.

The actual practice of the perfection of wisdom centers on an understanding that the nature of all persons, phenomena, concepts, and entities is simply emptiness, for when a bodhisattva "coursing in the perfection of wisdom" looks into such Buddhist categories as the five aggregates or defilement and purification, they see that "all these dharmas are entirely empty,"[287] utterly lacking any intrinsic existence or own-being. Seeing this basic fact and settling into a nonconceptual, "empty" meditative state, the bodhisattva becomes detached from all categories, thereby attaining freedom. Not surprisingly, this thoroughgoing negation comes to be applied to categories of significance to Buddhist karmic eschatology. Thus, in emptiness there is no defilement nor anyone who could be defiled, nor, conversely, is there any merit or anyone who could garner merit, which is declared to be "just worthless / And likewise empty, insignificant, void, and unsubstantial."[288] On the "enlightened" side of the ledger, the Buddha asserts in the *Aṣṭasāhasrikā* that there is no being who can be awakened, and that, furthermore, "full awakening is hard to win" because "it cannot possibly come about... in reality it is not there."[289]

This sort of categorical negation is echoed in countless other Perfection of Wisdom texts, such as the *Vajracheddikā Sūtra* (*Diamond-Cutter Discourse*), which consistently undermines such notions as sentient beings, body and mind, merit, buddhas and bodhisattvas, the adornment of pure lands, the marks of a great being, and even the Buddha's Dharma itself,[290] and urges its readers to see conditioned things as "stars, a fault of vision, as a lamp, / A mock show, dew drops, or a bubble, / A dream, a lightning flash, or cloud."[291] Similarly the *Prajñāpāramitā-hṛdaya Sūtra* (*Heart Sūtra*) negates a long list of basic Buddhist categories, asserting that "in emptiness" there are no five aggregates, six sense faculties, six sense objects, eighteen sense fields, twelve links of dependent origination, four noble truths, gnosis, or attainment.[292] Furthermore, the *Pañcaviṃśatisāhasrikā-prajñāpāramitā* (*Discourse on Perfect Wisdom in Twenty-five Thousand Lines*) specifically negates the idea that there exist positive and negative karmic acts, or any of the realms of saṃsāra, or awakening; indeed, everything from the hells all the way up to buddhahood is denied.[293]

Such ideas are found in countless Mahāyāna sūtras outside the Perfection of Wisdom literature, too. For example, the *Bhadramāyākāra-vyākaraṇa* (*Prophecy Regarding the Magician Bhadra*) asserts that the Tathāgata recognizes that "there are no such dharmas as coming [into this life], going [to the next life], or saṁsāra," while the *Acintyabuddhaviṣaya-nirdeśa* (*Teaching on the Inconceivable State of Buddhahood*) insists that because all dharmas are empty,

> there are no realms. If there are no realms, there are no elements of earth, water, fire, or air; there is no ego, sentient being, or life; no Realm of Desire, no Realm of Form, no Realm of Formlessness... no realm of saṁsāra or nirvāṇa.[294]

In the *Vimalakīrtinirdeśa* (*Teaching of Vimalakīrti*), the Buddha instructs Śāriputra to ask Vimalakīrti where he had resided in his previous birth. This leads to an exchange in which Vimalakīrti forces Śāriputra to acknowledge that nothing dies or is reborn, any more than a magical creation dies or is reborn. "'Death,'" says Vimalakīrti, "is the end of performance, and 'rebirth' is the continuation of performance"—but each is just a performance.[295] The same sūtra also undermines our ability to determine just what sorts of beings we live amongst, observing, for instance, that "the Māras who play the devil in the innumerable universes of the ten directions are all bodhisattvas dwelling in the inconceivable liberation, who are playing the devil in order to develop living beings."[296] Taken at face value, none of these passages from the Perfection of Wisdom and other early Mahāyāna sūtras seems to bode well for traditional Buddhist cosmology, which appears, quite literally, to have been hollowed out.

For the most part, philosophically oriented Mahāyāna sūtras delight in negation and paradox, but do not argue systematically for their radical ontology—the stance they take on the true nature of things. Rather, such systematic argument became the province of the two major schools of Great Vehicle thought that arose in the early centuries of the Common Era: Madhyamaka and Yogācāra.

The Madhyamaka, or "Middle Way," school of philosophy is traced to the second-century south Indian philosopher-monk Nāgārjuna, who is credited in legends with recovering the Perfection of Wisdom sūtras from the undersea realm of the nāgas, where they had been kept since the Buddha's time, and making them public. Nāgārjuna does not mention these texts in the works credibly attributed to him, but the act for which he is famed is symbolically appropriate, since emptiness, the great theme of the Perfection of Wisdom, is very much the focus of his work. Nāgārjuna's most famous and influential text is the *Madhyamakakārikā* (*Stanzas on the Middle Way*), in which, over the course of twenty-seven versified chapters, he argues for the unsustainability—the intrinsic emptiness—of every major philosophical concept of his time. Employing such techniques as the dilemma and its fourfold equivalent, the tetralemma (*catuṣkoṭi*), and evoking the relativity of apparently independent concepts, Nāgārjuna negates such general notions as causation, motion, desire, agency, saṃsāra, suffering, action, time, and self, and such distinctly Buddhist categories as the five aggregates, the twelve sense bases, the eighteen sense spheres, the four noble truths, the tathāgata, and nirvāṇa. As we know, the Mainstream Buddhist vision of life, death, rebirth, and awakening rests on the validity of many of these concepts, so when Nāgārjuna comes along and argues, for instance, that no reasoning can actually prove that things arise either from themselves, something else, both, or neither, and that that exhausts all the possibilities, hence there can be no causation; or that notions of earlier or later rebirths within saṃsāra are undermined by the relativity of our temporal concepts; or that attempts to articulate the relation among agent, actor, action, and fruit inevitably issue in absurdity, hence are no more real than "the city of the gandharvas, . . . a mirage, a dream"; or that "there is no distinction whatsoever between saṃsāra and nirvāṇa"[297]—then traditional metaphysics and cosmology seem entirely to have lost their foundation, hence to be thrown into chaos.

Nor does Nāgārjuna spare traditional theories of knowledge: nearly half of his *Vigrahavyāvartanī* (*Dispeller of Disputes*), a short companion piece to the *Madhyamakakārikā*, is devoted to arguing that none of the generally accepted avenues of epistemic authority (*pramāṇas*)—perception, inference, analogy, or testimony—can be established, because (a) if valid cognitions are self-established, this entails a tautology, (b) if one valid cognition must be guaranteed by another, either of the same or a different type, an infinite regress results, (c) if valid cognitions are mutually established, then neither can be foundational or truly reliable, (d) if valid cognitions are established by their epistemic objects, then the difference between subject and object is effaced, and (e) if valid cognitions are simply asserted without reason, then all discussion must cease.[298] Hence, knowledge is impossible, and the metaphysical and natural processes supposedly comprehended by knowledge—including karma and rebirth—are placed in even greater jeopardy.

The Yogācāra ("Yoga-Practice") school arose shortly after the Madhyamaka, partly in reaction to the perceived nihilism of Nāgārjuna and his successors, but mostly as a result of meditative and philosophical explorations focused on the nature, structure, and functions of the mind, which Yogācāra thinkers saw not just as a primary causal factor in the cosmos but in some cases as the very substance of the cosmos as a whole. Although influenced by the Perfection of Wisdom sūtras' teachings on the illusion-like nature of the world and the deceptiveness of our mental fabrications, Yogācāra is most commonly based on a variety of other texts that appeared in the early centuries of the Common Era, including the *Saṃdhinirmocana* (*Unraveling the* [*Buddha's*] *Intention*) and *Laṅkāvatāra* (*Descent to Laṅkā*) sūtras and seminal treatises by Asaṅga and Vasubandhu (fourth to fifth century).

The *Saṃdhinirmocana* is among the earliest Yogācāra sūtras, and it introduces several key themes of Yogācāra thought, including the claim that it represents a *third* turning of the wheel of Dharma, which supersedes the apparent realism of the first turning and the apparent nihilism of the Perfection of Wisdom sūtras and Madhyamaka by providing a clear explanation of what exists and what does not, through utilizing the notion of the three natures, or characteristics, of phenomena.[299] What does *not* exist, according to the *Saṃdhinirmocana*, is the "imagined nature" (*parikalpita-svabhāva*) we impute onto dependently arisen phenomena (the "other-dependent nature," *paratantra-svabhāva*), which are unreal insofar as they are misapprehended, but real insofar as they are seen without such imputations, in their "perfected nature" (*pariniṣpanna-svabhāva*).[300]

Exactly what is wrongly imputed onto dependent phenomena would be debated by Yogācāra thinkers for many centuries. Some interpreters argued that our mistake, as in Madhyamaka, is to impute intrinsic existence to concepts and entities—including the standard categories of Mainstream Buddhism. More commonly, however, Yogācāras insisted that our error lies in seeing apparently external objects as separate from the consciousness that perceives them. The metaphysical corollary of this idea is expressed in the *Saṃdhinirmocana* through the positing of an "appropriating consciousness" (*adanavijñāna*), or "storehouse consciousness" (*ālayavijñāna)*, which is itself fundamentally unstained, but which nevertheless carries along karmic seeds from moment to moment and life to life and is the source of the six sense consciousness, as well as their objects.[301] The upshot of this is that all things in the cosmos, including "the appearances of the forms of sentient beings," are "representation-only" (*vijñaptimātra*).[302] A synonymous and perhaps even commoner term is "mind-only" (*cittamātra*). The *Daśabhūmika Sūtra* (*Discourse on the Ten Stages*) asserts that the bodhisattva intent on perfecting wisdom must realize that "the three realms are only mind,"[303] and, as the Buddha explains in the *Laṅkāvatāra Sūtra*,

> "the Bodhisattva-Mahsāsattvas...attain to the understanding that nirvāṇa and saṃsāra are one.... knowing that all beings... are not bound by causation, being beyond subject and object; [and further] seeing that there is nothing outside Mind...[and] that the triple world is of Mind itself."[304]

The *Laṅkāvatāra* also describes the storehouse consciousness in considerable detail, and identifies it with the tathāgata-matrix, or buddhanature, for it is that basic, primordially pure consciousness that—by being purged of the mistaken idea that anything exists outside mind and by contemplative transcendence of dualistic categories—will be transformed into the mind of a buddha.[305] The *Laṅkāvatāra* further specifies that it is the tathāgata-matrix "which is the cause of Nirvāṇa as well as that of pleasure and pain," and transmigrates from life to life.[306] The tathāgata-matrix is, as noted, synonymous with the storehouse consciousness, and is equivalent to the perfected nature posited in the *Saṃdhinirmocana*.

Like the Perfection of Wisdom sūtras, the Yogācāra sūtras do not typically argue their case so much as assert it, while providing clarifying analogies. It was left to scholarly figures like Asaṅga and Vasubandhu to provide a philosophical justification for the representation-only, or mind-only, view. In his *Mahāyānasaṃgraha*

(*Compendium of Mahāyāna*), Asaṅga defends the representation-only position by arguing, for instance, that it is evident to advanced yogīs that their meditative objects are mere appearances of the mind, and that because yogic perception is clearer than standard sensory or mental perception, the objects of standard perception must also be mere appearances of the mind. He adds that the appearance of externality is merely a function of an "afflicted consciousness" (*kliṣṭamanas*) that mediates between the storehouse consciousness and the six sense consciousness.[307] Asaṅga's half brother Vasubandhu—the same as the author of the *Abhidharmakośa*—argues even more forcefully for mind-only in his *Viṃśatikākārikā* (*Twenty Stanzas*) and its autocommentary, pointing out, for instance, that (a) the certainties we maintain in waking life all can be replicated in a dream, yet we know dreams to be unreal; (b) the fact that different sorts of beings—humans, deities, hungry ghosts, and so forth—see the same "external" object as water, nectar, or pus shows that, as it were, "there is no there there"; and (c) the atoms that are claimed by realist schools to be the building blocks of matter cannot be proven, for they fall apart under close analysis—and so, therefore, does the external world.[308] Hence, just as in Madhyamaka all things are reduced to emptiness, in Yogācāra all things turn out to be illusory appearances of the mind, and once again traditional Buddhist cosmology, with its realms of rebirth, seems to be at risk.

A third important strand of the Mahāyāna wisdom tradition, discourse on buddhanature,[309] represents a thematic focus rather than a distinct philosophical school. It emerged in significant part from Yogācāra explorations of the nature of mind, but is broader in scope, for it drew as well on presentations and analyses of emptiness in Perfection of Wisdom and Madhyamaka literature. Thus, such scriptures as the *Tathāgatagarbha* (*Tathḡata-Matrix*) and *Śrīmālādevīsiṃhanāda* (*Lion's Roar of Queen Śrīmālā*) sūtras, and various poetic treatises revealed to Asaṅga by the buddha-to-come Maitreya, especially the *Uttaratantra* (*Sublime Continuum*),[310] assert uniformly and unequivocally that all beings have the capacity to achieve buddhahood and that our basis for doing so lies in the "fundamental purity" of our minds, whose nature is clear, luminous, and empty of all saṃsāric stains—which in fact are merely accidental, temporary, or adventitious (*āgantuka*). Although the Buddha concedes in the *Śrīmālādevīsiṃhanāda Sūtra* that the process whereby pure awareness comes to be obscured with delusion is "difficult to understand," such obscuration does occur.[311] When delusions temporarily obscure it, our natural luminosity is referred to as the tathāgata-matrix; when the delusions have been removed by practice of the path, then, like the sun when clouds have dispersed or gold that has been separated from dross, what remains is a buddha's Dharma Body: empty, all-pervasive, and nondual, yet replete with all perfect qualities. As noted in the *Uttaratantra*,

> Buddhahood is inconceivable, permanent, steadfast, at peace, and immutable.
> It is utterly peaceful, pervasive, without thought, and unattached like space.
> It is free from hindrance and coarse objects of contact are eliminated.
> It cannot be seen or grasped. It is virtuous and free from pollution.[312]

Anyone "who has faith in this teaching, and practices it single-mindedly," says the Buddha in the *Tathāgatagarbha Sūtra*, "will attain liberation and true, universal enlightenment, and for the sake of the world...will perform buddha deeds far and wide." [313] Because the mind of a sentient being and that of a buddha have the same nature, and that nature is indistinguishable from the way things are in the most fundamental sense—permanent, empty, luminous, primordially pure, and so forth—it is sometimes suggested in the buddhanature literature that every being—perhaps even every *thing*—is primordially awakened, already buddha.[314] If that is so, then once again the classic dichotomy between saṃsāra and nirvāṇa seems threatened, cosmological details like realms and karmic processes apparently rendered superfluous, and our motivation for practicing the path potentially undermined.

A final tradition worthy of mention is that of the *Avataṃsaka Sūtra*, which, while also not a philosophical school as such, became the basis of the Huayan school in China and the Kegon school in Japan. The *Avataṃsaka* is among the longest of all Buddhist sūtras, amounting to nearly fifteen hundred pages in its sole complete English translation.[315] As Paul Williams notes, however, the text's single title "is apt to give a misleading impression of unity. In fact, the sūtra as it stands is a heterogenous work, a collection of texts some of which were circulated separately," and only later combined, with fill-ins as needed, to create a single work.[316] The two best-known "chapters" of the *Avataṃsaka* are also perhaps the earliest and the likeliest to have started as completely independent sūtras: the *Daśabhūmika* (cited above) and the *Gaṇḍavyūha* (*Arboreal Display*). In any case, the *Avataṃsaka* incorporates Madhyamaka insights into emptiness, Yogācāra perspectives on mind-only, and discussions of primordial purity in the buddhanature literature, but goes beyond them to present a vision of reality in which all times are contained in a single instant, and all things are contained in—and reflect—all other things. A classic image from the sūtra illustrates this idea: that of Indra's net, a vast interwoven complex in which each intersection of rope is held together by a jewel, which in turn reflects every other jewel in the net.[317] Other images from the *Avataṃsaka* and its derivative traditions that further illustrate the idea include the Buddha's hair pores, in each of which are found countless buddhas, in each of whose pores still more buddhas are to be found; the tower of the future buddha Maitreya, which similarly incorporates countless towers within towers within towers; and a room full of mirrors, in which each mirror reflects all others. In short, the reality-realm (*dharmadhātu*) is one infinite, unobstructed, interpenetrating whole.[318]

From one perspective the reality-realm is simply the infinite interrelation of all things, perhaps a radical extension of the idea of dependent origination. From another, deeper perspective, however, all things are actually the infinitely luminous Dharma Body of the Buddha, which "fills the cosmos, without end," such that "the nature of all the infinity of things / is in that body completely."[319] A buddha's Dharma Body—which is indivisible from any other Dharma Body, and is buddha as buddha actually is—is at various points in the sūtra equated to space, emptiness, and the mind—which "is like an artist, / able to paint the worlds."[320] This has two important implications: first, despite our conceptual construction of aggregates, elements, realms, causes and results, and good and bad, reality is an undifferentiated unity; and second, because that unity is buddha, "the nature of things is fundamentally pure."[321] This perspective carries echoes of the sūtras and treatises devoted to buddhanature, mentioned above. If, however, as stated or implied in the *Avataṃsaka* and the buddhanature traditions, everything (and each of us) is buddha, hence primordially pure, then karma and rebirth, along with the whole cosmology and eschatology of which they are the linchpin, seem to be swallowed up in a vision of universal perfection, hence are unworthy of serious attention—and the consequences of this for ethics, and indeed the entire Buddhist path, seem potentially catastrophic. After all, if we're all already buddha, why bother?

Implications of Mahāyāna Wisdom for Karma and Rebirth

Do Mahāyāna ontology and metaphysics actually negate traditional Buddhist cosmology and eschatology? The answer is unequivocally "no," but to understand this "no," we must appreciate the crucial distinction—maintained explicitly or implicitly throughout all Mahāyāna literature—between two truths, or realities: ultimate truth (*paramārtha-satya*) and phenomenal or conventional truth (*saṃvṛti-satya*, *vyāvahārika-satya*). As Nāgārjuna puts it in the twenty-fourth chapter of his *Madhyamakakārikā*, replying to an opponent who claims that the teaching of emptiness subverts all the Buddha's teachings, including the three jewels of refuge, the fruits of the religious path, and even the four noble truths:

> The Dharma teaching of the Buddha rests on two truths:
> conventional truth and ultimate truth.
> [Those] who do not know the distinction between the two truths . . . do not understand reality in accordance with the profound teachings of the Buddha.
> The ultimate truth is not taught independent of customary ways of talking and thinking.
> [Without] having acquired the ultimate truth, nirvāṇa is not attained.[322]

Nāgārjuna goes on to make a crucial point: it is by seeing emptiness as a negation of all conventionalities that his critics misunderstand it. Taking emptiness to entail nihilism, says Nāgārjuna, is as dangerous as "a serpent wrongly held or a spell wrongly executed."[323] Then, in one of the great reversals in philosophical history, Nāgārjuna argues that not only does emptiness not obviate the conventional but in fact it is only emptiness that can assure worldly conventions, for "All is possible when emptiness is possible. / Nothing is possible when emptiness is impossible."[324] The reason this is so is that (a) the opposite of emptiness is intrinsic existence (*svabhāva*), which is by definition permanent and independent, (b) we know the conventional world to be marked by impermanence and dependence, so (c) only if things are empty can they actually function as we know them to do.

This, Nāgārjuna points out, entails that there is a profound equivalency between dependent origination and emptiness: in effect, dependent origination is a "positive" way of referring to emptiness, while emptiness is the "negative" formulation of dependent origination.[325] As a result, argues Nāgārjuna, *none* of the Buddha's basic teachings is negated; rather, emptiness is what makes them possible. He spells out the implications of this "rescue of the conventional" in his autocommentary to *Vigrahavyāvartanī* 70:

> For whom there is emptiness there are all natural and supernatural things. Why? For whom there is emptiness there is dependent

> origination. For whom there is dependent origination there are the four noble truths. For whom there are the four noble truths there are the fruits of religious practice and all special attainments. For whom there are all special attainments there are the three jewels, the Buddha, Dharma, and Sangha.[326]

"For whom there is all this," Nāgārjuna concludes, good and bad actions and their results, the realms of rebirth, and the transcendence of rebirth—indeed, "all worldly conventions"—are established. Two footnotes on Nāgārjuna's argument are in order: first, the twenty-sixth and penultimate chapter of the *Madhyamakakārikā* is entirely given over to a completely straightforward exposition of the twelve links of dependent origination; and second, the only Buddhist text mentioned in the *Madhyamakakārikā* is the Mainstream Buddhist *Mahākatyāyana Sūtra* (*Great Discourse to Katyāyana*), which, in either its Pāli or Sanskritic version,[327] describes the "middle way" (*madhyama*) in terms of the twelve links. In this sense, Nāgārjuna's great text may be as much a commentary on the *Mahākatyāyana* as on the Perfection of Wisdom sūtras.

Although the reasoning outlined here is unique to the Madhyamaka tradition founded by Nāgārjuna, it is reflective of the stance adopted by all the wisdom traditions we have examined in this section. Thus, whether the "ultimate" truth we must grasp is emptiness as in the Perfection of Wisdom literature and Madhyamaka, mind-only as in Yogācāra, the natural luminosity of mind as in buddhanature discourse, or the fact that "all is buddha" as articulated by the *Avataṃsaka*, in no case do these perspectives cancel out the conventional teachings of the Mainstream and Mahāyāna traditions, including their rebirth eschatology. Thus, most major Mahāyāna sūtras are set in a vast assembly of beings that includes visitors from almost every sentient realm imaginable (including, occasionally, the lower ones); the reality of karma and rebirth (however conventional) are universally assumed; and the twelve links of dependent origination remain the best way to explain how it is we suffer in saṃsāra and how we can escape it. Let us cite three quick examples of the explicit acceptance of dependent origination.

A late Prajñāpāramita text extolling the 108 names of the Perfection of Wisdom lists among those epithets "the full meditational development of dependent origination." The *Saṃdhinirmocana Sūtra* straightforwardly asserts that, the ultimate notwithstanding, it is through hearing about dependent origination that beings know compounded phenomena to be impermanent, "unstable, unworthy of confidence, and changeable, whereby they develop antipathy" toward saṃsāra and set out toward awakening. And the *Daśabhūmika Sūtra* describes sixth-stage bodhisattvas, who specialize in perfecting wisdom, and do so, in part, through thinking through the twelve links "in order of progression."[328] Furthermore, there are a number of Mahāyāna sūtras and treatises that straightforwardly present Buddhist karmic eschatology without a whiff of paradox or negation. For instance, in the *Pratibhānamatiparipṛcchā Sūtra* (*Discourse on the Questions of Pratibhāna*) the Buddha lays out clearly and in detail the karmic causes that lead to particular sorts of rebirth, while in the anonymous *Ṣaḍgatikārikā* (*Stanzas on the Six Realms*), the realms of saṃsāra are described in lavish detail.[329]

In short, the apparent negation of traditional Buddhist categories and cosmology in Mahāyāna wisdom literature is merely apparent. Saṃsāra and nirvāṇa, heaven and hell, karma and its results, and dependent origination may be empty of intrinsic existence, merely imagined, or simply part of buddha—but they are very much a part of the structure and functions of the conventional world experienced by unawakened beings. And it may be that in order to attain the wisdom necessary for buddhahood, we must cease grasping at them as if they were *ultimately* existent—for grasping and attachment, as we know, are keys to the perpetuation of rebirth—but we ignore their *conventional* reality at our peril. Indeed, whether the cosmos is seen as empty of intrinsic existence, mind made, or just buddha, or viewed from the pluralist standpoint of Mainstream Abhidharma, the realms are real enough and traditional descriptions of karma and its results reliable enough, that we'd best be mindful of what we do, say, and think, lest we be shocked to awaken after death in an unpleasant abode we thought was fictional in every sense.

CHAPTER 9

Indian Tantric Buddhist Views of Rebirth

If Mahāyāna Buddhism may in part be understood as a radicalization of Mainstream ideas and practices, the Buddhist esoteric traditions—which go under such names as the Tantra Vehicle (*tantrayāna*), Diamond Vehicle (*vajrayāna*), and Way of Mantra (*mantranaya*)—represent a corresponding radicalization of the "ordinary" Mahāyāna. Esoteric texts and traditions began to appear in India around the seventh century C.E., and they increasingly came to define how Mahāyāna was articulated and practiced, to the point where, by the year 1000, not long before the near-disappearance of Buddhism from the subcontinent, some standard Mahāyāna traditions were sometimes hard to find in the subcontinent—as a case in point, the scholar and missionary Atiśa Dīpaṃkāra Śrījñāna (982–1054) had to travel to Sumatra to find a particular set of teachings on the awakening mind. This probably exaggerates the degree to which Mainstream and standard Great Vehicle Buddhism were eclipsed, for we have evidence of their vitality right up until the early thirteenth century, but it is likely that whatever success Mahāyāna eventually came to enjoy in India was due at least in part to texts, practices, and teachers spawned by the esoteric movement.[330]

Origins and Nature of Buddhist Tantra

There is no clear line of demarcation between standard and esoteric Mahāyāna texts and traditions. Many of the features most associated with the tantras—visualizations of buddhas and other deities, descriptions of divine palaces or maṇḍalas, the recitation of mantras, consecrations or initiations (*abhiṣeka*) conferred by gurus, and complex rituals in which buddhas and other divine forces might be summoned and utilized—were common features of both earlier Mahāyāna Buddhism and the Hindu and Jain traditions with which Buddhists shared the Indian subcontinent. Still, around the middle of the first millennium, Buddhist dhāranī—or spell—texts began to appear in which the magical evocation of buddhas and other divine beings was paramount, and these eventually led to the appearance of tantras—texts purported to have been taught by the Buddha during his earthly career and then hidden, or revealed by him later in one of his Form-Body manifestations. The earliest tantras (seventh to eighth century), which later were classified (at least according to one scheme) as ritual or action (*kriyā*) tantras, performance (*caryā*) tantras, or yoga tantras, were clearly derived from Mahāyāna images, ideas, and practices, and were distinguishable from them only insofar as they tended increasingly to focus on (a) the requirement for initiation into a small circle of disciples by a qualified guru or vajra master (*vajrācārya*), and (b) an emphasis on "deity yoga" (*devatāyoga*), a procedure for identifying oneself with the body, speech, mind, and environment of the particular buddha one will someday become, seeing oneself and others in divine form, uttering and hearing all speech as mantra, realizing in every moment the pure and empty nature of oneself and all things, and seeing one's surroundings as a maṇḍala or pure land. The yoga tantras, many of which centered on the cosmic buddha Mahāvairocana, were taken to China in the eighth century, where they became the basis of Zhenyan (True Word) Buddhism and its later Japanese offshoot, Shingon.

Late in the eighth century in India, texts began to appear that would eventually be classified as Mahāyoga tantras—of which the *Guhyasamāja* (*Secret Assembly*) is the most prominent. Slightly later, Yoginī tantras began to appear—of which the *Hevajra*, *Cakrasaṃvara*, and *Kālacakra* are key. The Mahāyoga and Yoginī tantras—which sometimes are lumped together under the rubric of unexcelled yoga tantra (*yoganiruttaratantra*), have strong resonances with Hindu tantric texts and traditions from the same era, and scholars continue to debate the actual direction of influence between the Buddhist and Hindu esoteric traditions—it probably worked both ways. The literature inspired by these later tantras—which includes commentaries and independent treatises, as well as poetic songs attributed to their charismatic advocates, the oft-transgressive great adepts (*mahāsiddhas*)—is notable for their evocation of images and practices involving both wrathful action and sexual bliss and for their focus on meditations conducted within the subtle body (*sukṣmaśarīra*) that interpenetrates our coarse physical body, and is assumed in yogic and esoteric traditions to be the true locus of the "alchemy" that will eventually transmute our ordinary body, speech, and mind into those of a buddha. The Mahāyoga and Yoginī tantric traditions (along with those of the action, performance, and yoga tantras), would eventually be transmitted to Tibet, where they shaped Buddhist practice to an extraordinary degree—far more than the yoga tantras ever affected Buddhism in East Asia.

Tantric Metaphysics

Although Buddhist tantra is better known for systems of practice than for fine-grained philosophical analysis, it was deeply influenced by the Mahāyāna philosophical traditions discussed in the previous chapter. Thus, the realization of emptiness stressed in the Perfection of Wisdom sūtras and Madhyamaka becomes the contemplative basis for reducing oneself and one's world to nothing and recreating them in divine form. The Yogācāra emphasis on all things being mind-only assures the practitioner that reality is malleable, and that a transformation of the mind will lead to a change in reality—not only for oneself but for others, too. The buddhanature tradition's insistence that buddhahood is assured because of the natural luminosity of the mind gives us a strong focal point for transformative practices, and becomes something of a "trademark" of tantric literature—especially the songs of the great adepts. The implication in the *Avataṃsaka* and other Mahāyāna texts that all of reality is, in fact, simply buddha in manifest form provides the inspiration for tantric cosmogonies in which the whole cosmos is seen as an emanation of a primordial gnosis where emptiness, awareness, and bliss are inseparably fused.

Thus, for instance, a text often associated with the Mahāyoga tantras, the *Mañjuśrīnāmasaṃgīti* (*Litany of Names of Mañjuśrī*), says of buddha-wisdom, "It is the supreme nature of all entities, / the bearer of the nature of all entities; / unarisen, [yet] with manifold meanings, / it holds fast the essence of all things."[331] Another Mahāyoga tantra, the *Guhyasamāja*, proclaims even more pointedly: "Naturally luminous are dharmas, primordially pure, like space; / there is no awakening or realization, and this vouchsafes awakening."[332] And the *Hevajra*, a Yoginī tantra, is the most explicit of all, when in it the Buddha declares: "Whatever things there are, moving and motionless, all these things am I. . . . The whole of existence arises in me, / In me arises the threefold world, / By me pervaded is this all, / Of nought else does this world consist."[333] Put another way, "saṃsāra is [Hevajra's] phenomenal aspect, and he is the Lord, the savior of the world."[334] And because Hevajra's own nature is emptiness, awareness, and bliss, and he is, furthermore, everything, it stands to reason that

> all beings are buddhas. . . . There is not a being that is not enlightened, if it but knows its own true nature. The denizens of hell, the pretas and the animals, gods and men and titans, even the worms upon the dung-heap, are eternally blissful in their true nature. . . .[335]

Along similar lines, the great adept Tilopa sings of the realization he has come to through tantric practice: "I am the cosmos, I am the Buddha, I am the unadorned, / I am unthinking—I've broken existence!"[336]

These metaphysical expressions, particularly in the *Hevajra*, are reminiscent of a sort of monism found in theologies devoted to the great Hindu gods Viṣṇu or Śiva, and so seem even more dramatic than the claims found in Mahāyāna sūtras. In fact, however, they do not really depart much from the perspectives found in many pre-tantric texts, hence do not undermine Buddhist rebirth eschatology any more than the texts we considered in the previous chapter. Thus, regardless of whether *ultimately* the cosmos is empty, or merely mind, or primordially pure, or buddha, *conventionally* the six realms, karma and its results, and the links of dependent origination very much apply. Some tantric cosmologies add flourishes to the traditional structure—for instance, by the introduction of buddhafields devoted to specific tantric deities and the addition of a hell even lower than Avīci, the vajra hell, in which we may be born for breaking our tantric vows—but for the most part, the basic outlines are left intact. So, too, is the foundational Buddhist assumption that it is meaningful and important to think in terms of a basic divide between saṃsāra and nirvāṇa, delusion and awakening. That is why the *Guhyasamāja*, much like the Perfection of Wisdom literature, speaks of awakening's being vouchsafed by the fact and by the realization that all things are empty—if the distinction between delusion and awakening were utterly invalid, awakening would not have to be guaranteed. Similarly, within the context of asserting the primordial buddhahood of all beings, the *Hevajra* carefully notes that in order to recognize their innate state of awakening, beings have to know their own true nature—and this, again, implies that all is not right with us or the world, for there is a gap between what we are and what we understand. That gap, presumably, must be bridged through tantric practice.

Tantric Practices

As suggested above, much of Buddhist tantric practice may be viewed as an extension of standard Mahāyāna ritual procedures, from which it varies primarily in its concern to *enact* the Great

Vehicle understanding of ourselves and the world as being divine. Thus, the contemplative practices prescribed in the visualization rites (*sādhana*; literally, "methods of actualization") of the action, performance, and yoga tantras seek primarily to change our mode of *seeing*, by reducing our environment, other beings, and our own body, speech, and mind, to emptiness, then—in a kind of dress rehearsal for enlightenment—reimagining our own body, words, thoughts, and actions as those of the buddha we will someday become, our environs as that of a buddha's maṇḍala, and other beings as the buddhas, bodhisattvas, and other beings who inhabit that maṇḍala. This much is common to most tantric traditions, including those of the Mahāyoga and Yoginī tantras, where such procedures are referred to as the "generation stage" (*utpattikrama*). Where these later and "higher" tantras most clearly separate themselves from the rest is in their discussion of the "completion stage" (*saṃpannakrama*), the final steps that must be taken before we shift from *seeing* ourselves as buddha to *being* buddha. It is in the completion stage that we focus primarily on work within the subtle body, with its channels (*nāḍī*), breath-related energies (*prāṇa*), drops (*bindu*), and the channel intersections called cakras (literally, "wheels"). Although completion-stage practices vary from one tantric system to another, they frequently require forcing the breath-related energies from the "outer" channels into the central channel (*avadhūti*), experiencing various levels of bliss (*ānanda*) as the energies are moved up and down there, then bringing the breath-related energies to the heart cakra—at the center of which is an "indestructible drop," which contains the subtle consciousness and breath-related energy from which we begin a particular rebirth at conception and which at death, when all other mental and physical activity has ceased, pass on to the next life. Within the indestructible drop, we use our meditative powers and realization of emptiness to transform our mind and body into the luminous Dharma Body and illusion-like Form Body of a buddha, respectively. We no longer imagine ourselves as buddha; we *are* buddha.

As described in Indian and Tibetan commentarial traditions, the generation and completion stages are intimately connected to issues of birth, death, and rebirth, as well as to aspects of our eventual awakening. Thus, the three basic phases of a sādhana or generation-stage practice correspond to three "existential moments": reducing ourselves to emptiness purifies ordinary death and sows the seeds for attainment of a buddha's Dharma Body; emerging out of emptiness as a buddha-deity's generative syllable purifies the intermediate state and plants the seeds for attainment of an Enjoyment Body; and embodying ourselves as the deity purifies rebirth and plants the seeds for attainment of the Emanation Body. Furthermore, once we have generated ourselves as a buddha, we recite the mantra of the deity we have become, sending out rays of light and/or streams of nectar that purify the delusion and suffering of sentient beings throughout the three spheres and the six realms of saṃsāra, and those purified beings are reabsorbed into our own divine form. In this way, we imagine that all beings transcend ordinary death and rebirth, just as we will.

On the completion stage, the process whereby the breath-related energies are brought into the central channel of the subtle body, then drawn into the heart cakra, mimics the various physical and mental events that transpire at the time of death, which involve the dissolution of various material elements and physical abilities, the collapse of ordinary mental processes, and the attainment of various "visions." These visions culminate in the clear light or luminosity (*prabhāsvara*) witnessed at the time of death, and this luminosity, which is the very nature of mind itself, will, if properly grasped, become the basis for liberation. In advanced completion-stage meditation, the practitioner repeatedly "pre-enacts" the death process, never actually dying but coming to know the details so thoroughly that when death does actually come, they can—if not already awakened—use the occasion either to attain buddhahood or control their next rebirth. For those less adept in the most advanced contemplations, the tradition offers the optional practice known as transference (Skt. *vyāvana*, T. *'pho ba*), whereby at the time of death one projects one's consciousness—or has it projected by a guru—into the heart of Amitābha, residing in his western paradise of Sukhāvatī, or into the presence of some other buddha.

The ultimate outcome of the completion stage, the nondual, luminous gnosis of bliss and emptiness that is equivalent to a buddha's Dharma Body, is often referred to in Vajrayāna literature as the "Great Seal" (*mahāmudrā*), and it is sometimes suggested in the tantras and their commentaries—and especially so in the songs of the great adepts—that the complex meditations and rituals entailed in tantric practice may be short-circuited by an instantaneous attainment of that gnosis through dropping all conceptual elaboration (*prapañca*) and directly seeing the primordial nature of mind. Thus, as the adept Saraha sings:

> No tantra, no mantra, no reflection or recollection!
> Hey fool! All this is the cause of error.
> Mind is unstained—don't taint it with meditation;
> you're living in bliss: don't torment yourself.[337]

A term of increasing importance in Indic Buddhism, the Great Seal became even more vital in Tibet, especially among the traditions that developed there after the year 1000, during the so-called later spread (*phyi dar*) of the Dharma on the plateau, namely, the Kagyü, Sakya, Kadam, and the Kadam's eventual successor, the Geluk. During the earlier spread (*snga dar*) of Buddhism (seventh to ninth century), a great adept from northwest India, Padmasaṃbhava, is credited with introducing a somewhat similar system of direct meditation on the mind's true nature, that of the Great Perfection (Skt. *mahāsaṅdhi*, T. *rdzogs chen*), which stressed seeing our "original purity" (*ka dag*), and profoundly shaped theory and practice in the Tibetan order that traces itself to Padmasambhava's visits, the Nyingma, or Old Tradition. We will say more about the Great Perfection and the Great Seal when we address Tibetan Buddhism (chapter 13) and will remark here only that they stand in a clear line of development that leads from the Perfection of Wisdom sūtras through to the Mahāyoga and Yoginī tantras. Hence, whatever their rhetoric, they undermine neither the classic cosmology of early Buddhism nor the ideas and practices of Mahāyāna, whether "standard" or tantric.

As noted earlier, one of the distinguishing features of the Mahāyoga and Yoginī tantras is their transgressive focus on wrathful and sexual images and practices. This, in turn, reflects the tantric tradition's extension of the Mahāyāna doctrine of skillful means to even greater extremes. Thus, any number of tantras devote considerable attention to methods for ritually evoking divine powers so as to pacify obstructive forces, enhance one's attributes, attract other beings, and destroy opponents. These could be, and of course often were, interpreted "psychologically" and "spiritually," but they sometimes were seen in more ordinary terms, too, such that a great adept was considered capable of taming demons, gaining psychic powers, attracting women, and killing enemies. The sexual imagery for which the tantras are so famous also may be interpreted symbolically, as indicating, for instance, the union of compassion and wisdom, but there is no doubt that initiation ceremonies for the Mahāyoga and Yoginī tantras included ritual sexual intercourse and the ingestion of sexual fluids, and that once consecrated, a tantric practitioner might engage in sexual yoga with flesh-and-blood consort (*mudrā*) of the opposite sex. Indeed, the lifestyle adopted by Indian adepts—often referred to as "performance," or "tantric conduct" (*caryā*)—typically involved their living with a consort in liminal places like forests or cremation grounds, following low-caste occupations, behaving eccentrically, transgressing traditional ethical norms, and participating regularly in ritual feasts (*gaṇacakra*; literally, "clan circles") that included singing, dancing, sexual intercourse, and the consumption of meat, alcohol, and the "five nectars": urine, excrement, semen, blood, and marrow.[338] As Saraha sings:

> Behaving like a crazed elephant and acting dumb,
> Behaving without regard to dos and don'ts like an elephant
> plunging on impulse into a pond: his mind perpetually crazed,
> he performs the basest of deeds yet is free....[339]

All these practices, of course, presuppose initiation by a guru, but because the practices are so precious, rare, and profound, a disciple cannot be initiated unless they have shown themselves worthy of receiving the tradition, and are willing to take to heart the first of the great vows of the higher tantras: complete obedience to the spiritual master. As a result, tantric lore is replete with stories of the trials to which students were subjected by their prospective teachers. The most famous of these are the tests endured by the pandit Nāropa (1016–1100) at the hands of his master Tilopa (988–1069), each of which involved what we nowadays would consider physical abuse. Yet so intent on receiving tantric instruction was Nāropa that he bore every hardship, and in the end was initiated and taught, going on to become a great master in his own right.[340]

Many of these practices are truly norm defying, and the degree to which they pose ethical challenges should not be understated. Yet, as instances of skillful means, they do not destroy Buddhist ethics or truly threaten karmic eschatology, any more than did the buddha- and bodhisattva-actions described in early Mahāyāna sūtras—for like those actions, these tantric deeds rest on the assumption that one may undertake transgressive practices only if qualified to do so by virtue of superior development of discipline, compassion, and insight into the true nature of things.

Because their intention is pure and their knowledge both vast and profound, advanced tantric practitioners produce only positive karma (or no karma at all), regardless of how unwholesome their actions appear to be. Thus, the powers of pacification, enhancement, attraction, and destruction may be used by those with sufficient wisdom and compassion—but only by them. Sexual yoga is to be practiced only at certain points in the completion stage of the highest tantras, and in those contexts, it is for the purpose not of ordinary sexual satisfaction but for channeling energies and evoking the bliss that is part of the fundamental nature of mind. The tantric lifestyle undertaken by many of the great adepts does not reflect a complete rejection of social norms so much as the temporary adoption of a non-monastic way of life that assists the practitioner in breaking through dualities and other mental fixations in a lived and visceral way.[341] Finally, the harsh trials imposed on prospective disciples by certain gurus simply reflect their understanding of precisely what is needed by those who would study with them, and while these may seem quite dramatic, they are very much on the same continuum with the Mahāyāna Buddha's decision to give different teachings to different disciples based on their differing cultural contexts, intellectual capacities, and psychological tendencies. And because the guru's actions are motivated by the awakening mind and compassion, they too are pure, and operate within, rather than outside of, the classical Buddhist system of rewards and punishments.

Women in Mahāyāna and Tantra

As noted above, the first of the tantric vows taken by disciples at the time of initiation is to obey the guru. The fourteenth and final vow is "not to disparage women." This instruction seems, on the face of it, to represent a nearly complete turnaround from the notion of the female rebirth as an unfortunate one, encountered so frequently in the literature of Mainstream Buddhism. To understand the vow better and consider its apparent distance from early Buddhist attitudes, we must step back and briefly survey Mahāyāna and tantric views of the advantages and disadvantages of a female rebirth.

There certainly are passages in early Mahāyāna sūtras that seem to undermine gender distinctions and celebrate women's potential not only for attaining liberation but for serving as spiritual teachers.[342] The most famous subversion of gender distinctions comes in the *Vimalakīrtinirdeśa Sūtra*, where Śāriputra challenges the spiritual attainment of a goddess living in Vimalakāirti's house by asking why she does not change out of her female state. She replies that she has sought her "female state" for twelve years and has not found it. She then uses her magical powers to make Śāriputra appear in her form and vice versa, bringing home the point that "men" and "women" are just appearances and that, as she says, "In all things, there is neither male nor female."[343] The goddess, imbued as she is with wisdom, is in effect serving as Śāriputra's teacher. The fact that females, even lay females, may be Buddhist teachers is made more explicit in the *Śrīmālādevīsiṃhanāda Sūtra*, where much of the teaching on buddhanature is conveyed by the queen who gives her name to the sūtra. Female teachers are notable, as well, in the *Gaṇḍavyūha Sūtra*, where fully twenty of the fifty-three gurus visited by the young male pilgrim Sudhana are women. Of these, over half are goddesses, but their number also includes a nun, several lay devotees, the mother and wife of the Buddha, and—most intriguingly—a courtesan named Vasumitrā, who taught the Dharma amidst saṃsāric impurity, but, as a Chinese commentator observes, "she appeared to be a woman, yet in ultimate reality one is neither male nor female; she is just portrayed as female to represent the compassion of the real universe."[344] Incidentally, in the realm of worship, the Mahāyāna tends to be somewhat more accepting of goddesses than the Mainstream schools; as we know, the female bodhisattva Tārā is a major Great Vehicle deity, and the Perfection of Wisdom was personified as female, being frequently depicted in sculptures and celebrated in hymns of praise.

All this, however, begs the question whether a female can be a buddha *in female form*. The answer in the Mainstream tradition, as we know, is an unequivocal "no," and the view expressed even in gender-distinction-defying Mahāyāna sūtras is less than clear. Thus, in the *Vimaladattāparipṛcchā Sūtra* (*Discourse on the Questions of Vimaladattā*), the eponymous heroine, who is showing herself to be very wise indeed, is told by the arhat Maudgalyāyana, "No one can ever attain supreme enlightenment in female form." Her response is to make a solemn vow before the whole assembly that she will in fact become a fully awakened buddha, and states that if her pledge is valid, the worlds will quake and she will be transformed into a sixteen-year-old boy. This is precisely what happens, but the sex change she undergoes seems to undermine rather than uphold the idea of a female buddha, though the sūtra does not say so.[345]

Similarly, in a famous passage in the *Saddharmapuṇḍarīka Sūtra* (*Discourse on the Lotus of the True Dharma*, usually called the *Lotus Sūtra*), the wisdom-bodhisattva Mañjuśrī describes to the assembly an eight-year-old nāga princess he has met in her undersea kingdom, who is, he declares, wise, skilled, and compassionate—indeed, "capable of attaining bodhi" instantaneously. Another bodhisattva challenges Mañjuśrī's claim on the grounds that buddhahood cannot be attained instantly, for Śākyamuni himself took many eons to reach it; unstated, but obvious to the audience, is the traditional idea that neither children, nāgas, or females can become a buddha, whether gradually or instantly. At that, the nāga princess appears in the assembly. When Śāriputra challenges her level of awakening, saying that "a woman's body is soiled and defiled, not a vessel for the Law," the princess proclaims that she will become a buddha, immediately. She then turns into a man and in an instant carries out all the bodhisattva practices and becomes a buddha.[346] As in the *Vimaladattāparipṛcchā*, female buddhahood seems imminent, only to be snatched away by a last-minute gender change.

While the texts we have cited are unequivocal in their challenge to gender dichotomies, it is far from clear that they seek to undermine gender *discrimination*—and in any case, they represent only a small minority of Mahāyāna texts in which the nature of the female rebirth is considered. Most references to women we encounter in Great Vehicle literature conform to the rather misogynistic rhetoric common in the Mainstream traditions. Thus, the *Udayanavatsarājaparivarta Sūtra* (*Discourse on the Tale of King Udayana of Vatsa*) describes the various defects of women, concluding that "the dead snake and dog / are detestable, / but women are even more detestable than they are."[347] Similarly Śāntideva's (c. 685–763) verse treatise, the *Bodhicaryāvatāra* (*Entry into Enlightened Conduct*), which is one of the most beloved of all Mahāyāna texts, includes in the chapter on meditation a long section in which women's repulsiveness is described in lurid detail, with a particular focus on the foulness of the female body: it appears attractive but is understood through analysis to be nothing but a decaying bag of bones, a pile of meat, a stinking cesspool, unworthy of attention, let alone of avid pursuit.[348] Examples could be multiplied endlessly, but these suffice to bring home the point that Mahāyāna was far from unequivocally feminist. And the key reason for this, as for the misogyny of the Mainstream traditions, is not hard to discern: it is rooted in ingrained patriarchy and androcentrism, but also in the fact that most Buddhist texts were written not only by men but by monks—for whom, as we know, women are eternally "a problem." As with the Mainstream tradition, however, we must recall that Mahāyāna certainly admitted that women had real spiritual capacity as women—in this case, to practice the bodhisattva path and attain some form of spiritual liberation—but that they could be buddhas in female form is dubious at best.

It is, then, to the tantric traditions that we must turn for confirmation that a buddha can be female in form, and here, at last the evidence seems unambiguous. The origin story of the bodhisattva Tārā, whose widespread popularity carries over from standard Mahāyāna into the Vajrayāna, tells of her having been born eons ago as a devout princess named Prajñācandrā, who, when advised by monks to pray for a male birth, replied,

> "Since there is no such thing as a 'man' or 'woman'... this bondage to male and female is hollow.... Those who wish to attain supreme enlightenment in a man's body are many, but those who wish to serve the aims of beings in a woman's body are few indeed; therefore, may I, until this world empties out, serve the aims of beings with nothing but the body of a woman."[349]

Tārā fulfilled her vow, and is regarded by her devotees as a savioress (one meaning of her name) who rescues beings from worldly perils and as a sometimes-peaceful, sometimes-wrathful remover of all obstacles to successful action, including demons and other interfering spirits. She also is worshipped as the mother of the buddhas—identical in nature and realization to Prajñāpāramitā, the Perfection of Wisdom personified female in form.[350] More to the point, the first of a list of thirty-two names by which she is known is Buddhā; with the Sanskrit long *a* feminine ending; among her other epithets are Dharma Body, the Nonabiding One, and Sugata.[351]

Within the Mahāyoga and Yoginī tantra traditions, feminine imagery and female figures are ubiquitous. Many of the Mahāyoga traditions, especially the *Guhyasamāja*, feature a variety of female deities, including yoginīs, wrathful and powerful "sky-goers" known as ḍākinīs, mother-goddesses, daughters of awareness-holders, yakṣa maidens, consecration goddesses, offering goddesses, and so forth.[352] These tantras also posit for the buddhas who inhabit maṇḍalas female consorts who symbolize the transformation of the physical elements as the buddhas symbolize the transformation of the five aggregates,[353] as well as flesh-and-blood consorts—described in considerable detail in terms of age, caste, physical features, adornment, and so forth—with whom the tantra's adherents will practice sexual yoga.[354] As their name might indicate, the Yoginī tantras give even greater prominence to female figures. In such systems as the Cakrasaṃvara and Hevajra, the maṇḍalas include a significant number of female deities, and buddha-consorts, yoginīs, and ḍākinīs receive considerable attention, serving as interlocutors in the texts and being celebrated for their powers. The buddha-consorts are particularly noteworthy. The consort of Hevajra, Nairātmyā ("No-Self"), is—like Prajñāpāramitā and Tārā—praised as a manifestation of the true nature of reality, which is the union of bliss and emptiness:

> She is symbolized by the letter A, and it is as Wisdom that the enlightened conceive her.... She is the Innate itself, the divine yoginī of great bliss. She is the whole maṇḍala, and comprehends the five wisdoms. She is the "I," the Lord of the maṇḍala. She is Nairātmyāyoginī, the sphere of thought in essence.[355]

The consort of Cakrasaṃvara, variously known as Vajravarāhī ("Adamantine Sow") or Vajrayoginī ("Adamantine Yoginī"), is similarly celebrated in the tantras devoted to that male form of buddha, and then, early in the second millennium C.E., shortly before the eclipse of Buddhism in India, she becomes the focus of her own cult, a buddha in her own right who becomes largely independent of her male counterpart, much like such great Hindu goddesses as Durgā and Kālī, who originally were associated with Śiva.[356] In Tibet, she was most often known as Vajrayoginī, and practices related to her became an important element of all the major traditions. She was the main meditation deity (*yi dam*) for any number of practitioners, who sought to attain buddhahood in her form through the generation and completion stages and, if falling short of buddhahood, to be reborn in her paradise of Khecara. It hardly needs saying that she fully qualifies as a buddha.

Given the importance of these female deities in the later tantric systems, it is not surprising that the literature of the great adepts who practiced them is full of stories of encounters with yoginīs and ḍākinīs, who often provide instruction at a critical juncture on the adept's path. Although most of the great adepts were male, there were accomplished female practitioners, too, whose stories and texts have been handed down through the ages. Given the androcentric nature of medieval Indian society and literature, there no doubt were many more female adepts than the historical record shows. Miranda Shaw goes so far as to argue that the Yoginī tantras may have originated among circles of women.[357] That may or may not be—the evidence is far from persuasive—but there is no doubt that something has changed when an early Yoginī tantra, the *Sarvabuddhasamāyoga* (*Union of All the Buddhas*) can declare, "Women... are the supreme treasure, / enjoying everything of the substance of space,"[358] and the great adept Padmasaṃbhava, as cited in Tibetan tradition, can admit:

> The basis for realizing enlightenment is a human body. Male or female—there is no great difference. But if she develops the mind bent on enlightenment, the woman's body is better.[359]

Passages like this make it easy to understand why the nondisparagement of women became one of the key tantric vows, and make it seem that in the later tantras Buddhists are finally placing female rebirth on a par with the male.

A final caution is in order, however, for these various Indic "celebrations of the feminine" did not necessarily betoken a dramatic change in women's status, either in society at large or in Buddhist communities—even tantric ones. In the West, it is often assumed that metaphysical or ontological equality ("all persons are created equal") naturally entails social or political equality ("therefore, the races and genders ought to be treated equally"), but this was not, for the most part, the case in premodern India. Thus, goddesses have been an important element of Indic religions for close to two thousand years—sometimes even being considered superior to male deities and worshipped in preference to them—yet their prominence in myth, ritual, contemplative practice, and visionary experience did little to move women closer to social "equality" in the modern sense. Picturing the divine as female certainly enriched South Asian religious traditions, and may have provided personal meaning and inspiration to both women and men on the subcontinent—but it did not set off a gender revolution any more than the development of a cult of the Virgin Mary altered the gender equation in Christianity. Similarly, the vital participation of women in tantric sexual rituals might seem to indicate a kind of male-female mutuality not typically assumed in Indic religious circles.[360] It is, however, unclear from the surviving literature whether tantric consorts—typically described as female—only could serve thus if they were at the same spiritual level as their male partner or whether they were regarded as mere instruments of male advancement, their own level of previous or subsequent attainment being quite irrelevant. If the latter is the case, then once again what seems like an indicator of gender equality would turn out to be considerably less. Nevertheless, there is no doubt at all that Mahāyāna metaphysics equalized men and women by recognizing the emptiness of gender dichotomies, and that tantric mythology, ritual, and practice, along with tales of accomplished female adepts, provide a basis for modern feminist readings of Buddhist tradition, and inspire women and men today to value the female rebirth and bring about changes in religious communities that premodern Buddhist women in India never enjoyed, and could hardly imagine.[361]

CHAPTER 10

Is Rebirth Real?

Indian Buddhist Arguments

Most of the Indian Buddhist discourse on rebirth we have examined thus far is descriptive or explanatory: accounts of the realms of saṃsāra, assertions of the ways in which delusion and karma lead to particular postmortem outcomes, analyses of how the factors of dependent origination lead from one life to the next, and assurances that the "radical" ontologies and metaphysics of Mahāyāna and Vajrayāna do not in fact undermine the conventional cosmology articulated by Mainstream traditions. For the most part, this discourse assumes the truth of claims about rebirth without attempting to prove them.

Although rebirth was widely asserted in South Asian societies from the mid-first-millennium B.C.E. on, it was—as we know from early Buddhist accounts of materialist philosophers—far from universally accepted, and the specifically Buddhist explanation of rebirth was often disputed by members of Hindu and other schools that propounded rebirth, on the grounds that if the common Buddhist denial of self is true, then rebirth is an incoherent idea. As a result, from early on, at least some Buddhist thinkers felt the need to justify both the idea of rebirth in general and their particular formulation of it in particular. They did so on a variety of grounds, offering arguments on the basis of spiritual experience, pragmatism, moral considerations, analogy, or formal rational analysis. In this chapter, proceeding more or less chronologically, I will explore a number of these arguments, with an emphasis on presentation rather than evaluation.

Experiential, Pragmatic, Moral, and Analogical Arguments

The most basic, and probably the earliest, Buddhist argument for the truth of Śākyamuni's cosmology in general and the reality of rebirth in particular is one we have encountered before. Recall that in canonical "first-person" accounts of the Buddha's awakening, such as that of the *Bhayabherava Sutta*, he vouchsafes the reality of rebirth through his meditatively acquired power of retrocognition and the structure and operations of saṃsāra, including, crucially, karma, through his divine eye—also a result of his contemplative prowess.[362] Even more plainly, in the *Devadūta Sutta*, after describing the general way in which karma leads to rebirth and then detailing the tortures of those reborn in hell, the Buddha declares, "I tell you this not as something I heard from another recluse or brahmin. I tell you this as something I have actually known, seen, and discovered by myself."[363] These and similar claims scattered throughout the Nikāya/Āgama literature and later systematized by Abhidharma traditions, all may be regarded as "experiential" arguments for karma and rebirth, in that their "evidence" is the Buddha's own direct, unimpeded, suprasensory knowledge of the way things really are in the cosmos. Much is made in Mainstream texts of the fact that the Buddha's teaching is "visible here and now, immediately effective, inviting inspection, onward leading, to be experienced by the wise for themselves."[364] The key phrases here are "inviting inspection" (P. *ehi passako*; literally, "[inviting] to come and see") and "to be experienced by the wise for themselves," each of which makes it clear that the Dhamma is something that each person must verify for themselves through practice.

Furthermore, such personal verification is superior to all other ways of ascertaining how things work. As the Buddha puts it in the *Kālāma* (or *Kesaputtiya*) *Sutta* (*Discourse to the Kālāmas* [or

Kesaputtiyas]), in response to a query on how proper behavior is to be ascertained:

> "Do not go by oral tradition, by lineage of teaching, by hearsay, by a collection of scriptures, by logical reasoning, by inferential reasoning, by reasoned cogitation, by the acceptance of a view after pondering it, by the seeming competence [of a speaker], or because you think: 'The ascetic is my guru.' But when you know for yourselves: 'These things are wholesome; these things are blameless; these things are praised by the wise; these things, if accepted and undertaken, lead to welfare and happiness,' then you should live in accordance with them."[365]

Presumably, the things the Kālāmas may come to know for themselves include precisely those details of the structure and processes of the cosmos realized by the Buddha on the night of his awakening. This is so because although the Buddha is a special kind of arhat in terms of his historical role, his meditative attainments—including retrocognition and the divine eye—are open to anyone with the time and discipline to follow the path through to completion. Thus, any disciple who accepts the Dhamma's invitation to "come and see" whether it is true as advertised may verify it in their own experience through commitment to the attitudes, ideas, and practices taught by the Buddha. Anyone, in short, can ascertain the reality of karma and rebirth, as well as the prospect of attaining liberation, through living a proper Buddhist life, gaining proficiency in meditative absorption, and coming to see what the Buddha saw. Assertions about "the way things are" that are based on contemplative experiences beyond the ken of ordinary people—we might call them mystical claims—are not, of course, without their problems (we will touch on some of these later), but experiential arguments were in the past, and remain today, basic to Buddhists' ways of defending their worldview, including their belief in karma and rebirth.

Incidentally, *experiential* arguments should not be confused with *experimental* arguments, which are rejected by early Buddhists in the realm of metaphysics and cosmology. As we saw in chapter 3, the *Pāyāsi Sutta*[366] describes a materialist king's attempt to *dis*prove rebirth through arguing that no soul is observed to leave the body at the time of death and that no one has returned from the dead to report on an afterlife. The Buddhist assumption is that what carries over from one life to the next is, in one way or another, consciousness, which by definition is immaterial, hence unobservable. There is, thus, no question of Buddhism being a form of empiricism, at least in the common Western sense of the term, whereby all knowledge is derived from sense-experience.[367]

Although the Buddha of the *Kālāma Sutta* dismisses the value of any source of knowledge other than direct experience, it is quite evident that from the earliest times, Buddhists also utilized "logical reasoning," "inferential reasoning," and "reasoned cogitation"—as well as oral tradition, the claims of scripture, and the authority or charisma of a teacher—to arrive at proper knowledge of the way things are, that is, to arrive at right view. Perhaps out of respect for the Buddha's frequent eschewal of disputation, as in the *Sutta Nipāta*, these arguments were not always laid out explicitly, but the early literature is nonetheless peppered with rational arguments of one sort or another that help to make plausible the notions of karma and rebirth. Three major kinds of arguments are evident in the early literature: pragmatic, moral, and analogical.

Modern authors sometimes describe the Buddha as a "pragmatist" because of his insistence that philosophical speculation with no practical bearing on our progress toward liberation is fruitless. Whether this is an appropriate designation for Śākyamuni or not, there are a few occasions on which he seems to have offered an argument for acceptance of rebirth that we might call pragmatic. The most famous such argument occurs in the *Apaṇṇaka Sutta* (*Discourse on the Incontravertible*), where the Buddha suggests a useful strategy for thinking about other teachers' denials of karma, rebirth, causation, immaterial realms, and the cessation of suffering. With regard to karma and rebirth, the rationale is as follows:

> "If there is no other world, then on the dissolution of the body this good person will have made himself safe enough. But if there is another world, then on the dissolution of the body, after death, he will appear in a state of deprivation, in an unhappy destination, in perdition, even in hell. Now...let me assume that there is no other world: still this good person is here and now an immoral person, one of wrong view who holds the doctrine of nihilism. But on the other hand, if there is another world, then this good person has made an unlucky throw on both counts: since he is censured by the wise here and now, and since on the dissolution of the body, after death, he will reappear in a state of deprivation, in an unhappy destination, in perdition, even in hell." [368]

The Buddha goes on to suggest similar strategies for those inclined to believe in rebirth and to those disinclined or inclined to accept the efficacy of karma, the reality of causation, and the possibility of attaining nirvāṇa. Along the same lines, the *Kālāma Sutta* outlines "four assurances" enjoyed by one who chooses to act wholesomely: if there is another world, then one will be reborn in a good destination, while if there is no other world, then one still is happy here and now; if suffering does come to evildoers, then one will avoid suffering by avoiding evil, while if no suffering comes to evildoers, one is purified nonetheless.[369]

The key phrase in the *Apaññaka* passage quoted above is "an unlucky throw," for this likens the uncertain disciple's approach to that of a gambler. And this, in turn, anticipates the suggestion by the French philosopher Blaise Pascal (1623–1662) that, in the face of uncertainty, we "wager" on the existence of God: if we bet on the existence of God and behave in a way prescribed by scripture, then if God exists, we will be rewarded, and if he doesn't, we lose nothing; whereas, if we bet against God's existence and live immorally, we lose nothing if he doesn't exist but lose a great deal if he does exist. In short, beset by metaphysical uncertainty, we do best to act on the assumption that, in the Christian case, God exists or, in the

Buddhist case, that karma and rebirth are real—for to do so places us in a win-win situation, while if we fail to do so, we lose both in this life and, if it exists, the next.

Another type of argument for the reality of karma and rebirth encountered in the early literature is what we might call the "moral justice" argument. This involves the claim that if the cosmos is morally just, then only Buddhist metaphysics, cosmology, and karma theory can explain how this is so. Although not common in the suttas/sūtras, such arguments, stated in either negative or positive form, do turn up in the Jātakas and some Abhidharma texts. In the *Mahābodhi Jātaka*, for instance, we find the future Buddha rejecting several non-Buddhist moral theories, each of which, he says, fails to explain retribution for evil and implicitly relieves beings of their karmic responsibility, hence undermines morality. Chaos theory (*ahetuvāda*) is rejected on the grounds that it destroys the connection between act and fruition. Theism (*issarakaraṇavāda*) is rejected because it shifts the moral burden from the individual to God and because in a cosmos created by God, the presence of evil means that God is either impotent or himself evil. Determinism, materialism, and an Indian form of Machiavellianism also are rejected because, like chaos theory and theism, they remove moral responsibility from the individual and eliminate justice from the cosmos.[370] In a similar vein, Vasubandhu argues in his *Karmasiddhiprakaraṇa* (*Treatise on Action*) that if rebirth, or transmigration, does not exist—if a death-time consciousness is not followed in the same series by a rebirth-linking consciousness—then the relationship between action and its result will be severed. On a more positive note,

> ...if transmigration exists, there [will] be—perhaps in another life—a relationship between the action accomplished here and its fruit of retribution, and so the relationship between actions and their results will not be impeded. Thus, there is most certainly transmigration because it assures the relationship between action and its result.[371]

Like the arguments of Platonists, Christians, Muslims, Hindus, and other religious folk, these Buddhist arguments all presuppose that (a) there is moral justice in the cosmos, and (b) such justice requires that individual moral responsibility is meaningful and an afterlife exists. Buddhist thinkers, of course, would add that such justice only is possible if moral responsibility and the afterlife are described in terms of karma and rebirth, which operate according to distinctively Buddhist categories and causal theories—for, as argued in the Jātakas, all other theories fall short.

Buddhist literature is replete with similes, metaphors, and analogies, and while the purpose of such figures of speech is illustrative rather than argumentative, we might say that when it comes to metaphysics, such images do sometimes function as arguments, in the sense that an everyday example drawn from our own experience may help us understand how a metaphysical fact beyond the range of our perception is actually plausible. Claims about karma and rebirth certainly are metaphysical, and in attempting to defend or assert them, Buddhist thinkers sometimes resorted to analogies. The text most famous for such analogical reasoning is the *Milindapañhā*, the Pāli treatise, mentioned in chapter 4, that consists of conversations between the Buddhist monk Nāgasena and the Indo-Greek king Milinda. The king asks Nāgasena a great number of questions on various aspects of Buddhist doctrine and practice, and the monk frequently employs analogies to illustrate his answer. Unsurprisingly, karma and rebirth are among the topics addressed. Thus, in answer to the king's question about the nature of saṃsāra, Nāgasena explains that, having died here, a being is born elsewhere, and that dying there, they are born in yet another place—just as a man, having eaten a mango, plants its seed, which grows into a tree, which produces its own seeds, such that "there would be no end to the succession, in that way, of mango trees."[372] To Milinda's inquiry as to whether one who is to be reborn knows they will be reborn, Nāgasena replies that it is so—just as a farmer who plants a crop and observes that it has rained will know that a crop has been produced.[373] Conversely, Nāgasena compares a person's knowledge that they will not be reborn—when that is in fact the case—to a farmer's knowledge that when he has ceased planting and harvesting and his granary is no longer being filled, "the cause, proximate and remote, of the filling of the granary had ceased."[374]

Another text that resorts to analogical argument is the Mahāyāna sūtra known as the *Bhadrapālaśreṣṭhiparipṛcchā* (*Questions of the Chief Merchant Bhadrapāla*), which is primarily concerned with the elucidation of the nature and functions of the mind, especially at the time of death. When Bhadrapāla asks what consciousness is and how it may be reborn, the Buddha tells him that because consciousness is invisible, its nature and functions are difficult to discern. However,

> "The consciousness moves and turns, transmigrates and expires, and comes and goes like the wind. Wind has no color or shape and is invisible, yet it can [generate and] stir up things and cause them to take on different shapes.... Consciousness is without color, shape, or light, and cannot be manifested. It shows its various functions only when [proper] causes and conditions are met.... When a sentient being dies, the elements... together with consciousness, all leave the [old] body.... [Similarly,] when the wind passes over exquisite flowers, the flowers remain where they are, while their fragrance spreads far and wide. The substance of the wind does not take in the fragrance of the exquisite flowers.... By virtue of a wind, we see and feel the effects of the wind, whose power spreads the fragrance far and wide."[375]

The sūtra goes on to invoke various other analogies to illustrate the nature and functions of the mind, likening consciousness's migration to another body to the sudden appearance of a face in a mirror or a rider's changing horses, the uncertainty of mind's location in the body to a pregnant woman's ignorance of the features her newborn will display, the powers of mind to affect the world to a puppeteer's control of a marionette, karma's effect on consciousness to the infusion of herbs into fine butter, and so forth.[376] As with the

Milindapañhā, the *Bhadrapālaśreṣṭhipraipṛcchā* is not attempting to frame a formal argument for rebirth but simply supplying analogies that can help to explain how we might understand it, hence more easily come to accept the idea—and in that sense, the provision of analogies is, at the very least, an argumentative strategy.

Rational Arguments: Nāgārjuna, Dharmakīrti, and Śāntarakṣita

The experiential, pragmatic, moral justice, and analogical arguments just cited all make a case for the truth of Buddhist karmic eschatology, and do so in a manner that is, broadly speaking, philosophical or rational, even if they do not attempt anything like a formal proof. Despite the Buddha's warning to the Kālāmas not to take stock in logical reasoning, inferential reasoning, or reasoned cogitation, Buddhist thinkers did offer rigorous and formal proofs of their cosmology, and it is to such proofs that we turn in this section.

One argument, which we encountered in chapter 8, was Nāgārjuna's famous claim, in his commentary to verse 70 of the *Vigrahavyāvartanī*, that because emptiness and dependent origination are interchangeable, emptiness guarantees that all valid worldly conventions are indeed valid—and that among these conventions are claims based on everyday perception and knowledge, as well as certain metaphysical claims, including the truth of the four noble truths, the reality of karma and rebirth, and the attainment of various fruits of the spiritual path. Nāgārjuna's claim is quite ingenious, and certainly establishes that the doctrine of emptiness is anything but nihilistic, but his readers—whether Buddhist or outside the fold—must have recognized that while the argument assures that dependently originated worldly conventions *in general* are valid, it does nothing to vouchsafe any *particular* instantiation of dependent origination. Thus, while arguing that valid worldly conventions are indeed guaranteed by emptiness, Nāgārjuna does not *argue for* the validity of Buddhist worldly conventions; rather, he simply assumes it.[377] Buddhist ideas of valid worldly conventions, however—especially in the realms of metaphysics, cosmology, and eschatology—were far from uncontested in the Indian philosophical world, and as Buddhists engaged with members of other traditions, from materialists, to Jains, to various Hindu schools, it was inevitable that they would have to go beyond Nāgārjuna and actively defend their particular vision of mind, life, and cosmos.

Gestures toward such a defense are found piecemeal in the works of a number of early first-millennium thinkers, including Vasubandhu and Asaṅga, as well as the Mādhyamika philosophers Āryadeva (second to third century) and Bhāviveka (sixth century), but it was only in the second half of that millennium that a full, systematic defense of the Buddhist worldview was offered. The author of that defense was Dharmakīrti (seventh century), whom we encountered during our discussion of Buddhist causal theories in chapter 5. Dharmakīrti is traditionally regarded as the grand-disciple of Dignāga (sixth to seventh century), the originator of the mature tradition of Indian Buddhist logic and epistemology, which is marked by sophisticated analyses of various avenues of epistemic authority—especially perception and inference—and modes of proper argumentation (*pramāṇa* and *tarka*, respectively). Most of Dharmakīrti's works are preoccupied with developing Dignāga's ideas on such matters. His most influential work, the versified treatise known as the *Pramāṇavārttika*, written early in his career, devotes three of its four chapters to technical discussions of inference for the sake of oneself (*svārthānumāna*), inference for the sake of others (*parārthānumāna*), and perception (*pratyakṣa*). One chapter, however—variously reckoned as the first or second—focuses on a "proof of epistemic authority" (*pramāṇasiddhi*), that is, on a demonstration that the Buddha is a reliable guide—or epistemic authority—for the spiritually curious. Unlike many of his Buddhist predecessors, Dharmakīrti does not base his argument on appeals to mystical experience, pragmatic considerations, an ideal of moral justice, or analogy; rather, he tries to make his case on the basis of logical argument rooted in commonly accepted observations about the world. Applying the methods of formal inference generally accepted by Indian philosophical schools of his era, he argues that the Buddha is epistemically reliable because (a) he has attained full awakening and (b) what he teaches on the basis of that awakening, the four noble truths, is true. In the process, Dharmakīrti frames the most sophisticated rational defense of rebirth proposed by any premodern Buddhist—a defense that still has many proponents today.

The take-off point for Dharmakīrti's chapter is the first half of the first verse of Dignāga's *Pramāṇasamuccaya* (*Compendium on Epistemic Authority*), which pays homage to the Buddha on the basis of his being (1) one who has "become epistemic authority" (*pramāṇabhūta*), (2) the compassionate one (*jagaddhitaiṣina*; literally, "one who desires the welfare of the world"), (3) the teacher (*śastṛ*), (4) the well-gone one (*sugata*), and (5) the savior, or protector (*tāyin*).[378] In a way, Dharmakīrti's chapter is a single 285-verse argument that the first of these five epithets is appropriately applied to the Buddha, with the other four epithets serving as logical reasons for the assertion. The argument actually proceeds in two different phases, each of which occupies around half the chapter. In the "forward system of explanation," Dharmakīrti argues for the Buddha's reliability on the basis of his being compassionate, which leads to his becoming a teacher, well-gone, and a savior—in other words, because he was able, over the course of time, to develop the perfect qualities attributed to an awakened being. In the reverse system, the Buddha's status as an epistemic authority is established first through his being a truth-telling savior, as a result of which he must also be well-gone, a teacher, and compassionate—in other words, because what he teaches, the four noble truths, is demonstrably true. Although Dharmakīrti defends rebirth in both parts of the chapter, his most detailed argument is laid out in the course of the forward system of explanation.

Dharmakīrti begins the "proof of epistemic authority" chapter by positing and defending a definition of epistemic authority as a fresh, uncontradicted cognition (verses 1-6). He then asserts—and this is the logical thesis of his entire argument—that "the Muni is such an epistemic authority" (verse 7a). Dharmakīrti then demonstrates that because of the permanence attributed to him, the creator God (*īśvara*) posited by the Hindu Nyāya school not only cannot be taken as an epistemic authority but must be regarded as non-existent (verses 7b–28), whereas the Buddha may rightly be regarded as trustworthy on spiritual matters because he has "become epistemic authority" by virtue of knowing what is to be shunned and done (*heyopadeya*) on the path to liberation (verses 29–33). Having established the Buddha's reliability as his logical thesis, Dharmakīrti states, in verse 34, "the proof is compassion, which [arises] from repeated practice." An opponent, most likely a materialist, objects, "that is unproven, because of the mind's dependence on the body." Dharmakīrti's reply to the materialist sets in motion everything that is to come: "That is not so, because we deny such dependence."[379] The logic behind this terse exchange is this: If compassion—and, implicitly, wisdom, power, and other positive qualities—must be developed through repeated practice to the highest possible degree in order to be a buddha's compassion, wisdom, and so forth, it is impossible that such qualities be developed over the course of one, brief lifetime. Hence, the attainment of buddhahood requires the existence of multiple lives, that is, of rebirth. But the reality of rebirth hinges on a discussion of the mind-body problem, since if the mind, as claimed by materialists, is utterly dependent upon the body, it will cease when the body dies, whereas if the mind can be shown to be independent of the body in significant respects, then survival of death may be assured.

Over the succeeding eighty-five verses (34–119), Dharmakīrti sets forth a complex argument that seeks both to undermine materialist proofs of the mind's dependence upon the body and to demonstrate that the mind must be sufficiently independent of the body so as to permit rebirth. Here, we can only summarize it briefly.[380] In refuting materialist claims that the mind is so utterly dependent upon the body as to make survival of death impossible, Dharmakīrti points out the absurdities entailed by such a position, noting, for instance, that if that were the case, then as long as a body is present, so must mind be—with the consequence that mind must be present in a corpse; conversely, the removal of the body need not entail the destruction of the mind, any more than removal of the fire that has baked a pot leads to the disappearance of the pot. A further absurdity in the materialist position, says Dharmakīrti, is that if the mind has the body as its principal cause, then every change in the body ought to produce a corresponding change in the mind—yet we know that the mind does *not* change in lockstep with changes in the body, for the mind can continue perfectly well even when physical processes such as respiration, the function of one or another sense-faculty, or the use of limbs is severely compromised. To put it in the more technical language employed by Dharmakīrti, the physical cannot be the substantial cause (*upadāna-hetu*) of the mental because a substantial cause is that which, when transformed, becomes a substantial result (as a seed becomes a sprout), and this cannot be said of the body-mind relation. Nor can the body be an indispensable cooperative condition of mind—an assistant condition (*sahākāriya-pratyaya*) in the absence of which the result cannot occur (as moisture or sunlight for the growing of a plant)—since it is clear that various mental qualities are not automatically entailed by changes in physical processes.

The key to Dharmakīrti's positive argument for rebirth lies in his invocation of the notion of a homogeneous cause (*sabhagahetu*), that is, a cause of the same general type. A common example of a homogeneous cause is an apple seed, which inevitably will produce an apple tree, and not a mango, papaya, or any other sort of tree. By the same token, says Dharmakīrti, the physical only can arise from the physical, and the mental from the mental, because although each is an entity, or substance (*vastu*), they are entities so different in *kind* that they cannot be related as substantial cause and result or special assistant condition and result. And what makes them so dramatically different is that mind is by nature immaterial and cognitive, while the body is material and insentient. Dharmakīrti concedes that the body, the senses, and various physical processes *a*ffect the mind, but that these can *e*ffect the mind he finds impossible.

In this sense, he proposes a form of interactionist dualism: it is interactionist because it allows for the influence of body on mind, and vice versa; it is dualist because it insists that, in the deepest sense, body and mind are different and separable—and indeed, at death, they separate, with the body left behind to decay while the mind passes on to a new existence.

The mechanics of death and rebirth are explored in greater detail in other texts we have cited, but Dharmakīrti establishes the general possibility of past and future lives by noting that if mind only can have mind as its substantial cause, then the first moment of consciousness in this life—at the moment of conception—must have been preceded by a causal event of the same type, hence by a previous moment of mind, and that moment, perforce, must have been the last mind moment of a previous life (or the intermediate state). When we work back through the same sequence, we quickly realize that our previous life must have been preceded by still another life, and so forth ad infinitum. Thus, our sequence of lives, which is itself definitive of saṃsāra, is proved to be beginningless. Projecting forward, then, the final mind moment of this life will serve as the directly antecedent substantial cause for the first mind moment of our next life, so future lives must be possible, as well. There is an important qualification to the claim about future lives, however: the final mind moment of a given life will be followed by the first mind moment of a subsequent life only if it is an *attached* mind or, more broadly, an unliberated mind. If, in Dharmakīrti's parlance, one has become an arhat in this life, then one's final mind moment will lack the necessary conditions for rebirth—ignorance and craving—hence will have no sequel. Thus, while saṃsāra is beginningless, it is not endless.

These, then, are the main contours of Dharmakīrti's argument. Once he has clinched it, he goes on (in verses 120–131) to entertain, and refute, an objection to the effect that even if multiple lives exist in which we might increase our compassion and other qualities through repeated practice, those qualities cannot be developed to the nth degree required for buddhahood—any more than jumping ability, while subject to improvement, can be developed to the point when one can jump a mile; or boiling water will somehow not boil away if the flame under it remains continuously lit. Dharmakīrti's response is consonant with his earlier discussion of the substantive differences between mind and body: he points out that the opponent's examples are both physically based, hence are inapplicable to the development of *mental* qualities. Thus, while each new jump attempt requires starting from the ground up, compassion, wisdom, and other positive mental qualities need not always begin anew, but can build on one another, proceeding ever higher. Similarly, the water boiling away in the second example lacks a stable basis, hence is destined to disappear, whereas the positive mental qualities one develops on the Buddhist path are solidly based in the attainment of a stable meditative absorption on the way we and all things really exist: as devoid of self. And because, as Dharmakīrti argues elsewhere (verses 205–209), the mind is by nature clear and aware—hence revelatory of truth—a perception of the truth cannot be supplanted by its opposite. Thus, positive mental qualities are indeed stable and capable of infinite development, and spiritual liberation is therefore possible.

Dharmakīrti's argument for the reality of rebirth and the possibility of liberation was deeply influential among Indian Buddhist thinkers, who commented upon it in detail and sometimes borrowed elements of it for their own independent treatises. The most significant of these treatises was the 3,646-verse *Tattvasaṃgraha* (*Compendium of Principles*) by the eighth-century master Śāntarakṣita (725–788), which examines, and criticizes, the philosophical claims of a range of non-Buddhist schools. Its chapter on Lokāyata materialism is in most respects a rehash of many of the main arguments proffered over a century earlier by Dharmakīrti, but it does add a novel touch in suggesting that, beyond what Dharmakīrti posited, a further reason for accepting the existence of past lives is the behavior of newborn infants, who manifest a wide range of desires, emotions, and mental states: hunger, frustration, love, hatred, and so forth. Feelings and mental states, says Śāntarakṣita, only can arise through previous habit and repetition, yet in a newborn they are:

> ...entirely devoid of any habit and repetition during the present life; what then is the cause of their appearance...if there is no other life?....These feelings appearing in this life must be regarded as appearing...through the force of the habitual appearance of similar feelings in the past.[381]

Although Śāntarakṣita does not extend his argument to other examples, such as the unusual musical talent displayed by certain children, or their claims to remember events in previous lives, he certainly could have done so. Even without such elaboration, his argument is reminiscent of Plato's appeal, in his *Meno* and *Phaedo*, to the idea that we know and learn things in our present life through a process of "unforgetting" (*anamnesis*) things we have known in a previous existence. In this sense, there is a subtle but important linkage between the arguments found in the two great "karmic eschatologies," the Indian and the Platonic.

Rebirth without a Self

Although Buddhist thinkers constructed most of their arguments for rebirth in response to skeptical attacks on the idea framed by metaphysical materialists, they consistently faced attacks, too, from members of Hindu and Jain schools who accepted the reality of karma and rebirth but argued that the basic Buddhist denial of a permanent self renders karma and rebirth either impossible or meaningless. Their objection is this: if the idea of no-self is deduced from the fact of impermanence, and impermanence entails the absence of a continuous individual identity even from one moment to the next, we are left wondering how a discontinuous "I" can be said to maintain any coherence within this life—let alone take rebirth in another realm and experience there the results of actions performed by "me" in this life. On the Buddhist view, it would have to be said that one person dies and another is reborn, and that one person performs actions and another experiences the result—and this makes a mockery of both personal identity and moral responsibility, not to mention the whole karmic eschatology broadly accepted by South Asian traditions. If such wrangling tempts us to ask, "So what?" we must recall that debates over self in Indian philosophical schools are far from merely academic exercises: most Hindu schools, for example, insist that spiritual liberation (*mokṣa*) is impossible without a recognition of and identification with the reality of the self (*ātman*) or person (*puruṣa*), while Buddhists insist, conversely, that without realizing the ultimate nonexistence of any such self or person, we will ignorantly continue to generate the craving and grasping that keep us enmeshed in saṃsāra. Thus, Buddhist attempts to explain how the no-self doctrine did *not* make karma and rebirth impossible or meaningless are vital elements of the tradition's self-presentation and self-defense. In defense of the metaphysical coherence of their doctrine, Buddhists have employed two major kinds of "argument": analogical and phenomenological. We will describe each of these briefly, in turn.

As with the analogical arguments described above, attempts to reconcile the doctrine of no-self with the reality of karma and rebirth use a generally accepted worldly convention to exemplify an unseen—and perhaps unseeable—metaphysical process. And, as before, the *Milindapañhā* is the early text most replete with suggestive analogies. In a classic conversation, King Milinda asks his interlocutor, "He who is born, Nāgasena, does he remain the same or become another?" "Neither the same nor another," replies the monk, who then proceeds to illustrate this apparent paradox by asserting that, as an adult, a person is both the same as and different from who they were as an infant. This, in turn, is clarified through two further examples: a lamp that is lit at sundown and burns throughout the night, and milk that is extracted from a cow, then in succession turns to curds, then butter, then ghee. The flame in the final watch of the night is not identical to the flame in the first watch of the night, yet is in some sense continuous with it; similarly, the ghee that is the final refinement of the liquid drawn from the cow is not the same as that milk, yet exists on a continuum with it. "Just so," says Nāgasena, "is the continuity of a person or thing maintained. One comes into being, another passes away; and the rebirth, as it were, is simultaneous. Thus, neither the same nor different does a [person] go on to the last phase of [their] self-consciousness."[382]

Nāgasena also confronts the moral question. Asked by Milinda what, precisely, is reborn, he replies "name-and-form," or mentality-materiality, that is, the five aggregates, and goes on to explain that although the name-and-form that is reborn is not the same as that which died, it is through previous karma that the new name-and-form arises. "But," asks the king, "would not the new being be released from its evil karma?" "Yes," says Nāgasena—but only in the case of an arhat; in the case of an unliberated person, the very fact that they have been reborn is a signal that they are not yet free from karma. To illustrate this point, Nāgasena provides several more illustrations, including that of a man arrested for stealing another man's mango, who argues his innocence by claiming that the mango he stole was not the mango originally planted by the owner. Similar pleas of innocence are entered by a man who, in winter, lights a fire in a field for warmth and is arrested after the fire consumes the entire field; a man who lights a lamp atop a house so as to eat his meal and is arrested when the whole village eventually burns; and a man who is accused of adultery when he steals another man's wife while her husband is on a journey. In every case, an appeal to the ontological difference between an earlier state of affairs and the later one will be unacceptable, for there *is* sufficient continuity between the planted mango and the stolen mango, the warming fire and the field-consuming fire, the dinner lamp and the fire that burns the village, and the woman ritually wed to her husband and the woman stolen by the adulterer. In each case, the king is asked in whose favor he would decide a legal case, and each time he supports the plaintiff. "Just so," says Nāgasena, "it is one name-and-form that finds its end in death, and another that is reborn. But that other is the result of the first, and is therefore not entirely released from its evil deeds."[383] Through these analogies, then, the *Milindapañhā* establishes the plausibility—if not the certainty—that the no-self doctrine does not undermine either personal identity or morality.

The other approach to the problem used by Buddhist thinkers is to describe in phenomenological detail the actual processes whereby a person maintains relative identity within ultimate difference, particularly in the transition between one life and the next. We have already described some of these accounts—many of them found in the Abhidharma literature—in chapter 5, but will reexamine them briefly here from the perspective of the demand, posed by Hindus, Jains, and others, that Buddhists justify their acceptance of karma and rebirth in light of their denial of continuous individual identity. It must be conceded that Buddhists are far from unanimous in their technical accounts of how rebirth occurs, least so, perhaps, in their ideas of what, precisely, passes from one life or another, but they do all take as axiomatic the basic claims that (1) all compounded phenomena are impermanent, (2) all external and internal phenomena (*dharmas*) are without self, (3) the way the world works is best described through the theory of dependent origination, and (4) karma and rebirth are particular, eschatologically significant, instantiations of dependent origination.

As we know, the Sanskrit term *dharma* (P. *dhamma*)—often translated as "factor" or "phenomenon"—is a key to understanding Buddhist metaphysics, for dharmas have been, since the earliest days of the tradition, the basic elements of existence, the irreducible building blocks of reality, the "lexicon," as it were, of Buddhism. Although different Buddhist schools enumerated and organized dharmas in different ways, all lists tend to include such conditioned phenomena as the four physical elements; the five aggregates; the various sense spheres; multiple kinds of wholesome, unwholesome, and neutral mental states; as well as such unconditioned phenomena as meditative cessations, space, and nirvāṇa. Dharmas are dependently related through various types of causes and conditions. Again, enumerations and definitions differ from one school to another, but these causes and conditions are the vital "grammar" that explains how the world functions the way it does. At the same time, it is axiomatic that all conditioned dharmas are marked by impermanence, which means, too, that they lack any kind of "self" or permanent, intrinsic identity. It was the Buddhist insistence on impermanence and no-self that led to criticisms from non-Buddhist schools to the effect that such theories made impossible any explanation of personal identity, memory, moral responsibility, or spiritual progress—whether from moment to moment or from one life to the next.

Recognizing the challenge that their notions of impermanence and no-self posed for offering a coherent account of the world, Buddhists devised various ways of thinking about impermanence and describing how continuity and coherence are assured in spite of it. In the early Mainstream schools, two major theories of impermanence arose. The realist Sarvāstivādins, as represented in Vasubandhu's *Abhidharmakośa*, asserted that dharmas were indeed impermanent but that each moment of a given dharma was itself divisible into discernible sub-moments of arisal, abiding, decline, and cessation. The Sautrāntikas, however—as represented by Vasubandhu in his commentary to his own *Abhidharmakośa*—point out that the Sarvāstivādin account leads to an infinite regress, for each of the sub-moments of which a moment consists would itself have to be subdivided by its arisal, abiding, decline, and cessation, and so would each of those sub-sub-moments, ad infinitum.[384] By contrast, the Sautrāntika view, which met with general if not universal acceptance, was that when the Buddha asserted that all dharmas are impermanent he only can have meant that they are *radically* impermanent: having arisen, they abide for the shortest conceivable time, and then cease; in effect, they arise and cease *almost* simultaneously, existing only long enough to leave a trace in the world such that they could said to have existed. Because the Sautrāntika concept of radical impermanence was the most widely adopted by later Buddhists, it was in the context of this theory that they sought to explain why personal identity, memory, moral responsibility, and spiritual progress still made sense.

Thus, over the course of the tradition's first millennium, Indian Buddhists developed a number of different concepts—often, but not always, classified as dharmas—to help explain how continuity in general and rebirth in particular are possible. Theravādins described a factor known as the *bhavaṅga*, literally, the "basis of existence" or, with imagery added, the "basic stream of existence," which is sometimes associated with the fundamental clarity and purity of mind, and whose main function is to assure that when a moment of consciousness has ceased, what replaces it is a consciousness in the same continuum, both during life and, crucially, at the moment of death and rebirth.[385] The Sarvāstivādins posited a compositional factor not associated with the mind (*cittaviprayuktadharma*) called "the obtainer" (*prāpti*), which guarantees that mental events within a particular mental continuum "obtain" from one moment to the next, and that the one who has performed a particular action will, either in this life or a future life, "obtain" the proper result.[386] One of the most popular of all Indian Buddhist schools, the Pudgalavāda, posited a "person" (*pudgala*) that was neither permanent nor impermanent, and—by virtue of its non-impermanence—helped to assure continuity from moment to moment and life to life.[387] Finally, as we have seen, the Yogācāra school of the Mahāyāna posited a storehouse consciousness (*ālayavijñāna*), which served as a sort of undercurrent to, and source of, not just sensory consciousnesses and a distorting "afflicted mind" but the material world, as well. In the Yogācāra view, it is the storehouse consciousness that provides moment-to-moment and life-to-life continuity to an individual sentient being's mental continuum.[388]

Although accounts of the functioning of these continuity-assuring factors were developed to an elaborate degree within the schools that posited them, and painstaking attempts were made to show that such concepts did not violate the axioms of impermanence and no-self, each was open to the criticism, from other Buddhists, that it nevertheless represented an attempt to smuggle in a self through the philosophical back door by eliding the basic Buddhist assertion of the radical impermanence, or momentariness, of all conditioned dharmas. We cannot examine these intra-Buddhist critiques here, but will simply note that the thinkers who most consistently *upheld* radical impermanence, although for different reasons, were the Sautrāntikas and Mādhyamikas.

The Sautrāntikas—whose views on natural processes are represented, in differing ways, by both Vasubandhu and Dharmakīrti—freely admit that a consequence of radical impermanence is, in fact, that there is no *real* continuity between one moment of a sentient being's mental continuum and the next, nor between one life and the next, and that identity is therefore a complete fiction (*prajñapti*). Yet things do not fall apart, for the simple reason that any given momentary instance of either a mind or physical matter will be followed by a nearly exact replica of itself in the subsequent moment. This is so because—in a manner reminiscent of Newton's first law of motion—there exists in each flashing moment a sort of inertial force, a forward momentum, that assures that the next moment will follow in sequence from the previous moment—within the same "continuum"—unless it is acted on by other forces. Thus, one jar-moment will be followed by another jar-moment unless it is shattered by a hammer, while—most crucially for our purposes—one moment of "my" mind will be followed by another moment of "my" mind as long as the desire for self-perpetuation—craving for existence—remains in force; when that desire is eliminated, as in the case of an arhat, then "my" mental continuum will cease. Despite their radical stance, the Sautrāntikas, like other schools, do provide their own way of helping to make continuity comprehensible, through the notion of *vāsanā*, usually translated as tendencies, proclivities, or impressions, and related etymologically to the notion of perfuming. Thus, each moment of mind is "perfumed" with the tendencies established at some point in the past, and will be thus perfumed until their basis is undermined through the destruction of defilements.

Being most intent on ontological and epistemological refutation, many early Mādhyamikas—including Nāgārjuna himself—did not much concern themselves with attempts to give a positive account of how the world works against the background of impermanence and no-self or emptiness. As we have seen, however, Nāgārjuna, in the course of positing emptiness as the nature of all entities and concepts, clearly asserts that the converse of emptiness is dependent origination, which either in general form as a theory of causation or specific form as the twelve links provides the most adequate possible account of the world and our life within it. Beyond that, perhaps, he thought it unwise to go, so we cannot know precisely how he might have analyzed impermanence or explained how relative continuity may be maintained in the face of impermanence and emptiness. Later Mādhyamikas—those eventually designated as Svātantrikas, or autonomists—did at times draw on the conventional explanations found in other schools. Thus, such figures as Bhāviveka (c. 500-578) and Jñānagarbha (eighth century) freely adopted Sautrāntika views in framing their accounts of conventional reality, while others, like Śāntarakṣita and Kamalaśīla, opted for Yogācāra terminology in their analyses of the conventional world. On the other hand, Mādhyamikas like Buddhapālita (c. 470-550), Candrakīrti (c. 600-650), and Śāntideva—who later would be labeled as Prāsaṅgikas, or consequentialists—remained true to Nāgārjuna's noncommittal position on how dependent origination actually works, being content to identify relative truth with agreed-upon worldly conventions—none of which can sustain analysis from an ultimate standpoint, and which, in any case, are not perhaps worthy of deep investigation.

To be clear, none of the accounts and explanations we have cited in this section amounts to a full-throated "proof" of rebirth like that proposed by Dharmakīrti. Rather, each in its own way is simply an attempt to show that the basic facts of impermanence and no-self do not obviate personal identity, memory, moral justice, or rebirth, and to show, too, that it is possible, through Abhidharma-style analysis, to frame a positive account of reality that—in the manner of Western philosophers such as David Hume (1711-1776) and Derek Parfit (1942-2017)—allows identity, memory, justice, and rebirth to be explained without resorting to "substance-language." Whether any of these accounts is fully satisfactory was much debated by both Buddhists and non-Buddhists, and is not for us to decide in the present context.

CHAPTER 11

The Spread of Buddhism, and Theravāda Views of Rebirth

Although the main direction of Buddhist discourse on rebirth was set by the South Asian traditions, Buddhist institutions largely disappeared from present-day India, Pakistan, and Bangladesh in the thirteenth century C.E., undone by centuries of shrinking patronage and the sudden violence unleashed by Turkic Muslim invaders, who swept through north India starting in 1192, destroying all manner of "idolatrous" institutions on the Gangetic plain, including Buddhist monasteries. And although a few holdouts kept monastic life alive in isolated pockets in north India, and Buddhist outposts continued to flourish for a time in the south, these were relatively insignificant, and it would not be until the twentieth century that Buddhism resumed its role as a cultural force on the mainland in India. In the meantime, however, the Dharma had been carried, by land and by sea, to many other parts of Asia, so the decline of Buddhism in India did not mean the end of the tradition. Indeed, a map of the Buddhist world in 1300 would have recalled an aerial view of certain South Asian banyan groves, where the original tree is gone but the space where it stood is surrounded by offspring trees that started with aerial roots long ago sent down by the now-dead mother tree.

Wherever Buddhism spread outside India, monks and other missionaries carried with them texts, intellectual traditions, stories, images, material artifacts, and rituals that had been developed in India, introducing to a wide range of cultures a set of ideas, practices, and institutions that were alien in most respects. These included Buddhist cosmology and metaphysics, notably the rebirth eschatology; images of buddhas and bodhisattvas, who inspired virtue and spiritual striving from ordinary people and might also serve as savior figures; the monastic ideal and the structures and lifeways of the saṅgha; the classic Buddhist monument, the stūpa; and a range of religious techniques with something for everyone, from magical incantations, to popular rites, to advanced contemplations. Wherever Buddhism traveled in Asia, its cosmology and eschatology proved particularly potent and persuasive, and its practitioners typically came to be regarded as the experts *par excellence* in matters relating to death, funerals, and the afterlife—to the point where Buddhism sometimes was caricatured as being mostly a funeral religion. It was far more, of course, but its success throughout Asia was not unconnected to its practitioners' apparent mastery of both thanatology and thaumaturgy.

Buddhism's Expansion Outside India

At the risk of oversimplification, it is possible to view the history of Buddhist expansion outside India as consisting of three great waves. The first, according to legend, began in the third century B.C.E., during the reign of the Maurya emperor Aśoka, who dispatched Buddhist missionaries northwestward to Central Asia, where the Dharma would flourish for a thousand years, and also sent his own son and daughter, both Buddhist monastics, south to Sri Lanka, to implant the teaching—the *sāsana*—among the Sinhalese peoples of the island, who themselves trace their ancestry to north India. The efforts of Aśoka's offspring led to the conversion of the Sinhalese king, the establishment of monasteries in and around the north-central capital of Anuradhapura, and the eventual predominance of an early Buddhist school known for upholding the "doctrine of the elders": Sthaviravāda in Sanskrit, or Theravāda in Pāli,[389] which rooted its ideas and practices in the Pāli canon. Although the fortunes of the Theravāda would wax and wane in Sri Lanka (there were long periods when Mahāyāna and tantric traditions flourished), it became the hegemonic form of Buddhism there in the twelfth century C.E., and from there spread to various parts of mainland Southeast Asia, eventually becoming the dominant religious tradition among the Burmese, Khmer, Thai, and Lao peoples inhabiting the region; it also took root among some Vietnamese and Malays. Like those of the Sinhalese, each of those cultures has its own long and complicated religious history (which in some cases, as in Sri Lanka, included periods of strong Hindu and/or Mahāyāna influence), but nowadays—united above all by their adherence to the Pāli canon—they make up what is generally called the Theravāda world.

The second great wave of Buddhist expansion began in the first and second centuries C.E., partly under the aegis of the north Indian Kuśan-Dynasty king Kaniṣka, who sent Buddhist monks and nuns northward on the trade routes that wove from the subcontinent into Central Asia—already under Buddhist influence—thence eastward into China. Multiple Buddhist traditions—along with their material culture—were transported from India and Central Asia to China. The Chinese—often aided by polyglot Central Asian scholars—translated vast numbers of Indian Buddhist texts into Chinese, providing for literate Buddhists in the Middle Kingdom an authoritative set of scriptures they might consult. In time, Mahāyāna texts and traditions came to predominate in China over those of the Mainstream schools—with a dash of tantra added during the eighth century. Chinese Buddhists respected their Indian antecedents but developed their own traditions, including schools based on the *Lotus* (Tiantai), *Avataṃsaka* (Huayan), and Pure Land sūtras (Jingtu Zong), and a school that focused primarily on meditation, Chan—the Chinese pronunciation of *dhyāna*, the Sanskrit term for meditative absorption. As the seminal civilization of East Asia, China extended its cultural influence to other lands in the region, so when, in the second half of the first millennium C.E., Buddhism spread to Korea, Japan, and Vietnam, the texts and traditions developed in China—including the Indian Buddhist canon translated into

Chinese and several Chinese doctrinal schools—tended to be the most important, although, like the Chinese themselves, Buddhists in these areas developed their own distinctive forms of Buddhist theory and practice. A secondary development during the first millennium C.E. was the export of Mahāyāna forms of Buddhism along Indian Ocean sea routes, to Cambodia, the Malayan peninsula, and the Indonesian archipelago. (Indian seafarers also made their way to China.) In Cambodia, Great Vehicle traditions flourished alongside Hindu forms until the ascent of Theravāda in the thirteenth century, leaving behind such masterpieces as the temple complex of Angkor Wat. On the Malay peninsula and the Indonesian archipelago, Mahāyāna lasted until the arrival of Islam early in the second millennium, bequeathing to the world such splendors as the great stūpa at Borobudur, on the island of Java.

The third great wave of Buddhist expansion dates to the seventh century C.E., when a series of kings from the Yarlung Valley in central Tibet unified the warring clans in their area and created a Tibetan empire, which dispatched armies and emissaries to neighboring lands, and undertook a Tibetan "civilizing project" that featured the importation of Buddhism, and Buddhist culture, as a unifying system of thought and practice. Although Chinese and Indian Buddhism both were important in the initial development of a Tibetan form of Dharma, Indian influences came to the fore late in the eighth century, so that henceforth the Tibetans primarily imported—and then translated—texts and traditions that came to them across the Himalayas from north India, rather than from their eastern neighbor. As in China, the imported texts and traditions included those of multiple Mainstream and "standard" Mahāyāna schools, but because Indian Buddhism between the eighth and twelfth centuries had a more strongly tantric flavor than the Buddhism that most influenced the Chinese, that was the style that came to predominate in Tibet. Thus, when Tibetan Buddhism spread to Mongolia, Ladakh, Bhutan, Sikkim, and other Inner Asian regions during the second millennium C.E., and even exerted influence at the Qing-Dynasty Chinese court (1644–1911), the version of the Dharma that was transmitted to those lands was the tantra-inflected style of late Indian Mahāyāna Buddhism, as translated into the Tibetan language and viewed through a distinctly Tibetan filter.

In this and the following two chapters, we will look briefly at the way rebirth was imagined and described in each of these three Asian Buddhist cultural regions, with special attention to the "seminal" sites from which Buddhism spread: Sri Lanka for the Theravāda world, China for the East Asian, and Tibet for the Inner Asian. Before we do so, however, a brief note is in order about the issue of "global" vs. "local" in Buddhist societies. Buddhism in India was a multifarious tradition, showing considerable disparities from region to region, school to school, and text to text, but it is not unfair to characterize normative South Asian Buddhism as united by particular terms of discourse, ritual practices, institutional structures, and images of the ideal person or society. In this sense, there is a Buddhist "imaginary," or a Buddhist "aesthetic," that carries through from one place and time to another,[390] and a key element of this imaginary, or aesthetic, is the vision and description of a cosmology that is best understood in terms of action, retribution, and rebirth—what Obeyeskere calls Buddhist karmic eschatology. Thus, as Buddhism was "translated"—carried across—from one culture to another, primarily by monks who belonged to the Buddhist elite, most of the unifying features of the Buddhist imaginary, or aesthetic, were carried over, too, helping to provide the "global" Buddhist themes on which various "local" changes would be rung. Thus, the notions of karma and rebirth were considered axiomatic in virtually every premodern Buddhist culture, but because Buddhism's success invariably depended on the degree to which originally Indic ideas and practices could be made comprehensible and appealing in a non-Indic setting, Buddhists in each culture added their own emphases, flourishes, and local touches to the normative, global vision they received, whether it came to them directly from India or through the intermediary of another Buddhist culture.

One important variable in the reception and interpretation of Buddhist karmic eschatology in this or that culture is the degree to which that culture, on the one hand, already possessed its own deeply imbedded imaginary or aesthetic, a long-established set of ideas, institutions, and practices to which Buddhism then had to adapt in order to gain a following or, on the other hand, the culture and polity were still in their formative stages and utilized Buddhism to shape ethnic, institutional, linguistic, social, and religious identity—in which case the model involved adoption more than adaptation. No culture perfectly fitted either of these models, but it is probably fair to say that the society of the Han Chinese was the prime example of a long-established culture to which Buddhism had to *adapt* in major respects, while those of, for instance, the Sinhalese in Sri Lanka and the Tibetans on their Inner Asian plateau were cultures profoundly shaped by the presence of Buddhism, and tended to *adopt* its ideology and praxis wholesale—although because Buddhism never is imprinted on a cultural blank slate, Buddhists in these areas also had to adapt to preexisting social and cultural conditions. To reiterate, however, karma and rebirth were accepted in all premodern Asian Buddhist cultures more or less as formulated in India; hence, it is upon the local emphases, flourishes, and variations added to that formulation that we will mostly focus in the discussions that follow.

The Case of Sri Lanka

In the terms just discussed, the peoples who accepted Theravāda Buddhism—the Sinhalese in Sri Lanka, the Burmese in Myanmar, the Khmer in Cambodia, and the Lao and Thai in Laos and Thailand—belonged to "adoption cultures," in that Buddhism became, for each, a formative influence in the development of a coherent identity for the ethnic group that accepted the Dharma. In every case, of course, there were multiple cultural traditions already at play, so those exporting Buddhism still had the task of making the Dharma compelling and comprehensible according to local notions and norms, but for the most part Buddhist ideology and praxis became a vital element of the local group's identity. Still, local history and local forces did help determine the precise shape taken by Buddhism in any given Theravāda setting, such that each "national" version of Theravāda introduced elements that marked a departure from Indian traditions, as well as from those of other Theravāda cultures. In what follows, we will focus primarily on the example of Sri Lanka.

Much of what we know of ancient Sri Lankan history must be deduced from various archeological sites scattered across the island, which show evidence that from early times Sri Lanka lay at a crossroads of various peoples, including those of aboriginal, south Indian, and north Indian origin. Such literary evidence as we possess comes from considerably later, in the form of several triumphalist chronicles composed by monks from the influential Theravādin monastery in Anuradhapura, the Mahāvihāra. These chronicles, especially the *Mahāvaṃsa* (*Great Chronicle*), tell of the Buddha's visits to Sri Lanka during his lifetime; the arrival on the island, in the year of the Buddha's death, of Vijaya, the north Indian progenitor of the Sinhala people; the establishment of Buddhism during the reign of Aśoka; the struggle by a second-century B.C.E. Buddhist king Duṭṭhagāmini to wrest control of the island from a south Indian Tamil king; and Duṭṭhagāmini's subsequent construction of a great stūpa in Anuradhapura—the first of many that would dot the landscape around the capital.[391] It is important to note that, from the very outset, Sri Lanka was inhabited at one time or another not just by Theravāda, Mahāyāna, and tantric Buddhists but practitioners of indigenous religions and of one or another Hindu tradition, particularly those of Tamil provenance. Islam began to make inroads in the late first millennium C.E., and even later, Portuguese, Dutch, and British colonial occupiers brought various forms of Christianity to the island, leading to the rich ethnic, religious, and linguistic mix to be found in the modern-day nation of Sri Lanka.

Thus, although Theravāda Buddhism is possibly the earliest form of Buddhism in Sri Lanka, and has been the dominant form of Buddhism there since the twelfth century C.E., we would be mistaken to think that the cosmology and eschatology of the Theravāda found on the island is an exact replica of that found in the Pāli canon—which itself, as we have seen, is not always consistent, and did not always translate out into "real life," whether for monastics or laypeople. Certainly, given the Pāli texts' influence on Theravāda everywhere, the vision of the five or six realms of saṃsāra, and the long, difficult progression of sentient beings from one karmically fueled rebirth to another until nirvāṇa is attained is the normative outlook adopted by all Sri Lankan Buddhists, but in practice, this outlook is complicated by influences drawn from other Buddhist traditions and from outside Buddhism. Indeed, Sri Lankan Buddhist temple complexes from the ancient, medieval, and modern periods all show evidence of extraneous influences. Archeologists have unearthed remains of Hindu Śaiva temples in the ruins of the great north-central capitals of Anuradhapura and Polonnaruwa, and starting in the fourteenth century, temples built in various parts of the island have displayed a common pattern: the incorporation of various deities from outside Theravāda into the sacred precincts.

These deities include the Hindu god Viṣṇu, who is often said to be the protector of the island; Nātha, who is a form of the Mahāyāna bodhisattva Avalokiteśvara; Saman, a solar and mountain deity that may be of indigenous origin; Paṭṭinī, a goddess originally from south India; Kataragama, a Sri Lankan version of the Hindu war god, Skanda, or Kartikeyya; the terrifying goddess Kālī; the demonic Hūniyam; and Vibhiṣana, the virtuous brother of Ravaṇa, the Laṅka-based villain of the epic *Rāmāyaṇa*. (The female bodhisattva Tārā and the female personification of the Perfection of Wisdom, Prajñāpāramitā, also seem to have been worshipped during the efflorescence of Mahāyāna in the first millennium, though not afterward.) Although there have been shifts over time in the relative prominence of these deities, with some gaining importance as others become otiose, in one combination or another they figure significantly in Sri Lankan Buddhist cosmology, art, and ritual practice. In the ritual realm, a classic instance is the Esala Perahera, a multiday festival held annually in the central-highlands city of Kandy, in which a tooth relic of the Buddha, housed in the nearby

Dalada Maligawa temple, is paraded through the streets on the back of an ornately bedecked elephant, accompanied by dancers, musicians, and devotees not only of the Buddha but of other deities with temples in the vicinity: Nātha, Viṣṇu, Kataragama, and Paṭṭinī.[392]

The importance of such deities derives from the curious paradox at the heart of Theravāda ideology: the Buddha was, of course, the greatest of all beings, but by virtue of his attainment of parinirvāṇa, he has, at least in principle, removed himself forever from the vicissitudes of saṃsāra. As a result, he has no real power to aid us, except by his inspiring example, the scriptures he left, and the teachings and other services provided by the saṅgha he founded. He certainly can be of no help when it comes to mundane matters, whether of national, local, or personal importance, and it was to fill this vacuum that Sri Lankan Buddhists attributed great worldly powers to a range of deities, from mighty nation protectors such as Viṣṇu and Nātha; to gods that might affect their immediate health, safety, and fortune, such as Paṭṭinī and Kataragama; to the countless nameless demons who made mischief with their lives, possessed them at times, and had to be placated if normalcy was to be restored.[393] It should be added that, just as in India, the Buddha's absence is not as complete as the texts would have us believe, for in Sri Lanka as elsewhere, something of Śākyamuni's power is said to remain in relics preserved in the stūpas that memorialize him and the images of him found in temples. Indeed, one of the most popular of all Sri Lankan rituals, the *pirit* (P. *paritta*), or protection, ceremony, features the recitation by monks of a collection of magically potent Pāli suttas, accompanied by the act of connecting a thread to a Buddha statue, then winding it through the congregation, to each of whose members it confers a sort of spiritual charge, or blessing.

These "pragmatic" variations notwithstanding, the normative Indian Buddhist cosmology and eschatology have long held sway over both monastics and laypeople in Sri Lanka, and, especially in the premodern period, the realities—and inhabitants—of heaven, hell, and the other realms of saṃsāra were taken for granted as part of the "furniture" of the wider world to which humans belong.

The reality of rebirth and the realms in which we might be reborn were reinforced in various ways, not only through recitation of, and commentary upon, selected texts from the Pāli canon, including the *Petavatthu* and *Vimānavatthu*, but also through lectures on karma and rebirth delivered by monks to devout laypeople on new- and full-moon days, and the creation of temple murals that depict the tortures of hell in gruesome detail, carefully linking each punishment with the evil act that brings it about. On a more positive note, the Jātakas, the stories of the Buddha's previous births, form a centerpiece of both preaching and temple art, serving at one and the same time to reinforce the doctrines of karma and rebirth and inspire both laypeople and monastics to emulate the Bodhisattva's striving, through all manner of lives and circumstances, to perfect various virtues and place himself at the threshold of awakening. In terms of everyday practice, especially in premodern times, laypeople assumed that meditation was reserved almost exclusively for monks and that arhatship was beyond reach in their present life—but that sincere observance of the moral precepts and generous donations to the monastic order (or, failing that, a deathbed intention for a higher rebirth[394]) would assure in the next life a human or godly rebirth, where they might be better positioned for spiritual practice. Virtue also is cultivated through such rituals as the Bodhi Pūjā, an offering ceremony directed to the Buddha's tree of awakening and to the deities believed to inhabit it. At the ritual's conclusion, the participants attempt to transfer their accumulated merit to those deities—and although, as we have observed, such a transfer is impossible in light of karma theory, it is itself an expression of a virtuous and altruistic intention, hence meritorious for the person wishing to transfer their merit.[395]

The notion of merit transfer also figures in Sri Lankan Buddhist funerals and their follow-up rites, all of which are conducted by monks.[396] Thus, at a funeral, after contemplating impermanence and offering robe-cloth to the monks, the relatives of the deceased pour water from a pitcher into a cup placed on a saucer until it overflows, while the monks intone these verses from the Pāli canon:

> Just as the water fallen on high ground flows to a lower level.
> Even so, what is given here accrues to the departed.
> Just as the full flowing rivers fill the ocean,
> Even so, what is given here accrues to the departed.[397]

Similarly, either three days or a week after the funeral, a monk will be invited to "preach for the benefit of the dead." He will offer a sermon on a suitable topic, at the conclusion of which the merits accrued by those in attendance are transferred to the departed. Merit transfer is also at the heart of an almsgiving ceremony, called the "offering in the name of the dead," which is typically held three months after the funeral. Although it is hard, if not impossible, to know where a given person has been reborn—and we must recall that for Theravādins, rebirth occurs immediately after death—a presupposition of these rites is that the deceased may have been born as a hungry ghost and therefore needs to be nourished and appeased before they can move on to a better rebirth.[398] As scholars have observed, these ceremonies are very similar to Hindu *śrāddha* rites, which involve the ritual feeding of the dead. We might also observe that in Theravāda settings, the hungry-ghost realm seems to stand in for the intermediate state asserted by most other Buddhist schools to intervene between death and the next rebirth.

In normative Theravāda, *nibbana*, or nirvāṇa, is defined as complete liberation from rebirth, and those few monks or nuns who did aim for arhatship recognized that although morality was a necessary condition for liberation, it was not a sufficient condition, for mastery of meditation—the processes yielding both mental serenity (*samatha*) and extraordinary insight (*vipassanā*)—also was required. Serenity was achieved through single-pointed concentration on one or another external or internal object; these might include the breath, a Buddha image, various parts of the body, geometric discs, or—significantly for our purposes—the four divine abodes, or immeasurable attitudes: love, compassion, sympathetic joy, and equanimity, which the meditator is to imagine extending to all beings throughout the cosmos. Within Buddhist cosmology, of course, this entails consideration of the five or six realms of rebirth, and may involve, as well, a supplementary reflection on the wholesome and unwholesome deeds that lead to rebirth in those realms. As we know, advanced states of concentration lead naturally to such psychic powers as the recollection of past lives and the clairvoyant vision of the operation of karma in determining the rebirths of sentient beings. Insight is attained through intellectual and experiential investigation into "the way things are." This may initially involve bare, present-moment-centered mindfulness of the rise and fall of mental and physical events—this is the aspect of insight meditation most emphasized in the modern "mindfulness movement"—but in a larger context, these "immediate" experiences of the body, sensations, and thought were filtered through such general categories as the four noble truths, the twelve links of dependent origination, or such "marks of existence" as impermanence and lack of self. For those of a philosophical bent, the detailed descriptions of mind and matter—including explanations of the realms of saṃsāra and the functioning of karma—to be found in the Abhidhamma literature provided a fine-grained analysis of how persons and things "work," despite their neither being nor possessing a permanent self.

An important caveat regarding the last paragraph deserves mention: while the Theravāda ideal, in Sri Lanka and elsewhere, remains arhatship, it is asserted within normative tradition that the degeneracy of the age in which we live actually makes it impossible for anyone to attain complete liberation at present—and that this situation has obtained for quite some time. Not everyone accepts this claim, but even those who believe there may be arhats among us have to concede that, on the one hand, no true arhat will claim to be an arhat, and, on the other, while ordinary people like us may deduce from the behavior of certain accomplished monks, nuns, or laypeople that they *could* be fully liberated beings, short of becoming spiritually accomplished ourselves, we cannot be certain, for in Buddhism the dictum always has been: "it takes one to know one." This, in turn, leaves hanging the question whether release from rebirth—as opposed to attainment of sublime states of mind—truly is an option for Theravāda Buddhists, or has been an option any time recently.

Women in the Theravāda World

As we have with relation to early Buddhism and the Mahāyāna, we will briefly consider here the Sri Lankan Theravāda view of the human female rebirth. Sri Lankan society is an Indic society, with strong influences from both north Indian and south Indian traditions, hence for the most part patriarchal. And like any other Indic Buddhism, Theravāda is itself also patriarchal, and its literature and outlook on the world largely androcentric. Thus, Sri Lankan Buddhist assumptions about the nature of women, their proper social role, and their spiritual potential are mostly aligned with the perspective of normative Theravāda, to the effect that (a) women's nature is defined in large part by their sexual appetite, emotional lability, and skill at manipulation; (b) their proper social location is in the domestic sphere; and (c) while, like men, they are capable of attaining arhatship, they never can hope to become buddhas. The insistence that a woman can become an arhat, which goes back to the time of the Buddha, does place women on a nearly equal plane with men in matters of the highest importance, but because it is generally assumed that monastic life is the primary, if not the sole, avenue to liberation, it would be important for Sri Lankan nuns to form a strong and well-supported order.

The bhikkhunī ordination tradition was, we are told, brought to Sri Lanka during the time of Aśoka, but it seems never to have thrived there, and disappeared from the island late in the first millennium, during a time of turmoil and warfare brought on by invasions from south India. Women could, and occasionally did, live a monastic life as ascetic but unordained laywomen, but until the twentieth century, joining the saṅgha was an option largely closed to females. As in other patriarchal cultures, of course, female voices did make their way to the surface in Sri Lanka, whether in the songs and stories of the early Indian Buddhist nuns found in the *Therīgāthā*, or in Sinhala language retellings of the lives and deeds of great Indian nuns and laywomen, such as Mahāprajāpatī, Viśākhā, and Uttarā, or in poems that recount the sufferings of Yaśodharā, the wife whom the Buddha abandoned when he entered the ascetic life. Like many other Buddhist stories, these tales typically include revelations about the characters' past lives and the karma that leads to fortunate or unfortunate rebirths, but they do cast women and their lives in a mostly positive light.[399] Also, as in India, there were goddesses such as Paṭṭinī and Tārā that evinced some degree of devotion, but just as in the Indic cases examined earlier, Sri Lankan Buddhists' worship of female deities did not translate into social advancement for ordinary women and did not change the discourse suggesting that a female rebirth was inferior to that of a male.

Regional Extensions

The observations we have made regarding Sri Lankan Buddhism may cautiously be applied to the Theravāda cultures of Southeast Asia, as well.[400] Like that of the Sinhalese in Sri Lanka, the cultures of the Burmese, Khmers, Thais, and Lao were deeply shaped by normative Theravāda texts, ideas, and practices, but as in the case of Sri Lanka, Theravāda was not the sole influence on the development of culture. Thus, the Burmese culture was affected not only by Theravāda but by Mahāyāna and tantric currents, the Khmer absorbed significant elements of Hinduism and Mahāyāna before Theravāda came to prominence, and the areas of Vietnam in which Theravāda gained a foothold bore the imprint of Mahāyāna traditions that originated in China. Being more recent than the others, the Thai and Lao cultures were shaped to a greater degree by Theravāda, but they, like others in Southeast Asia, accepted Buddhism as an overlay to indigenous traditions going back into prehistory. As a result, the cosmologies of these Buddhist cultures were enriched in one way or another by the addition of deities unknown to Indian Buddhism, and while Theravāda Buddhist ideas and practices—including the classical karmic eschatology in its theoretical, ethical, and ritual dimensions, as well as the tradition's intellectual and contemplative tools for transcending rebirth—became normative, dominant, and definitive, in each setting proponents of Theravāda inevitably had to contend with traditions from outside the Buddhist fold, just as any missionary religion must when it enters new territory.

One distinctive feature of Southeast Asian Buddhist societies—evident in the premodern era, but especially notable in modern times—was the development of a "merit economy," wherein considerable wealth was channeled into donations to the saṅgha rather than invested in businesses, the state, or other "classic" finance-dependent institutions. The rationale for this was karmic: the merit gained through such generosity might not bring the donor material rewards in this life but would help assure them a better rebirth in their next life.[401] Although most frequently remarked upon in Southeast Asian contexts, the "merit economy" has been a feature of Buddhist social life to one degree or another wherever the saṅgha has flourished—which is to say, nearly everywhere in Buddhist Asia.

Finally, the observations we made about the status of the female rebirth in Sri Lanka apply to the Southeast Asian cases, as well: the cultures were patriarchal and androcentric and the female saṅgha—even when it was established—was rarely of significance, while at the same time, women's spiritual potential was asserted in principle, and the voices of exemplary females, whether from Indian or local sources, did run as an important undercurrent beneath the mainstream male dominance typical of the cultures in question.

CHAPTER 12

East Asian Views of Rebirth

Buddhist East Asia, comprising the eastern half of present-day China, as well as Korea, Japan, and much of Vietnam, displays a mixture of adoption cultures and adaptation cultures. Like their counterparts in Sri Lanka and much of Southeast Asia, Koreans, Japanese, and Vietnamese had their life-world and sense of ethnic identity shaped to a significant degree by Buddhist ideas and practices, making them, arguably, adoption cultures—although just like their counterparts in the Theravāda regions, these East Asian Buddhists superimposed the Dharma upon earlier traditions, and the influence of those pre-Buddhist traditions, and of later non-Buddhist forces of one sort or another, undermines the idea that "adoption" of Buddhism ever is completely straightforward. Just as Sri Lankan Buddhists and, by extension, those in Southeast Asia drew their main inspiration from India, so did Buddhists in Korea, Japan, and Vietnam look above all to the Buddhism of the "seed" civilization of East Asia, that of China. Because of Buddhism's Indic origins, the subcontinent was considered by all Buddhists to be the motherland of the Dharma, but the forms of Buddhism transmitted to the peripheral regions of East Asia were, at first, almost entirely Chinese.

As suggested earlier, China itself is probably best regarded as an "adaptation" culture, in which Buddhist missionaries arriving from India and Central Asia encountered a longstanding, powerful, and sophisticated civilizational apparatus, which could not simply be converted to Buddhism wholesale. Rather, Chinese Buddhists had to accept that certain aspects of Chinese culture were nonnegotiable and adapt their teachings and practices to reflect the reality they encountered on the ground; only then could Buddhism begin to make a significant impact in China. Because China is in many respects the seminal culture of East Asia, and because it exemplifies the notion of a Buddhist adaptation culture, in the following section we will focus on the Middle Kingdom's reception and adaptation of Indian ideas and practices surrounding rebirth, karma, and other key religious doctrines and practices.

The Entry of Buddhism into China

As mentioned in the previous chapter, Buddhism first penetrated China in the first or second century C.E., when Buddhist monks and merchants from India and Central Asia made their way eastward along caravan routes into the domains of the Han Dynasty, which was then in decline. Unlike their counterparts elsewhere, Buddhists newly arriving in China found an established civilizational apparatus that stretched back well over a millennium, and included a sophisticated written language, a history of larger or smaller imperial dynasties, and two well entrenched religious traditions: Confucianism, with its focus on the proper ordering of society, individual ethical behavior, and the maintenance of ritual; and Daoism, with its philosophical paradoxes, its exploration of the basic principle of the cosmos, the Dao, and its shamanic, contemplative, and alchemical practices for achieving immortality. There also were remnants of an early sacrificial religion, as well as an ever-vibrant folk tradition, with its teeming pantheon and popular ideas and practices, most of them aimed at alleviating this-worldly ills.

None of this rich legacy was going to simply give way before the brilliance of the Dharma, and Buddhists seeking a mission field in China faced a number of daunting obstacles. The first, and arguably most significant, of these was simply the fact Buddhism was a foreign, or "barbarian," religion, hence suspect to those many Chinese who considered any import from outside the Middle Kingdom deeply suspect. What's more, many of the Buddhist ideas and practices brought to China ran against the grain of longstanding Chinese values and practices. The Buddhist insistence on renunciation of lay life in pursuit of individual spiritual awakening cut against the grain of the Chinese tendency to regard life within society as of paramount value. Buddhist descriptions of karma-fueled rebirth into this or that realm of saṃsāra ran counter to the Chinese focus on the welfare of one's ancestors, who were believed to reside in an afterworld where they were accessible to the living through ritual means, not lost into some utterly different life beyond their descendants' ken. And the saṅgha, as an independent polity that controlled its own resources, could be seen as a potentially troublesome alternative center of power that might, in difficult times, threaten the hegemony of the imperial authorities. The odds were not entirely stacked against Buddhism, however. Its textual and intellectual tradition, while non-Chinese, was clearly the product of a sophisticated society, hence intriguing to Chinese intellectuals who encountered it. Its practices and practitioners often exuded both charisma and magical potency, which could prove appealing to those unconcerned by ideological niceties. Importantly, its philosophical paradoxes and its contemplative traditions were evocative of, if far from identical to, those of Daoism. And, perhaps, most importantly, the pedagogical flexibility exhibited by the Buddha and his successors assured that, for all its deep-seated principles, Buddhism was not an especially "creedal" religion but one capable of adaptation and transformation—whether in the short term or over longer stretches of time.

As noted, when Buddhism first entered China, the Han Dynasty was in decline. The Han had made Confucian tradition the bulwark of their rule, but as they gave way to a succession of other regimes that rose and fell from the third to seventh centuries C.E.—the Three Kingdoms, the Jin, the Northern and Southern Dynasties, and the Sui—the "official" influence of Confucianism waned, and this allowed Buddhism to gain a foothold, although in somewhat different ways in different parts of the country. In the north, where ethnically non-Han Mongols and other "barbarian" invaders often were in control, the Buddhism was more pragmatic and popular—though not without its scholarly side. In the south, where many Han intellectuals had fled, the more theoretical aspects of the Dharma proved a source of fascination—though popular practices were introduced, as well. In both cases, Buddhism enjoyed a certain degree of state support, although its place was not uncontested: Confucians and Daoists both challenged the legitimacy of the new religion, chiefly on the grounds that it was a foreign import, hence inherently inferior and dangerous. Nevertheless, despite the political and ideological vicissitudes of the middle centuries of the first millennium C.E., which included occasional persecutions, and although it never came to dominate Chinese culture as it did the cultures of many other Asian locales, Buddhism slowly but steadily gained ground in China, to the point where it shared equal religious billing with Confucianism and Daoism in the Chinese imagination. (It is worth remarking that in China, as in India and so many other complex cultures, distinctions among religions were maintained far more at the level of elite institutions than of popular practices.)

Among the ways in which Buddhism worked its way into the fabric of Chinese ideology and society was through the establishment of highly organized and disciplined monasteries; the translation of intriguing and impressive Indic and Central Asian Buddhist texts into Chinese; the appropriation of native deities and terminology to bridge the gap between Indic and Chinese ways; a willingness to identify the Chinese emperor as a buddha or bodhisattva; the creation of itineraries and practices focused on centers of pilgrimage; the development of daily, monthly, and annual rituals that could be meaningful to both monastics and laypeople; and the formation of various elite "schools" of thought and practice.[402]

These schools—which were by no means always distinct, let alone mutually exclusive—tended to be identified by their promulgation and interpretation of one or another Indian text or textual tradition. Among the earliest schools to appear were those focused on the monastic regulations of the Vinaya, Vasubandhu's *Abhidharmakośa*, and the *Satyasiddhi Śāstra* (*Treatise on True Attainment*) of

Harivarman (fourth century), three major Mādhyamika treatises (two by Nāgārjuna, one by his disciple Āryadeva), and the various sūtras and treatises associated with Yogācāra and the buddhanature doctrine. The buddhanature teaching, which was accepted by virtually all schools, was presented most effectively in the *Awakening of Faith in the Mahāyāna* (*Dasheng Qixin Lun*), a treatise attributed to the Indian literary master Aśvaghoṣa (author of the *Buddhacārita*, second century), but almost certainly of Chinese provenance. All of these schools left their imprint on Chinese Buddhist thought, but their preoccupation with Indian precedents limited their appeal, and they proved less influential in the long run than two somewhat later traditions: Tiantai, which focused on the *Lotus Sūtra*, and Huayan, which was concerned with the *Avataṃsaka*. Each of these schools produced a series of brilliant, synthetic thinkers who interpreted the basic teachings of the sūtras in creative and original ways, thereby hastening the process of making Indian Buddhist thought comprehensible in Chinese terms. They influenced the course of Buddhism not just in China but, when exported, in Japan, as well, where they were called Tendai and Kegon, respectively.

An even later school of lasting importance was Zhenyan, the "True Word" or Mantra tradition, which was introduced during a brief efflorescence of Indian tantric traditions in China during the eighth century, and had a significant impact on later Buddhist ideology and ritual. Most influential of all, perhaps, were the devotional Pure Land (Jingtu) school, which began around the fifth century, and the meditation-oriented Chan school, which rose to prominence in the late first millennium, during the late Tang and the Song Dynasties. Each claimed Indian provenance, yet each took Indian ideas and practices and made them accessible to Chinese audiences, more "popular" in the case of Pure Land, more intellectual in the case of Chan. We will say more about each of these shortly.

Rituals of Death and the Afterlife

In China, as in every other Asian culture to which Buddhism was introduced, the karmic eschatology developed in India was an essential part of the intellectual framework provided by proponents of the Dharma. Unlike in Sri Lanka and other adoption cultures, however, Buddhists arriving in China encountered long established ideas and practices surrounding death and the afterlife. As Stephen Teiser notes, "Before the growth of Buddhism and the development of organized Taoism, Chinese belief maintained a relatively fluid boundary between this life and the next. Human existence was viewed as a temporary conglomeration of the two dominant forces in the universe, *yin* and *yang*"—which were roughly equivalent to the ideas of matter and spirit, or body and soul, respectively.[403] At death, it was assumed, the lighter *yang* forces tended upward and the darker *yin* forces downward. In more immediate terms, "once they have died, people are found in or near their graves, visiting ancestral halls and family banquets, and lodged in specific sites like... the Yellow Springs."[404] In this same period, adds Teiser,

> a passion for immortality is also evident... ranging from the prolongation of life on earth to the search for an unending existence in heaven, various western paradises, or the islands of the east. Another important feature of the otherworld was that it was... organized along bureaucratic lines. Officers administered the empire of the dead, keeping records on every human being and taking charge of the spirit after death.[405]

Such a vision of the afterlife is broadly consonant with those found in many cultures, including that of Buddhist India, where a notion of postmortem reward or punishment for deeds performed in our earthly life provides some way of understanding what lies beyond the grave and why we end up where we do—whether temporarily or for eternity.

Thus, notes Teiser, when Buddhist cosmology and eschatology were introduced to China, they did not seek to supplant indigenous ideas so much as to supplement them, for "both indigenous Chinese and imported Buddhist conceptions viewed selfhood as a fluid process," not requiring a creator god or a fixed, eternal soul.[406] Also,

> to an originally fluid and multi-local vision of the afterlife, Buddhism added one more option: that the person could be reborn in another bodily form. [Similarly,] Buddhist notions of karma refined and completed a system of judgment after death that had been in place for centuries.[407]

With the arrival of Buddhism came detailed and sophisticated Indian teachings about saṃsāra, karma, and rebirth, and these certainly were accepted—if not always understood—by both monastic and lay Buddhists. Further, because they were not completely at odds with pre-Buddhist Chinese eschatology, they made an impression in Confucian and, even more so, Daoist circles. Buddhists, however, made their own adjustments. They often incorporated indigenous deities into their pantheon, and adapted their ritual practices to preexisting Chinese models. Within the general framework of their karmic eschatology, they adapted the Chinese vision of a bureaucratized afterlife, which eventually was enshrined in a short late-first-millennium apocryphal sūtra known as the *Scripture on the Ten Kings* (*Shiwangjing*). This text describes a postmortem "purgatory" presided over by ten officials, most of whose names are Chinese rather Indian in origin. These officials are responsible for meting out karmically appropriate rewards and punishments to the souls of the departed in the intermediate period between death and rebirth—which in this case lasts not for seven weeks but for three years. Typically, the souls are brought in for a "hearing" in the court of each of the ten kings, where they must defend their conduct. Bewildered as they are by the proceedings, souls often are represented by an advocate, the compassionate bodhisattva Kṣitigarbha (C. Dizang), who is reputed to have vowed in a previous life "to deliver all sentient beings from suffering, especially those trapped in the lower regions of rebirth."[408] Unsurprisingly, prayers to Kṣitigarbha and offerings to the ten kings feature prominently in the ritual portions of the *Scripture on the Ten Kings*; these prayers and offerings might be made before one's own death or, afterward, by one's relatives, so as to assure that when, at the end of three years, one receives one's next rebirth assignment, it is a heavenly one.

Of even greater eschatological significance in the Chinese Buddhist world are the texts and practices surrounding what generally is called the "ghost festival," which is held around the full moon of the seventh lunar month (typically in August), a moment that marks the end of the traditional rainy-season retreat undertaken by monks and nuns. It is reputed that on this occasion the gates of all the realms of rebirth are thrown open, and the departed are able to return to earth to visit their living relatives, who offer them incense; a banquet with empty seats for the visitors; material goods, including "spirit money," which is ritually burned; and, at the festival's end, paper boats bearing candles to light their way back to the afterlife. Although the deceased inhabiting any realm of saṃsāra are welcomed and feted, there is a particular focus on those spirits that have been consigned to the hungry ghost and hell realms. This is explained by the mythology underlying the festival, found in several Indic and Chinese sources. The most important is the *Ullambana Sūtra* (C. *Yulanpenjing*), an Indian Mahāyāna text that tells of the heroic, but unsuccessful, attempt by the Buddha's disciple Maudgalyāyana to rescue his mother from rebirth in the hungry ghost realm, and the compensatory practice he is taught by the Buddha: making food offerings at the end of the summer retreat to the saṅgha, who then transfer the merit to his mother, freeing her. Similar tales are found in the Sanskrit *Avadānaśataka*, where Maudgalyāyana instructs laypeople to practice as the Buddha had instructed him; the Pāli *Petavatthu*, which recounts Śāriputra's failed attempt to release his mother from a hungry ghost existence, and his ultimate success in doing so when he offers a feast to the monastic community and then transfers the merit to his mother; and a Chinese esoteric text in which Ānanda is visited by a terrifying hungry ghost who predicts the great disciple's own imminent death and rebirth as a preta, unless he makes appropriate offerings to all ghosts everywhere—which Ānanda is able to do when the Buddha teaches him a series of powerful preta-feeding mantras.[409]

As in India and Sri Lanka, these rituals for the departed play on the tension between, on the one hand, the removal from our purview of deceased loved ones, based on the seemingly iron-clad dictates of karmic law; and, on the other, the all-too-human need to retain some sense of communion with the departed—and to believe, as well, that karmic results can be mitigated through ritual, magic, or some form of divine intervention.

Later Debates, and Pure Land and Chan

In the ethical sphere, Chinese Buddhists debated a host of issues among themselves, of which two with implications for reflection on karma and rebirth bear brief mention. First, unlike their counterparts anywhere else in Asia, Chinese Buddhists opted decisively for a strict vegetarian diet. Despite the Buddha's own meat-eating—after all, he instructed his monks to eat whatever was placed in their alms bowls—and despite the carnivorous tendencies of the Chinese as a whole, Buddhists in China opted to accept the arguments scattered in a number of Indian texts, including the *Laṅkāvatāra Sūtra* and the *Mahāyānamahāparinirvāṇa Sūtra*, to the effect that consumption of animal flesh was an unmitigated moral evil, with dire karmic consequences. As a result, Chinese Buddhist monks and nuns maintain strict vegetarianism, while laypeople often do, as well, though not quite so consistently.[410] Furthermore, whether or not they are vegetarians, Chinese Buddhists (and Buddhists elsewhere in Asian societies) will on certain important ritual occasions purchase animals that they do not (as would be typical) slaughter for food but liberate them into the wild—a highly meritorious deed that nevertheless overlooks the irony that the animals had to be captured in the first place in order to be purchased and freed.

A second point of interest consists of discussions among the Chinese as to whether "grasses and trees"—that is, plant life—could ever attain spiritual awakening. Implicitly, if they can, then they must be sentient in some sense of the term, hence part of the scheme of karma and rebirth. As we know, unlike in Jainism, in the classical

Indic form of Buddhism, plants are not considered sentient beings, and they are not included among the realms of saṃsāra. However, certain Chinese Buddhist thinkers, especially in the Tiantai school, reasoned along lines like this: if everything in the cosmos is empty of intrinsic nature, and if emptiness is equivalent to buddhahood, then everything in the cosmos is buddha, is originally awakened mind. The Tiantai phrase that captures this idea is "three thousand worlds in one thought." Hence, grasses and trees—and for that matter, all natural and human-made things—also partake of true reality, also are buddha. Just as in India, so in China these Mahāyāna speculations did not result in any effacement or redrawing of the boundaries of saṃsāra, but they did add a new perspective to traditional Buddhist ways of conceiving of the cosmos and the entities within it, including the plant kingdom.[411]

As mentioned above, the two Chinese Buddhist schools that proved the most successful in the long run were Pure Land and Chan. Indeed, they were the only two schools that survived intact the great persecution of Buddhism in 842–845. The Pure Land tradition[412] rooted itself in Indian Mahāyāna sūtras that focused on the buddha of the western paradise of Sukhāvatī, Amitābha (Infinite Light) or, in slightly different iconographic form, Amitāyus (Infinite Life). Amitābha was a key figure in the Mahāyāna pantheon in both India and Central Asia, and aspiration to be reborn in Sukhāvatī is evident from texts and images found there, but it was in China that Pure Land theory and practice truly blossomed. Although Pure Land theologians such as Huiyuan (334–416), who established the first Pure Land monastery, atop Mount Lu, in 412, and Tanluan (476–542), who wrote detailed commentaries on the Pure Land sūtras and streamlined devotional practice, were great scholars and thinkers, the tradition spread largely because of its popular appeal.

Although the Indian sūtras describe a set of complex visualizations of Amitābha and his Pure Land that are supposed to allow practitioners to fix the buddha and his paradise in their minds and to assure them of being reborn in Sukhāvatī after death, the Chinese masters—while never abandoning the canonical visualization techniques—focused increasingly on the practice of reciting the name of Amitābha (C. *nianfo*). Although there are long spells that may be employed, the simplest and most common formulation is that attributed to Tanluan: "*namo amituo fo*," or "Homage to Amitābha Buddha." Although devotees were encouraged to utter the prayer constantly, counting out recitations on a rosary, it also was said that even one sincere repetition could assure one's rebirth in the Pure Land after death. Needless to say, such an approach to religious practice was immensely appealing to those who lacked the time, discipline, or circumstances to spend their life in study, meditation, or monastic life—although to repeat, many Pure Land masters were indeed great thinkers and contemplatives. Like the postmortem rituals described in the preceding paragraphs, Pure Land practice suggested that, despite the regularity of the mechanism of karmic cause and effect, the process could, to some degree, be short-circuited, for sincere recitation of Amitābha's name could assure that, immediately after death, the devotee would be ushered to Sukhāvatī—from which a return to saṃsāra is impossible.

In an origin story developed in China late in the first millennium, the Chan, or meditation, school[413] traces itself back to the Buddha's silent communication—"from mind to mind"—to his disciple Mahākāśyapa of a "special transmission outside the scriptures": a contemplative method for seeing directly into the nature of things, "without dependence upon words and letters." The practice, Chan tradition tells us, was handed down by over a score of Indian patriarchs (including Nāgārjuna and Vasubandhu) until it reached the twenty-eighth in the line, Bodhidharma, who in 525 C.E. took the tradition to China, along with a copy of the *Laṅkāvatāra Sūtra*. Early Chan masters established monasteries and garnered patronage for their institutions, while at the same time maintaining an aura of independence from worldly concerns. Although Chan thought was informed in various ways by such powerful traditions as Tiantai and Huayan, and while its focus eventually shifted away from the *Laṅkāvatāra* to the Perfection of Wisdom sūtras, the core of the tradition—at least in theory—always was its focus on meditation.

Over the centuries, through disagreements over succession, patronage, and practice, Chan divided into a supposedly more "gradual" northern school and a supposedly more "sudden" southern school, the latter of which became dominant and eventually split into five "houses." (Two of the five houses, Linji and Caodong, formed the basis for the two major Japanese Zen schools, Rinzai and Soto, respectively.) Through all its vicissitudes, the tradition generated a large and lively literature, including a "sūtra" attributed to the Sixth Chinese patriarch, and "founder" of the southern school, Huineng (638–713); a variety of lineage histories; brilliant poetry by the likes of Wangwei (699–759) and Hanshan (eighth century); and the collections of "public cases" or "encounter dialogues" (*gong'an*), or koans, in which charismatic and often cranky masters instruct their disciples by paradox, indirection, and sometimes violence, in order to help them break through their dualistic fixations and see their mind as it truly is: empty, brilliant, and primordially free.

Chan (and its successor traditions elsewhere in East Asia, especially Japanese Zen) has been much discussed, so we will note here only that, at least in its rhetoric, the tradition concerns itself very little with rebirth eschatology: so intent are its masters on enlightenment here and now that questions of the afterlife are mostly held in abeyance. However, there is no question that Buddhist cosmology—including the operations of karma, rebirth, and dependent origination—lurks in the background of Chan ideas and practices. Most of the Indian scriptures influential in Chan, including the *Laṅkāvatāra*, *Vimalakīrti*, *Vajracheddikā*, and *Śūraṅgama* (*Heroic March*) sūtras assume that Buddhist karmic eschatology is true to the way things actually work in the world. Indeed, the *Śūraṅgama* (which is most likely a Chinese apocryphon), lavishes attention on the relation among defilements, karma, and the various realms of rebirth—to which we will be subject as long as we do not recognize the pure and luminous buddha-mind that is our own inmost nature, and indeed, the nature of all things.[414] Such ideas are evident within Chinese Chan literature, as well. For instance, one of the most famous of all koans, the second case in the *Gateless Barrier* (C. *Wumenguan*) collection, features a long-ago Chan practitioner who is reborn as a fox five hundred times for claiming that he is exempt from the law of cause and effect.[415] Many other instances could be cited. Furthermore, Chan monasteries often participated in their own "cult of the dead," which involved, among other things, mummification of their deceased masters. Thus, just as neither the radical metaphysicians nor the tantric adepts of Indian Mahāyāna, their rhetoric notwithstanding, ever sought to upend the classical notions of karma and rebirth, so the dramatic negations and apparent mockery of everything holy by the masters of Chan simply reflect a skillful deployment of shock tactics in order to free a disciple's mind from dichotomous thinking and useless emotions, and directly realize the buddhanature within them.

It should be added in passing that although Pure Land and Chan are sometimes seen as polar opposites, with devotees of Amitābha relying solely on the power of an external deity, and Chan contemplatives relying solely on themselves, Pure Land masters did not eschew meditation, not did practitioners of Chan deny the importance of devotion—especially, but not solely, when it is directed to the spiritual master, without whose guidance awakening is impossible. What's more, in later times, Chan and Pure Land sometimes ended up in a sort of synthesis, whereby practitioners would practice both devotion to Amitābha and Chan meditation—and do so without any sense of contradiction. This is very much in keeping with the tendency, within Chinese religions more generally, to comfortably mingle not just popular-level practices, but even ideologies, as in the case of Buddhism's absorption of certain Daoist elements, alchemical Daoism's acceptance of some esoteric Buddhist ideas and practices, and Neo-Confucianism's borrowing of elements of Buddhist metaphysics.

The Place of Women

As before, we will conclude the main part of this chapter with a brief analysis of views of the human female rebirth. In China, as elsewhere in Asia, the culture has for the most part been patriarchal. In the classic Confucian scheme of the "five relationships," women are subordinated to men, as subjects to rulers, sons to fathers, and younger brothers to elder brothers. (Friends, on the other hand, enjoy mutuality). And although the "yielding" feminine principle, *yin*, is exalted in philosophical Daoism, and popular Daoism recognizes a host of female divinities, opportunities for women in public life nevertheless were as restricted in China as in most premodern cultures.

In the case of Chinese Buddhism, all the patriarchs of the great schools were male, and almost all these schools' literature was produced by males, so there is a decidedly androcentric shadow looming over our knowledge of Chinese Buddhist life. There are, however, some interesting countercurrents. Unlike in the rest of Buddhist Asia, in China the full-ordination tradition for nuns was established fairly early (429 C.E.), and has persisted—indeed, sometimes flourished—up to the present day. Some of the Chinese nuns were highly educated women from noble families, and a few of them displayed literary talents, writing classical poetry on a par with that of their better-known male counterparts.[416] Certainly, because of the widespread acceptance of the doctrine of buddhanature by Chinese Buddhists, women were assumed to be capable of awakening, if not necessarily of becoming a buddha in a female body. Further, one of the most significant of all savior bodhisattvas, the compassionate Guanyin (Skt. Avalokiteśvara), was widely worshipped in China in male form (as was the case in India) for nearly a millennium, but around 1000 C.E. was transformed into a female figure—perhaps because the qualities of compassion and mercy were so strongly identified in Chinese culture as "feminine" traits.[417] Finally, as in so many cultures, among Chinese Buddhists much of the everyday practice of religion was carried out by women, even if their activities and thoughts have been left unrecorded. Nevertheless, these countercurrents do not indicate anything approximating the modern ideal of gender equality, and Chinese Buddhist women, like their sisters elsewhere generally labored under the assumption that, of gendered human rebirths, theirs was decidedly inferior.

Regional Extensions

As mentioned above, Buddhism came to other East Asian cultures—Korea, Japan, and Vietnam—through the agency of Chinese culture. Where, however, Buddhist missionaries to China had to adapt to a long-established civilization, in other parts of East Asia they helped make the Dharma a formative influence on the emerging national identities of those who encountered it. As with the centralizing, culture-creating kings of Sri Lanka or Southeast Asia, early rulers of Korea, Japan, and Vietnam adopted Buddhism as a set of ideas, practices, and institutions that could help to unify a fractious society. In each case, as usual, there were pre-Buddhist indigenous traditions that had to be accommodated—for instance, Shinto in Japan or various shamanic traditions in Korea—but Buddhism remained a defining tradition for these cultures more often than not. At the same time, because the importation of Buddhism was part of a wholesale importation of Chinese culture writ large, elements of Confucian, Daoist, and Chinese folk traditions also entered into the mix. In any case, the Buddhist culture of China was transmitted to other East Asian cultures, which then, each in its own way, rang changes on the Chinese ideas and practices. In Japan, for instance, many of the schools that developed in China seeded counterpart traditions in the islands that would become vital, long-lasting institutions: Tiantai became Tendai, Huayan become Kegon, Zhenyan become Shingon, Chan became Zen, and the Pure Land school, Jingtu, became Jodo. Just as the Chinese altered Indian ideas and practice to suit their needs, so Japan and other East Asian cultures changed the traditions they inherited from China, producing their own distinctive variations on the ideas, practices, and institutions they received from the Middle Kingdom. Most crucially, they accepted the karmic eschatology that originated in India, and made it their own, so that while East Asian cosmologies—like those of the Theravāda world—may sometimes look quite different from their predecessor in India, the terms, the structures, and the overall sense of how things work in the world are quite similar, governed as they are by the vision—of karma and the six realms, saṃsāra and nirvāṇa, and the advantages and disadvantages of different sorts of rebirth—that is the currency of Buddhist life and thought everywhere the Dharma has taken root.

CHAPTER 13

Inner Asian Views of Rebirth

Buddhist Inner Asia includes the Tibetan cultural area—which comprises Tibetan-speaking portions of the People's Republic of China, Nepal, Bhutan, and Himalayan India—as well as parts of present-day Outer Mongolia and such ethnically Mongol regions of Russia as Buryatia and Kalmykia. Most of these could be classified as Buddhist adoption cultures, in that, like members of the Theravāda cultures of Sri Lanka and Southeast Asia and East Asian cultures outside China, the Tibetans and the peoples they influenced allowed Buddhism to shape their ethnic or national identity to a significant degree. The Mongols are arguably an exception, as Buddhism was adopted by the various tribes living north of the Tibetan plateau only after those groups, under the aegis of Genghis Khan (1155/62–1227), had already organized themselves into a powerful political and military force that left its mark on both the Asian and European worlds.

In any case, just as in other parts of Asia, Buddhist missionaries in Inner Asia encountered preexisting cultural ideas and practices that they could not simply overwhelm with their brilliance and sophistication, and, as elsewhere, the effectiveness of their promulgation of the Dharma depended upon their skill in employing local ideas and practices in the interest of advancing a Buddhist agenda. The seminal Inner Asian Buddhist culture is that of Tibet, and the Tibetans, like the Sri Lankans and Chinese, took their primary inspiration from India. But just as Korea, Japan, and Vietnam looked to China rather than India as their main source of Buddhist texts, institutions, and practices, so the Mongols and other Inner Asian groups "seeded" by Tibet were most deeply influenced by Tibetan forms of Buddhism, even while paying lip service to the Indian traditions on which the Tibetans themselves had directly drawn. Here, our main focus will be on Tibetan Buddhism—especially on the ways in which death, rebirth, and the afterlife were conceived on the Tibetan plateau.

The Development of Buddhism in Tibet

Buddhism first was brought to Tibet during the mid-seventh century C.E., when Songtsen Gampo (617–650), an ambitious king from the Yarlung Valley, southeast of Lhasa, unified the fractious nobility of central Tibet, sent armies far and wide, and decided that Buddhism—which at the time was practiced to the plateau's south in India and Nepal, to its west in Central Asia, and to its east in China—was not just a sophisticated religious system but might be used as leverage against recalcitrant nobles, who themselves tended to practice an amalgam of Tibetan folk beliefs and an older, shamanic tradition originally imported from further west, Bön. Songtsen Gampo had religious images brought from Nepal and China, sponsored the development of a Tibetan alphabet based on Indian models, and promulgated Buddhism at his court. Over a century later, a second great king, Trisong Detsen (742–797), expanded Tibetan military power as far as the Chinese capital, at modern Xi'an, and oversaw the founding of the first Tibetan Buddhist monastery, Samyé, in the Yarlung Valley—assisted in the process by the Indian pandit Śāntarakṣita (author of the *Tattvasaṃgraha*, mentioned in chapter 10) and Padmasaṃbhava, a great tantric adept from the western Himalayan region of Uḍḍiyāna. It was Trisong Detsen who seems to have set the Tibetans' sights toward the Indian rather than the Chinese Buddhist tradition, and to the scholarly and tantric traditions then thriving in the northern part of the subcontinent. Trisong Detsen's ninth-century successor Ralpachen (802–836) promoted Buddhism enthusiastically, underwriting the first significant Tibetan translations of Indian texts and taxing the populace in order to support the burgeoning monasteries—an unpopular move that led to his overthrow and murder. His successor, Langdarma (799-842), ruled only briefly, but in that span, he suppressed Buddhism, especially in central Tibet, driving many monastics back into lay life or into exile in outlying areas. This effectively marked the end of the Tibetan Empire, and what Tibetan Buddhist historians call "the earlier spread" of the Dharma.

The ensuing century is sometimes regarded as a sort of "dark age" by Tibetan historians, in that Buddhism was disestablished in the central part of the country, monastic life was tenuous at best, and contacts with India lessened—though they never ceased entirely. In the last part of the tenth century, under the sponsorship of a number of kings in western and central Tibet, the flow of teachers, texts, and ideas from India resumed, and in the ensuing centuries—referred to by Western scholars as the Tibetan renaissance and by Tibetans as "the later spread" of the Dharma—the work of translating Indian texts into Tibetan began anew, and a variety of religious orders sprang up, each of which assured its legitimacy by its connection to Indian masters and its institutional survival by the support of various factions within the nobility. The empire never would be revived, but, led by charismatic masters, or lamas (*bla ma*), these orders—the Kadam, Sakya, Kagyü, and Nyingma—would, to one degree or another, shape subsequent religious life in Tibet, and in some cases assumed considerable political, economic, and social power. In particular, the Sakya enjoyed a period of suzerainty under Mongol and Yuan Chinese sponsorship in the thirteenth and fourteenth centuries, the Karma branch of the Kagyü exercised considerable control in west-central, central, and eastern Tibet from the fourteenth to the mid-seventeenth century, and, first with Mongol help and later with the support of a succession of Qing emperors of China, the Kadams' successors, the Geluk, under the aegis of the Dalai Lamas of Lhasa, ruled much of the country (at least nominally) from 1642 until the Chinese Communist takeover in the 1950s. Over the course of this complex history, Buddhism became thoroughly enmeshed with Tibetan culture, to the point where the two sometimes were regarded as being synonymous, though of course they are not: as in every other Asian Buddhist culture, local elements—whether of the folk religion or other preexisting forms of ideology and practice (in Tibet, this would be Bön)—influenced Buddhist ideas and practices, even as Buddhism overlaid them with its hegemonic Indian cosmology, metaphysics, and eschatology, its institutions and value systems, and its catholic range of practices, aimed at everyone from common farmers and tradespeople, to merchants and princes, to monks, scholars, literati, and charismatic yogīs.[418]

The Tibetan Buddhist Cosmos

In the course of adopting Buddhism as their overarching religious ideology, Tibetans took on the Indian Buddhist karmic eschatology more or less *in toto*. As in other Asian cultures, indigenous deities, ideas, and practices were subsumed under the Buddhist superstructure. Thus, native Tibetan deities were "converted" into protectors, usually wrathful, whose role it was to defend the integrity of the plateau's land, water, air, and sacred sites—as well as the Dharma itself. And, as in other Asian Buddhist settings, the basic scheme of the six realms of saṃsāra—crowded as it already was with a panoply of beings—was supplemented by a focus on particular powerful imported Buddhist deities, in this case drawn from all three Indic traditions: Mainstream, Mahāyāna, and Vajrayāna. The great disciples of the Buddha celebrated in Mainstream Buddhism were revered in Tibet, as was a group of sixteen arhats whose worship was particularly prominent in China. Of Mahāyāna figures, the compassionate bodhisattva Avalokiteśvara—whose "sex-change" in China we mentioned in the last chapter—came to be seen in Tibet as both a progenitor and protector of the nation, as well as a figure that might be reincarnated in charismatic masters or powerful kings, and whose practices—especially the recitation of his mantra, OṂ MAṆI PADME HŪṂ—were well-nigh ubiquitous. Nearly as important were three other figures: the wisdom bodhisattva Mañjuśrī, the powerful and wrathful Vajrapāṇi, and Tārā, a goddess of multiple forms who was seen above all as a remover of obstacles. As in East Asia, Amitābha and Amitāyus were popular in Tibet, although they were not the focus of a particular school of thought and practice, nor did they gain the same degree of prominence as they did in China and the cultures it influenced. Other popular figures included the Medicine Buddha Bhaiṣajyarāja, the future Buddha Maitreya, and an assembly of thirty-five confession buddhas, as well as a variety of tantric buddha-deities, including Guhyasamāja, Hevajra, Kālacakra, Cakrasaṃvara, and Vajrayoginī, each in their own paradise, as well as lesser but still powerful tantric helper-deities like male "heroes" (*vīra*) and female ḍākinīs.

Also recognized in the pantheon were the great tantric adepts of Buddhist India and such deified Tibetan culture heroes as Padmasaṃbhava, Atiśa (982–1054), Milarepa (1040–1123), and Tsongkhapa (1357–1419), charismatic masters associated with the Nyingma, Kadam, Kagyü, and Geluk orders, respectively. It should be noted in passing that the line separating bodhisattvas from buddhas, and spiritual masters, or lamas, from the other two was often unclear in Tibet, where bodhisattvas might be regarded as being manifestations of buddhas, and lamas as being either bodhisattvas or buddhas. It is worth mentioning, as well, that just like Indian traditions, some Tibetan traditions (for instance, the Geluk) tend to see the whole cosmos simply as the product of the complex interaction of mental and physical events, while others (most notably the Nyingma) subsume everything to an "All-Creating King" (Kun byed rgyal po) or to a primordial, all-good, absolute buddha, often designated as Samantabhadra (Kun tu bzang po).

In addition to the classical Indian vision of the five or, more commonly, six realms of saṃsāra, Tibetans also took up the full South Asian account of karma and its results, which they analyzed in treatises, described in religious poetry, worked into their legal and medical systems, and depicted in their own versions of the "wheel of life" (described in chapter 7), with its graphic and symbolic presentation of the three poisons, the ups and downs of action and its fruits, the six realms, and the twelve links of dependent origination—all held in the grip of the Lord of Death, with a buddha standing outside the wheel pointing to the sole alternative: the practice of Dharma.

Another, more participatory, form in which Buddhist karmic eschatology was conveyed was in the game of Rebirth,[419] which is generally attributed to the great Sakya Pandita (1182–1251)—a master of the Sakya tradition who helped introduce Dharmakīrti's work (including his arguments for rebirth) to Tibet and was among the first Tibetan hierarchs to establish friendly relations with the Mongols. The game of Rebirth seems to be based on earlier Indian games like snakes-and-ladders, where through throws of a die the player progresses or regresses from one square to another (often by jumps) on a gridded board, seeking to reach a final, home square before the other players. There are numerous different Tibetan versions of the Rebirth game, as well as versions developed in Nepal, Bhutan, and Korea, and the number of squares varies considerably. In Sapan's version, which contains 104 squares, the hells occupy the lowest rungs, with the hungry ghost and other lower and higher realms of saṃsāra ranged above the hells; higher still are found various pure lands, and the stages of śrāvaka, pratyekabuddha, the Mahāyāna, and tantric paths. At the top are squares for the three buddha-bodies that are the outcome of the path, the performance of buddha-activities and, finally, having one's relics enshrined in a stūpa, where one will become "an object of reverence for the rest of the age." The game is educational not only in that players learn a great deal about the structure and details of Buddhist cosmology and soteriology from playing it (especially under the guidance of a knowledgeable teacher) but also in the way the throws of the die have been conceived, in such a way that one cannot move from one square to another unless the circumstances are right. Thus, one cannot directly jump from the Vajra Hell (the lowest square on the board) to buddhahood, or even to a place somewhere along one of the classical paths, without passing through other realms or practices. Furthermore, to get anywhere from one of the lower realms requires a good throw of the die—and in the case of the Vajra Hell one must throw a one once, a two twice, and so forth, up to six sixes, just to reach the realm of Yāma, the death-god—although from there, with a proper throw, one may begin the tantric path. All this gives the player an extraordinary appreciation for the ways in which karma works, both in this life and in future lives.

Tibetan Meditations on Saṃsāra and Its Denizens

Although rebirth was, and is, generally accepted in all Asian Buddhist cultures, the most sophisticated philosophical argument in its favor, that of the Indian pandit Dharmakīrti (surveyed in chapter 10), only took hold in the Tibetan tradition and those shaped by it. There, it has served as the go-to explanation of why Buddhist claims for rebirth must be true—and accepted as true by any person with the time and intelligence to follow it through to its conclusion. Needless to say, Dharmakīrti's argument is quite arcane, and likely to be understood only by a tiny minority of highly educated monastics. It is important fodder for scholastic debate, but known hardly at all by those not shaped by the complex educational traditions that Tibetans have prized for the past thousand years—traditions modeled on those of the great monastic universities of Buddhist India, such as Nālandā and Vikramaśīla. For most Tibetans, both lay and monastic, the fact of rebirth was axiomatic, and here, we will focus not on philosophical disputations but on meditative techniques—accessible to varying degrees to both monastics and laypeople—that demonstrate the Tibetan contemplative tradition's deep engagement with the beings that inhabit the various realms of rebirth and show, too, the tradition's various techniques for dealing with death and its aftermath.

Early in the second millennium C.E., inspired by the efforts of such Indian masters as Kamalaśīla (740–795) and Atiśa, both of whom visited Tibet late in life, the ascendant orders of the later spread of the Dharma in Tibet distilled from the vast array of texts and teachings they had received from the subcontinent a set of key doctrines, rearranged in an order suitable for reflection and meditation. This way of organizing the Dharma, best known as the "stages of the path" (*lam rim*),[420] typically begins with an initial reflection on, say, buddhanature, or the crucial role played by the guru in one's spiritual development, then goes on to treat in sequence the rarity and preciousness of rebirth as a human, the universality of impermanence and the inevitability of death, the sufferings of the lower realms of saṃsāra, the operations of karma, the unsatisfactory nature of even the upper realms, the details of the twelve links of dependent origination, and the six perfections of the bodhisattva: generosity, morality, patience, effort, meditation, and wisdom. Discussions of the last two perfections, in particular, provided an occasion for detailed discussions of—and sometimes arguments about—what constitutes effective or ineffective meditation and right or wrong view. Less commonly, masters in the various orders also produced texts in a genre called the stages of mantra (*sngags rim*), which sought to bring a similar sort of order to the plethora of tantric teachings that had made their way to the plateau from India over the span of the half-millennium from 700 to 1200 C.E.

As already suggested, the stages-of-the-path literature introduced those who followed its sequence of reflections—and these definitely included both monastics and laypeople—to the details of Buddhist rebirth eschatology, through providing detailed descriptions of the realms of saṃsāra and the dependently originated karmic processes by which we take birth in this or that postmortem destination. Practitioners were instructed to fear rebirth in the lower realms—seeking refuge in the Buddha, Dharma, and Saṅgha to forestall such a fate—and also to reject the blandishments of the upper realms by understanding that they, too, partake of the truth of suffering, and that only complete liberation from the wheel of rebirth can bring lasting satisfaction. However, this "Hīnayāna" path falls short of what sentient beings are capable of, for full buddhahood is our true destiny, and this can only be achieved through following the path of the bodhisattva. That path, as we have seen, is motivated above all by the aspiration to become a buddha so as to maximally benefit all sentient beings.

This awakening mind (T. *byang chub sems*, Skt. *bodhicitta*) is not merely a wish to be expressed but a practice to be cultivated, both in our everyday life and in our contemplative life. In everyday life, as well as in meditation, we must frame all our actions with the Mahāyāna spirit, beginning every action with the aspiration that it be for the benefit of others and concluding it with a dedication of merit for the welfare of sentient beings. In the ritual and meditative realm, sentient beings never are far from our minds. When we prostrate to buddhas and bodhisattvas, we visualize doing so alongside all sentient beings. When we make offerings to the buddhas and bodhisattvas, we sometimes do so by presenting to them the entire Mount Meru world system, with its inhabitants, objects, and environments. When we purify ourselves through recitation of, say, the hundred-syllable mantra of Vajrasattva, we see our own restored purity overflowing to other beings, visualized surrounding us, or above and below us, ranked by realm. When we develop the four immeasurable attitudes, we visualize sentient beings everywhere as the objects of our love, compassion, sympathetic joy, and equanimity. Nor is our own rebirth very far from our thoughts, either: nearly every ritual closes with prayers for auspiciousness, which typically include wishes for the welfare of the world and the express aspiration, in all our future lives, to meet our teachers again or be born in the presence of one or another buddha, bodhisattva, or tantric divinity.

Two specific contemplations recommended to those attempting to generate the awakening mind are of particular relevance. The first involves the attempt to equalize one's feelings toward a friend, enemy, and stranger by reflecting that because time is beginningless, each of us has had infinite previous lives and, in the course of these, every sentient being has at one time or another—indeed, countless times!—been our mother. We then reflect on the love and kindness shown us by our mother of this life, appreciate it, and extend it to the friend, enemy, stranger—and all other sentient beings. Finally, recognizing that we would do anything to help our own dear mother if she were suffering, and seeing that, in fact, all "mother sentient beings" are suffering in saṃsāra, we resolve to help all of them overcome suffering and attain true happiness. One possible way of effecting this contemplatively is through a second method, "giving and taking" (*gtong lan*), in which we visualize a vast gathering of sentient beings—known and unknown to us, human and non-human—arrayed before us in space, and practice a breath meditation in which, typically, we inhale the delusions and sufferings of these beings in the form of black smoke, which dissolves harmlessly within us, and then exhale to them all our love, compassion, and other positive qualities in the form of cleansing white light; at the end, we visualize all beings as fully purified and supremely happy, and they dissolve into us.

Comparable contemplations are found on the level of tantra, which, to repeat, suffuses Tibetan Buddhism, and is practiced at one level or another by everyone from laypeople, to monks and nuns, to tantric yogīs and yoginīs. Ordinary practitioners often are instructed simply to recite the six-syllable mantra of Avalokiteśvara, OṂ MAṆI PADME HŪṂ, with or without an accompanying visualization of the deity before one or oneself seen as the deity. In Tibetan tradition, each of the six syllables corresponds to one of the realms of saṃsāra. Thus, OṂ evokes the god realm, MA the asura realm, ṆI the human realms, PAD the animal realm, ME the hungry ghost realm, and HŪṂ the hell realms. As we utter it, each syllable is seen as sending a specifically colored light to the beings of the corresponding realm, liberating them from suffering and placing them in bliss. On the level of tantric "methods of actualization" (*sādhanas*)—which in the highest tantras are called generation-stage practices—we see ourselves as a buddha-deity such as Avalokiteśvara, Tārā, or Vajrayoginī at the center of a divine palace, or maṇḍala, and, after identifying physically, verbally, and mentally with the deity into whose practice we have been initiated, we typically are instructed to utter the deity's mantra in such a way that light or nectar, or a combination of the two, streams forth from the mantra circling at our heart and purifies sentient beings in the six realms and the ten directions, who then dissolve back into us.

The consummating practices on what in the highest tantric systems is called the completion stage are somewhat more interior in orientation than those of a sādhana or generation-stage practice, focused as they are on the channels, energies, and drops of the subtle body, but their object is to produce a buddha's actual Dharma Body and Form Body—and the latter, as we know, is that aspect of buddha that exists to serve the needs of others, so in that sense the completion stage also has sentient beings of the six realms very much in mind. On the side of tantric ritual, it should be noted that the most significant offering ceremonies—whether devoted to one's guru or to a particular deity—not only require multiple visualizations involving sending light to sentient beings, but after the solemn section of the ritual where the guru or deity is offered food and drink, which is blessed and distributed to the audience, the "leftover" food is taken outside for the hungry ghosts. This clearly echoes a ritual pattern we have observed in Indian, Theravāda, and East Asian Buddhism.

Tibetan Technologies Surrounding Death and Rebirth

As elsewhere in Asia, so in Tibet Buddhist traditions were regarded as especially knowledgeable and effective in dealing with death and its aftermath.[421] The stages-of-the-path tradition of reflection and contemplation placed the acknowledgment of impermanence and death at the very forefront, so anyone exposed to that tradition—almost everyone—would be well versed in recognizing that, as the Buddha reminded his followers on his deathbed, "all compounded phenomena are impermanent," and that the most significant existential implication of this is that we all someday will die. Furthermore, although death is certain, its time is not: we may be healthy and happy today, but we cannot be certain—as Tibetan masters like to say—whether tomorrow or the next life will come first. And, because, as we know, the quality of our next life depends both on the overall quality of the life we have led and on the specific state of mind that arises at death, dying is a matter of grave concern—an inevitable event for which we must prepare ourselves as much as possible. For those not sufficiently sobered by the prospect of death, meditations on bodily decay are recommended, either in visualized form or, if possible, through visiting a cemetery or charnel ground—and in Asia, such was seldom far away. It is worth mentioning that, like cultures everywhere, that of Tibet developed ritual practices—including prayers, meditations, and various magical techniques—for prolonging life,[422] so although death was accepted as inescapable, its timing was not. Deities regarded as especially effective for prolonging life were the buddha Amitāyus (whose name, recall, means "infinite life") and White Tārā.

Practitioners also were encouraged to familiarize themselves with the "signs" that might point to imminent death, including various conditions of the eyes, ears, stomach, flesh, and other body parts; the quality of their respiration; the content of their dreams; the look and smell of their semen or menstrual blood; and the qualities of their shadow. Careful observation of these and other phenomena, it was said, could instruct practitioners on both the time of their death and the location of their next rebirth.[423] Even more important were the signs that arise once the death process actually is underway. Classically, these are a set of bodily and psychological events that chart our transition from life, to death, to rebirth. They are described in terms of the sequential dissolution, or absorption (*thim*) of (a) the various physical elements that comprise our body, (b) our various physical and mental abilities, and (c) the five psycho-physical aggregates. Each stage is accompanied by a particular bodily sign, as well as by a series of internal visions: a mirage, smoke, fireflies, the light of a sputtering butter lamp, and an empty sky tinted first by white, then red, then black. After the black vision, when all our breath-related energies and drops have dissolved into the indestructible drop within the heart cakra, we experience a vision of clear light, or an empty luminosity, which marks the actual moment of death, when consciousness departs from the body. Empty luminosity is the true nature of our mind, glimpsed only fleetingly by non-contemplatives during life (e.g., during sneezing, fainting, or orgasm), but appearing quite starkly at the moment of death.[424]

While ordinary people are encouraged to learn all this, and may try to imagine it, serious tantric practitioners strive to "preenact" the process in their contemplations. Thus, as we have seen (chapter 9), the sādhana or generation-stage practice of reducing oneself to emptiness, then appearing as a seed syllable, then in the bodily form of one's chosen buddha-deity is a general way of purifying the processes of death, intermediate state, and rebirth, respectively, while manipulating energies, drops, and consciousness within the central channel of the subtle body in completion-stage practices quite explicitly takes the meditator through the stages of dying, right up to the threshold of the clear light of death itself. Through repeated practice, the yogī or yoginī becomes familiar with the whole experience of dying, and if they have not yet attained awakening at the time of death, they will be able to do so then, by recognizing the clear-light vision as the nature of mind and reality and transforming it into the Dharma Body of a buddha, as they transform their physical body into a buddha's Form Body.

The vast majority of us will not be able to train on—let alone master—the completion stage, hence are unlikely to recognize the clear light of death for what it is. Thus, we are enjoined to learn, as well, about what to expect in the intermediate state, or *bardo* (*bar do*), that follows the clear-light vision. As in certain Indian and East Asian traditions, the consensus among Tibetan teachers is that the intermediate state lasts up to forty-nine days, divided into seven seven-week segments, after which rebirth becomes inevitable. When one arises as a bardo-being, it typically is in the form of the being that one's karma projects for the next life—although the word "form" must be used advisedly, since the bardo "body" is mind made, and unhindered by material objects, but blown hither and yon by the winds of karma. The literature in Tibet on the bardo is voluminous. The best-known work is Karma Lingpa's (1326–1386) *Liberation through Hearing in the Bardo* (*Bar do thos grol*), which has been translated multiple times into English, first as the *Tibetan*

Book of the Dead—the name by which it is usually known.[425] Karma Lingpa's text describes a sequence of oft-confusing visions that the bardo-being encounters, including those of both wrathful and peaceable deities, and of different realms of saṃsāra. The bardo-being is consistently instructed to recognize these as mere projections of their own mind, and to realize the nature of mind as the nature of reality—thereby gaining liberation while in the intermediate state. By force of delusion and karma, however, most beings will fail to grasp the opportunity, and eventually—perhaps after a week or two, perhaps after the full seven—will, assuming the rebirth is to be from a womb, arrive in the vicinity of the copulating parents of its next life. As in Indian descriptions, in the case of a womb-based rebirth, the bardo-being desires the mother and loathes the father if male, and the other way around if female, and enters the mother's ovum at the moment the father's sperm reaches it, assuring fertilization. This is "rebirth" in the Buddhist sense, the first moment of a given life, designated as "consciousness" among the twelve links because it is the entrance of consciousness into the united male and female "drops" that incites the whole process of gestation and eventual emergence from the womb.

Passing through the bardo is the destiny of most beings, but given its terrors and vicissitudes, Tibetans often sought alternative ways to get through death and rebirth. The most popular of these is "transference" (*'pho ba*), which may be practiced by a reasonably skilled contemplative on their own or effected by a spiritual master (either in person or from afar) at the time of an ordinary person's death. In either case, the process entails a visualization and mantra recitation (whether by the contemplative or the master—or both) that brings about the forcible ejection of consciousness from the central channel at the crown of the deceased person's head, and the transfer of their consciousness into the presence of a buddha, such as Amitābha, in his pure land of Sukhāvati, or the future buddha Maitreya, in Tuṣita heaven.[426] For those advanced practitioners who have mastered the completion stage by attaining the clear-light vision through yogic means, death is quite a different matter.

(Indeed, tradition says, for them, it is like going on a picnic.) When their body no longer can support life, they willingly undergo the various stages of dying, and when they arrive at the culminating state of luminosity, they simply rest within the indestructible drop at the heart cakra, in contemplation of reality—a state called *thukdam* (*thugs dam*; literally, "mind-pledge," or "meditation"). Although their heartbeat and respiration have ceased, making them clinically dead, they typically show no signs of bodily decay and seem to maintain detectable warmth around the heart. Then, after a few days, or a week, or more, they complete their meditation and project their consciousness wherever they choose, whether to a pure land they may enjoy eternally or back into the world in a new form, where they may work again for the benefit of sentient beings.

Those Who Return: Tulkus and Revenants

A realized master who chooses to reenter the world is referred to by Tibetans as a *tulku* (*sprul sku*), or Emanation Body—a reference to the form a buddha takes, according to the Mahāyāna, in order to assist suffering beings. Although the possibility of a buddha assuming an Emanation Body was accepted wherever the Great Vehicle took root, and in an Indian or East Asian context a living master might honorifically be described as an "emanation" of this or that buddha, the systematic and widespread identification of living people as such emanations is, it seems, unique to the Inner Asian world. The idea originated in Tibet, but not until around the thirteenth century, when the Karma Kagyü order began to select its hierarchs not through the traditional practice of designating a relative or disciple of the deceased lama as their successor but by identifying the incarnation—the tulku—of the previous master.[427] The identification might be vouchsafed in various ways, whether through indications left before death by the lama in question, visions or dreams experienced by their disciples after their passing, or "tests" administered to children displaying unusual attitudes and abilities, who, if they were able to correctly identify ritual implements belonging to the deceased lama and/or recognize people the lama would have known in the previous life, were often adjudged legitimate. Not all tulku identifications were of children; at times, a lineage would retrospectively designate a distinguished master—or a generous patron—as a tulku. By the time the Chinese took over Tibet in the mid-twentieth century, there were hundreds, if not thousands, of tulku lineages—almost all of them male—found throughout the Tibetan culture area, some of national importance, some of merely local interest—but in every case, a person's identification as a tulku brought with it real prestige and often material goods as well.

The Karma Kagyü practice caught on with the other orders, and eventually the "tulku system," as modern scholars call it,[428] became the primary means for transferring not just spiritual authority but also wealth, property, and political power—which in the socio-religious culture of second-millennium Tibet, could be considerable. Among the most significant tulku lineages were the black- and red-hat Karmapas among the Kagyü, the Dalai and Panchen Lamas among the Geluk, and the Dudjom among the Nyingma. Because they were regarded as something akin to "living buddhas," tulkus were invested with a great deal of respect, given the best education possible, and expected to preside over their monasteries or other Dharma institutions as effectively as possible, performing rituals, dispensing blessings, and giving teachings to all those who sought them. The system was not—and is not—without its disadvantages, including the necessity of a potentially destabilizing regency period between the death of a previous lama and the majority of their successor, and the predictable occurrence of disputes as to which of several claimants to be the tulku of a particular lama was truly legitimate, hence heir to the prestige and power attached to the previous lama's estates. Incidentally, as consciously chosen reincarnates, tulkus were expected to remember details of their previous lives, and there certainly are references to such recollections in the biographical and autobiographical literature surrounding them,[429] but it also was understood that even in the case of great masters, the process of death and rebirth might "bury" certain memories, which, depending on circumstances, the lama might or might not ever choose to bring to the fore.

If tulkus are regarded as bodhisattvas who have chosen to reenter the world in order to benefit sentient beings, members of another class of "returners" have rather less say in their identity and role. These are the "revenants" (*'das log*)[430] people—usually women—who undergo a death experience; pass through the bardo; meet Yama, the Lord of the Dead; visit various realms of saṃsāra; and then—sometimes bearing a specific message from Yama for living beings—return to life to describe to the living what they have seen and to warn of the sufferings that await those who do not live a moral life. Once back in her reanimated body, a revenant often will undertake a career as a wandering preacher, traveling from place to place to describe the non-human realms (particularly the hell and hungry ghost abodes) that she has seen. Typically, she will claim to have become an incarnation of Avalokiteśvara, whose six-syllable mantra, as we have seen, can liberate beings from the sufferings of the six realms of saṃsāra. In this respect, the revenant is akin to another type of wandering preacher, the *maṇipa* (*maṇi pa*)—typically a male—who goes from town to town displaying instructive works of religious art like the wheel of life or depictions of deities or saints, and recounts edifying stories from Buddhist literature—often with Avalokiteśvara and his six-syllable mantra as the focus of the religious practices that he prescribes.

Such wandering preachers are found in nearly every religious tradition, and while revenants are not as common, the revenant's function as an intermediary between the dead and the living is one commonly assumed by the shaman in Inner Asian societies, including the *shen* (*gzhen*) of the Tibetan Bön tradition. As we have seen, early Buddhist literature is full of visits to the underworld by great disciples of the Buddha, and the Buddha himself could see into all the realms of saṃsāra using his divine eye, but for ordinary people to visit the afterlife and report on it was less common. Elsewhere in the Buddhist world, there is evidence of revenants in Chinese religious traditions,[431] but rarely elsewhere. Further afield, we may recall, Plato's "Myth of Er" hinges on the experience of a soldier who has died, seen the afterlife, and returned to tell of his experience, and this, in turn, recalls famous visits to the afterlife described in Western literature, most notably those of Odysseus, Aeneas, and Dante. There is an obvious resonance, as well, between revenants' accounts and those of modern people who report on their near-death experiences—and the profound effect it has on their understanding of life, death, and the afterlife.

The Great Perfection and the Great Seal

As mentioned briefly in chapter 9, an important element of Indian tantric Buddhist traditions was the description and prescription of contemplative techniques that appeared to "short-circuit" doctrine, ritual, and other "overcomplications" of religious life by insisting that the surest and swiftest way to gain awakening was simply to drop all elaboration of any sort and gaze directly at the empty, luminous, and blissful nature of our own mind—which is tantamount to buddhanature and the Dharma Body of a buddha. In Tibet, these techniques were often classified under the rubric of either the Great Perfection (T. *rdzogs chen*, Skt. *mahāsaṅdhi*) or the Great Seal (T. *phyag chen*, Skt. *mahāmudrā*).

The Great Perfection[432] is generally said to represent the highest view and meditative practice in the Nyingma tradition. It is traced to a set of Indian tantric texts and practices, and the masters who introduced them to Tibet during the early spread of the teaching there. Its most effective and prolific promulgator was the great tantric yogī Padmasaṃbhava, who taught it to his disciples during his sojourn in Tibet in the late eighth century and, before his departure, left behind a raft of Great Perfection "texts" that, centuries later, would be discovered as "treasures" (*gter ma*) hidden in the earth, or in pillars or walls, or in the mindstreams of latter-day Nyingmapas. The basic approach of the Great Perfection is to encourage those intent upon it to recognize their own primordial purity. According to Nyingma tradition, not only is each individual's mind naturally free and clear from the beginning, but the cosmos itself is an emanation of a primordial, all-good buddha, often identified as Samantabhadra. Great Perfection meditation is divided in various ways, but the mature tradition specified two crucial procedures that must be practiced by a serious contemplative: cutting-through (*khreg chod*) and transcendence (*thod rgal*). Cutting-through involves precisely the kind of direct meditation on the mind itself found in Chan or Zen Buddhism: the meditator eliminates all sense of duality between saṃsāra and nirvāṇa, good and evil, subject and object, or emptiness and form, and what is left when concepts have been dropped is simply our original nature. Transcendence entails a series of arcane yogic practices through which we see the world and act within it in a free and spontaneous way, unfettered by social or other conventions. As in Chan, so in the discourse of the Great Perfection conventional discussions of karma, rebirth, and the realms of saṃsāra often slip far into the background, leaving us to wonder whether they matter at all.

Whereas in India the Great Seal had multiple connotations—including a ritual gesture, the tantric visualization of oneself as a buddha-deity, a female consort employed in ritual sexual yoga practice, the outcome of the tantric path, and the true nature of mind and all phenomena—in a Tibetan context, it refers above all to the view, meditative practice, and conduct central to the Kagyü order—although the term is recognized and utilized by all the Tibetan traditions, with the Geluk giving it a place of considerable importance, as well.[433] Like the Great Perfection, the Great Seal is traced back to Indian masters—in this case to the mahāyoga and yoginī tantric systems and the great adepts who promulgated these tantras' practice through treatises, commentaries, and spontaneous songs of realization celebrating their unconventional—and sometimes quite transgressive—way of life and thought. Among the Kagyü, the Great Seal is recognized as the heart of the tradition. As a philosophical view, it is the recognition that all phenomena are empty—but that to recognize the way in which the mind is empty is special: in its true nature, the mind is empty of any sort of defilement but is naturally pure and luminous, in possession of all possible buddha-qualities, either potentially or in actuality. As meditation, the Kagyü Great Seal may entail a sudden, direct, liberating realization of the nature of mind or a more gradual series of four yogas leading to liberation: one-pointedness, which is equivalent to serenity meditation in other traditions; nonelaboration, which is the realization of the emptiness of persons and phenomena, including the mind; the single taste, which is experiencing all phenomena as partaking of ultimate reality; and nonmeditation, which is tantamount to buddhahood. The conduct ensuing from practice of the Great Seal is naturally virtuous, because it is based in recognition of the nature of reality, but—like the behavior of Indian tantric adepts, Chan masters, or Nyingma practitioners of transcendence—it may at times appear unconventional, or even mad, to those who are rule-bound and lack imagination. And, like that of the Great Perfection, the discourse of the Great Seal seems to underplay—and sometimes even ignore—Buddhist karmic eschatology, so that, again, we are left to wonder whether those intent on liberation through these special techniques really paid much attention to the traditional cosmology.

At this point, it will come as no surprise to learn that, in fact, the practice of the Great Perfection and the Great Seal no more undermined the classical Buddhist rebirth eschatology than did the radical ontological and metaphysical claims of the Mahāyāna, the antinomian pronouncements of the Indian tantric adepts, the intense focus on the present moment in Theravāda insight meditation, or the paradoxes—and even absurdities—that pepper the rhetoric of Chinese Chan and its counterparts elsewhere in East Asia. In every case—though especially so in Mahāyāna settings—the "rhetoric of immediacy"[434] employed within a given practice tradition masks that practice's place within a larger cosmological, metaphysical, and soteriological order. Thus, at least in the premodern era, each of these approaches to liberation operates within the framework of basic Buddhist assumptions about saṃsāra and nirvāṇa, the universality of dependent origination, the infallibility of karmic cause and effect, the mind's separability from the body, and the reality of multiple realms of rebirth. In the Tibetan instance, a closer examination of the contexts of Great Perfection and Great Seal meditation makes it clear that each of them is embedded within a larger "religious" context that presupposes the common assumptions held by virtually all Buddhist traditions, and requires of its practitioners a remarkable degree of devotion, compassion, contemplative skill, wisdom, and ritual competency. Indeed, the practice of either type of meditation usually requires special devotion to one's guru, a long series of preliminary reflections and rituals, and, often but not always, a tantric initiation—since the Great Perfection and the Great Seal both originated in tantric circles in India before being transmitted to Tibet.

Why, then, the rhetoric of immediacy, simplicity, and directness, why the dismissal of reason, ritual, and ethics? Simply, because liberation is predicated on a direct realization of the ultimate nature of reality, especially, in these cases, the nature of the mind. And while ultimate reality may be approached through devotion, ritual, or even reason, to actually realize it requires that the meditator transcend duality, conceptuality, and rationality. As deluded beings, we are reluctant to give up our fixed notions about things both profane and sacred, and so Buddhist masters over the centuries have provided dramatic, even shocking, ways of shaking us out of our complacency. But just as Nāgārjuna's thoroughgoing negation of philosophical categories did nothing to cancel traditional Buddhist cosmology but helped to undergird it, so Tibetan discussions—and practice—of the Great Perfection and the Great Seal must be understood as part of a larger, and quite typical, Buddhist attempt to leave behind the vicissitudes of birth, death, and rebirth and reach the safe "farther shore" of awakening—from which, because these are Mahāyāna traditions, the awakened ones may, and often do, choose once again to enter the fray.

The Female Rebirth in Tibet

Once again, we will conclude our main discussion with a brief consideration of the Buddhist view of being reborn female.[435] Because of the vast distances on the Tibetan plateau, the small population, and the pastoral, agricultural, and commercial preoccupations of Tibetan life, Tibet's traditional social, political, and economic systems were in many respects woven less tightly than those of, say, classical India or China, and at least superficially this meant that women often exercised public agency to a greater degree than their sisters elsewhere. However, like other premodern Asian societies, Tibet was basically patriarchal, such that, whatever degree of independence women may have expressed in certain realms, they were severely circumscribed with respect to political and social power, and rarely were permitted leadership in religious institutions. The patriarchal view of females is neatly summed up in one of the Tibetan words for "woman": *kyemen* (*skyes dman*), which literally translates as "low-born." Thus, the tradition of full female ordination never reached Tibet, and so (until recently), any Tibetan "nun" (*a ni*) one might encounter observed only the ten precepts expected of a male novice. In part because of their lesser status, but mostly because of their gender, Tibetan nuns received nowhere near the support or respect afforded the male saṅgha, so while their traditions never completely died out, they rarely flourished, either. Also, as noted earlier, almost all tulkus were male. And, although Tibetan Buddhism was deeply influenced by Indian tantric traditions, the root tantric vow not to disparage women seems to have been observed more in the breach than in actuality—especially by monks and ascetic yogīs.

At the same time, as elsewhere in Asia, women did find ways of asserting themselves in the religious realm, whether as oracles, revenants, or yoginīs. Sometimes a yoginī's power derived from her association with a powerful lama, as in the case of Padmasaṃbhava's consort, Yeshé Tsogyal, but sometimes she attained renown largely on her own, like Machik Labdrön (1055–1149), who founded a distinctive tradition of contemplation and ritual, Chöd (*gcod*, meaning "severance"), that spread to every Tibetan Buddhist order, and is practiced to this day. And, although the tulku system was quite androcentric, there were a number of female reincarnation lineages that developed over the years, the best known being the Dorjé Phakmo incarnation of Samding Monastery. Furthermore, as elsewhere in the Buddhist world, Buddhists in Tibet worshipped a considerable number of female deities, such as the female buddhas Tārā and Vajrayoginī, along with a host of ḍākinīs, worldly goddesses, demonesses, and protectors. As elsewhere in Asia, however, the prominence of female deities did not translate into anything resembling full social or religious equality for females, at least in the modern sense. Thus, the female rebirth was, in general, regarded as a lesser one in Tibet, just as it was in other Asian Buddhist cultures.

Regional Extensions

Some of the cultures to which Tibetan Buddhism spread in the second millennium C.E. were—despite the often-considerable distances involved, and despite the inevitable local variations—more or less of a piece with the language, society, politics, economy, and religion of the plateau. Thus, the Ladakhis in the far west, various Nepali groups like the Tamangs and Sherpas to the south, and the Bhutanese to the southeast, all adopted versions of the Buddhism dominant in the main centers of Tibetan civilization—often abetted by settlers who migrated from the plateau and introduced their version of Buddhism into the local religious mix. The languages spoken in Ladakh, the Sherpa regions of Nepal, and Bhutan may be mutually incomprehensible (or nearly so), but they all belong to the same language group and profess a version of Buddhism very much in line with that of the power centers of the Tibetan plateau, including, obviously, its rebirth eschatology.

The other major groups to which Tibetan Buddhism spread were various Mongol tribes to the north, who, despite their small numbers, exercised an outsized influence on Asian—and European—history, by dint of their extraordinary organizational and military capabilities. Prior to their rapid expansion under the leadership of Genghis Khan in the thirteenth century, the Mongols were a nomadic and pastoral people, whose religion was primarily shamanic in orientation. Their shamanism was never entirely overlaid by other traditions, but many Mongols did become Muslims, and even more became Buddhists, largely through the efforts of various charismatic Tibetan lamas, who understood the northern tribes to be a fertile mission field and, not coincidentally, an important source of patronage and protection. Deeply influenced by Tibetan Buddhism—especially, after the sixteenth century, by the Geluk order—the Mongols nevertheless developed their own style of Buddhism, which produced great scholars, charismatic tulkus, and impressive monastic establishments. They remained stalwart Buddhists right up until the Soviet-sponsored Communist takeover in 1924, and have taken up Buddhist practice again since the fall of the Communist state in 1990.

A final culture influenced by Tibetan Buddhism also bears mentioning: that of China. Although Chinese Buddhism, as we have seen, developed its own distinctive traditions over the course of nearly two millennia, various Han and non-Han groups within China found the Tibetan form of the Dharma quite attractive. In part, this may be attributed to the overall impressiveness of the Tibetans' intellectual, institutional, and ritual structures and practices, which contained elements that might appeal to either elite or popular practitioners, including Han Buddhists familiar with their own brand of Buddhism. As in the case of Mongolia, however, it was aided by the efforts of charismatic lamas (often ethnically Mongol) who traveled to China to go on pilgrimage, to teach, and to preach. Tibetan Buddhism was especially attractive to the non-Han groups that occasionally ruled in China, most notably the Mongols of the Yuan Dynasty and the Manchus of the Qing, for whom Tibetan Buddhism provided a counterforce to the Han institutions that tended to predominate in the Middle Kingdom most of the time. Interestingly, even after over seven decades of Communist rule in China, Tibetan Buddhism continues to appeal to a small, but often influential, group of people there, especially members of the intelligentsia, and it also has achieved considerable popularity in Taiwan.

CHAPTER 14

Rebirth and Modern Buddhism

All the texts and traditions surrounding rebirth we have investigated thus far are "traditional," or "premodern." As we have seen, whatever the rhetoric employed in a given place or time, it is highly likely that the classical Buddhist rebirth eschatology, with its "literal" account of the five or six realms of saṃsāra and the operation of karmic cause and effect in both this life and future lives, was taken as axiomatic. Certainly, some texts, traditions, or teachers placed the traditional cosmology in the foreground while others relegated it to the background, and we must not assume that every premodern Buddhist anywhere in Asia was obsessed with karma and rebirth in every waking moment. Nevertheless, it is probably fair to say that most Buddhists in most eras and areas took their tradition's karmic eschatology seriously, knew something about it, and were concerned—at least some of the time—with "winning" the game of rebirth, whether through observing moral rules, circumventing karma through magical means, or—all too rarely—striving for complete spiritual liberation. Among modern Buddhists, however, things are not nearly so straightforward, for it is everywhere a hallmark of modernity that received ideas about cosmology, metaphysics, and soteriology are brought into question—and this certainly has been true of Buddhist karmic eschatology and the doctrine of rebirth. In this chapter, we will discuss modernity and its relation to Buddhism, and briefly survey modern Buddhist attitudes on rebirth. In the final chapter, we will focus on some recent philosophical debates about rebirth and consider how we might think about rebirth in the twenty-first century.

Buddhism and Modernity

There is much debate about precisely what "modernity" is, where and when it begins, and how it relates to its supposed antonym, "tradition." I will not enter those debates here, but simply affirm the broadly consensual view that modernity is a social and intellectual condition introduced into a given cultural setting by direct or indirect contact with ideologies and technologies originating primarily in the post-Enlightenment West—particularly in its colonial or neo-colonial modality, with its accompanying promotion of corporate capitalism and/or socialism, ideals of social equality, employment of high-intensity technologies, and use of science as a touchstone for questioning, understanding, and mastering physical reality. Depending on local conditions, modernity has arrived in different places at different times, and has met with greater or lesser resistance from the upholders of the preexisting cultural beliefs and practices that are designated as "tradition," although even in "premodern" cultures, "tradition"—that which has supposedly been "delivered across" the ages—was constantly being contested and redefined.

One significant by-product of the onset of modernity is, of course, its challenge to premodern religious ideas, institutions, and practices. The cosmologies propounded by traditional religions are challenged by the scientific worldview; religious institutions are challenged by new sources of political and social authority, such as the nation state; and religious practices are increasingly viewed as optional activities that may be psychologically effective but are irrelevant to the operations of the cosmos. This being so, we might expect that religion would simply disappear from cultures that have entered modernity, and early social scientists such as Marx and Freud predicted exactly that. It has not worked out that way, however, for it turns out that, as Clifford Geertz astutely observed, the question for religious people in most modernizing societies "is less a matter of what to believe as how to believe it."[436]

This is certainly true for Buddhists. Whether in Asia or the West, modernity has challenged their traditional ideas, institutions, and practices as surely as those of other religious folk. Indeed, modern ways of thinking tend to cast doubt on the veracity of *any* of the four noble truths, since the karma-rebirth cosmology and metaphysics underlying the truth of suffering, as well as the assertions that there is a clearly identifiable source of suffering, that suffering can cease entirely, and that there is a distinct path to the cessation of suffering—all are questionable at best in light of the metaphysical materialism, epistemological skepticism, and fallibilist view of human nature generally assumed in the Western sciences and social sciences. In the case at hand, while rebirth may have been axiomatic for many traditional Asian Buddhists, it is far from a given for modern Buddhists, especially in the West. At the same time, because rebirth has been part of Buddhism's ideological apparatus since the beginning, it cannot easily be dismissed out of hand; contemporary Buddhists must confront it as surely as their Christian counterparts must confront traditional ideas of heaven, hell, and final judgment, not to mention the resurrection of Jesus. There is room for honest disagreement as to whether acceptance of a traditional presentation of rebirth is essential to being a "good Buddhist" or not but—to revert to Geertz's perspective—it is not so much a question of *whether* to believe in rebirth, since it is part of the conceptual framework inherited by all Buddhists, but *how* to believe it: whether to take it literally or figuratively.

Just as Christians, Muslims, and other religious people have responded to the challenges of modernity in various ways, so have Buddhists. Indeed, just as in other religions, it is easy to discern in modern Buddhism a spectrum of approaches that runs from literalism, through neo-traditionalism and modernism, all the way to self-conscious secularism.

- In terms of rebirth, *literalists* tend to assume that the karma-rebirth cosmology is real, the arguments for it persuasive, and the details of its operations more or less as described in traditional texts.

- *Neo-traditionalists* accept the reality of the system and many of the traditional arguments in its favor, but seek to understand its operation through an admixture of traditional and modern ways of explaining the world.
- *Modernists* think the traditional cosmology may or may not be literally true, but that arguments in its favor are unpersuasive, and that it is best understood in symbolic, psychological, or existential terms.
- *Secularists* believe that the concept of rebirth may not have been essential to the Buddha and in any case certainly should not preoccupy us, for the Dharma is a nonmetaphysically based way of life and of seeing the world that is psychological and ethical: in effect, secular humanism with a Buddhist lexicon.

With the exception of literalists, all others on the spectrum agree that the traditional cosmology requires some reinterpretation, and with the exception of secularists, all others agree that rebirth is an idea that must be accounted for—even if they disagree on how central it is to one's identity as a Buddhist. Modernists and secularists tend to agree that, whether one thinks rebirth is more likely or less likely to be the case, or more central or less central to the Dharma, some degree of agnosticism on the matter is probably warranted.[437] We will return to some of these issues later; in the meantime, however, it might be useful to get at least a general sense of the various ways in which modern Buddhists, whether in Asia or the West, have thought about rebirth.

Views of Rebirth in Modern Buddhism: 1800–1945

As we saw in chapter 1, the idea of rebirth was known, and sometimes espoused, in the West, whether by Pythagoreans, Platonists, unconventional Christians, Renaissance freethinkers, or Enlightenment-era esotericists. Unlike in the Indic and Buddhist world, however, belief in reincarnation never attained mainstream respectability, and to the degree that it has become a topic of interest in modern Western thought, it is probably due as much to Euro-American fascination with Asian ideas as to a revival of ancient Western esotericism.

Sporadic attempts by European intellectuals to come to terms with Buddhism can be traced back many centuries, if not millennia, but it really was around 1800 that the tradition began to receive sustained and serious attention, both in Europe and America.[438] Throughout the nineteenth century, scholars like Eugène Burnouf (1801–1852), Brian Hodgson (1801–1894), Hendrik Kern (1833–1917), and T. W. and Carolyn Rhys Davids (1843–1922 and 1857–1942, respectively) offered pioneering translations of Buddhist texts and accounts of Buddhism's history and ideology, while philosophers and literary figures began to reflect on Buddhist concepts, and at times to incorporate them into their own systems of thought. Although it has been suggested that the eighteenth-century Scottish philosopher David Hume may have been familiar with Buddhism because his analysis of perception, self, and phenomena seems to resemble that of Mainstream Buddhism,[439] it is in the works of nineteenth-century German thinkers that Buddhism overtly makes its debut in modern Western philosophy. G. W. F. Hegel (1770–1831), Arthur Schopenhauer (1788–1860), and Friedrich Nietzsche (1844–1900) brought Buddhist ideas under their purview, each in his own way. Hegel saw Buddhism's metaphysical "nihilism" and mystical apophasis as paving the way for the highest religious expression, Christianity; he notes that Buddhists accept "the dogma of the transmigration of souls," but shows little interest in its details, being rather more concerned with the elimination of transmigration that awaits in the "pure nothing" of nirvāṇa.[440] Schopenhauer famously acknowledged Buddhist influence on his conception of the world as "will and representation" and his articulation of the "nirvana principle" as the *summum bonum*; he reported the Buddhist belief in metempsychosis, and was inclined to accept the possibility in general, but asserted that if rebirth occurs, no characteristics at all of the previous being could be transmitted to the subsequent being, and suggested, as well, that Buddhists themselves did not intend rebirth to be taken literally but rather as a "popular" way of presenting their belief in a version of palingenesis: sentient beings as successive re-presentations of the Will.[441] Like Hegel and Schopenhauer, Nietzsche tended to regard Buddhism as nihilistic. He appreciated its emphasis on change and impermanence but regarded it as life-denying, hence as deficient in its own way as Christianity; at the same time, his critique of dogmatic philosophy and his "perspectivism" have been fruitfully compared with the approaches of Buddhist thinkers,[442] and his doctrine of eternal return has been likened to the doctrine of rebirth—though the two ideas differ in details, and Nietzsche admits no escape from eternal return, while Buddhists believe rebirth can be transcended.

Across the Atlantic, the American Transcendentalists, especially Ralph Waldo Emerson (1803-1882), Henry Thoreau (1817-1862), and Walt Whitman (1819-1892), read translations of Asian classics,[443] and propounded a broadly "spiritual" view of life and the cosmos that seemed to leave room for rebirth. Indeed, Emerson asserts in one of his earliest essays that "the transmigration of souls is not fable," explaining in a later work that "we are tendencies, or rather symptoms, and none of us is complete. We touch and go, we sip the foam of many lives. Rotation is the law of nature."[444] Unlike Emerson, Thoreau did not explicitly endorse the idea of rebirth in his published writings, but in letters to friends he recounted memories from lives he believed he had lived in the ancient Middle East, and noted in a journal that "as far back as I can remember I have unconsciously referred to the experiences of a previous state of existence."[445] In his great poem "Song of Myself," Whitman alludes to the possibility of rebirth a number of times, insisting, for instance, "round and round we go, all of us, and ever come back thither"; furthermore, "no doubt I have died myself ten thousand times before," and "shall come again upon the earth after five thousand years."[446] For the Transcendentalists, rebirth was of a piece with a metaphysical view of the cosmos, whereby the soul was a part of—and destined to reunite with—the absolute or, in Emerson's terms, the Oversoul. Such notions certainly were influenced by Indic—

especially Hindu—ideas, but also drew on the Western esoteric traditions whose undercurrents beneath the mainstream of Western philosophy and religion never had disappeared, and indeed, in the nineteenth century—perhaps as a reaction to the perceived encroachment upon the human soul by science—resurfaced in the form of a general fascination with parapsychology and the occult.

A similar mix of Indic and Western influences may be detected in an influential Euro-American intellectual movement that originated in the late nineteenth century, Theosophy.[447] Rooted in the purported visionary encounters between a Russian-born occultist and scholar, Helena P. Blavatsky (1831-1891), and "Mahatmas," or Hidden Masters, living in Tibet, Theosophy claims to reveal for the first time "the religion behind all religions," an emanationist monism that found its closest equivalents in ancient Egyptian religion, Neo-Platonism, Western esotericism, Hinduism, and Buddhism. Rebirth was a cardinal doctrine of Theosophy, although there—as in many modern Western versions of the idea influenced by evolutionary theory—movement from one life to the next was seen as progressive rather than cyclical, and there was no transmigration possible from one type of sentient state to another. Thus, humans could not become animals in the next life, nor vice versa; they only could become more spiritually evolved humans, that much closer to union with the absolute. At the hands of Blavatsky and her followers, including such luminaries as Henry Steele Olcott (1832-1907) and Annie Besant (1847-1933), Theosophy left a profound impression on intellectual and cultural circles in England, America, and India, and played a small but significant role in the revival of Hindu and Buddhist traditions in South Asia and in the anticolonial movements in India and Sri Lanka. Olcott spent considerable time in Sri Lanka, where he designed the still-used international Buddhist flag and wrote *A Buddhist Catechism*, which seeks to align traditional Buddhist cosmology and metaphysics with modern science, and propounds the reality of rebirth—though again, as a progressive and evolutionary process rather than a cyclical one.[448] A latter-day Theosophist of note, W. Y. Evans-Wentz (1878-1965), helped to bring Kazi Dawa Samdup's translations of Tibetan Buddhist ritual and contemplative texts (including the famous *Tibetan Book of the Dead*, discussed in chapter 13) to the attention of the English-speaking world in the 1920s and 1930s, and while explaining their contents in a distinctly Theosophical manner in his introductions and notes, he was among the first to make Tibetan cosmological and metaphysical writings available to a wider audience in the West.[449]

Views of Rebirth in Modern Buddhism: 1945-2020

Many other Buddhists, both Western and Asian, were active (or known) in the West in the first half of the twentieth century, among them Paul Carus (1852-1919), Dwight Goddard (1861-1939), Anagarika Dharmapala (1864-1933), Alexandra David-Neel (1868-1969), and D. T. Suzuki (1870-1966),[450] who emphasized rebirth to varying degrees, but all of whom advanced Euro-American appreciation for Buddhist ideas and practices in a modern idiom. It is really in the post-World War II era, however, that Buddhism began to make serious inroads in the West, not just in elite circles, but in the popular imagination, as well. And while it would be an exaggeration to say that the growth of Buddhism in the Euro-American world over the past seventy-five years has been inversely proportional to the emphasis placed on the doctrine of rebirth, it is indisputable that many of the figures who gained the greatest traction were those who downplayed traditional Buddhist cosmology and metaphysics—at the very same time that the growth of the so-called New Age movement brought rebirth-centered cosmologies and metaphysics, both Asian and Western, within the purview of large numbers of people to a greater degree than ever before.

Arguably, no single figure influenced Western views of Buddhism in the middle third of the twentieth century more than the multilingual and broadly trained Japanese scholar D. T. Suzuki, whose well-hewn writings on Zen conveyed an air of authority that, in the absence of other accounts or analyses, were hard to gainsay—and proved immensely appealing to several generations of Westerners trying to reconcile Buddhism with Western religion and philosophy. Much as Blavatsky and Olcott had presented Theosophy as an esoteric religion beyond religions, Suzuki presented Zen not only as the true essence of Buddhism but as a universal mystical perspective and practice, utterly beyond ritual, ideology, or any particular cultural forms—although he believed it best exemplified by Japanese culture. If, as noted in chapter 12, Zen tended to downplay past and future lives and other aspects of traditional Buddhist cosmology even in its premodern Asian settings, in Suzuki's writings that cosmology fell off the radar almost entirely: for him, Zen was Buddhism entirely in the present tense.[451] Suzuki, in turn, influenced a number of mid-century writers and thinkers, based mostly in America, who helped to turn Buddhism—Zen and otherwise—into an enduring feature of the Western cultural (or countercultural) landscape.

The most notable among them were Alan Watts (1915-1973) and the various members of the so-called Beat generation. Watts was an English-born scholar, writer, and lecturer who spent most of his life in America, and did much to popularize Zen, Daoism, and other Asian religions. He emphasized the mystical, experiential side of these religions, and while aware of traditional cosmologies, he tended to read them in this-worldly or psychological terms, noting, for instance, that sophisticated Buddhists "do not believe in reincarnation in any literal sense," instead seeing "the individual's multitude of lives... as the multitude of his physical and social relations."[452]

Even more influential—indeed, their works resonate to this day—were such Beat writers as Jack Kerouac (1922-1969), Philip Whalen (1923-2002), Allen Ginsberg (1926-1997), Gary Snyder (1930-), and Diane di Prima (1934-2020).[453] Each of them understood and practiced Buddhism in their own way. Kerouac, in his novels, poems, and notebooks, portrayed himself as a modern-day bhikkhu-bodhisattva who lamented the sufferings of the world and longed to be off "the slaving meat-wheel" of saṃsāra,[454] but vowed to save all beings by showing them the natural freedom of their own minds. Whalen studied Buddhism seriously for most of his life—his poems are replete with Zen references—and he eventually became abbot of the Hartford Street Zen Center in San Francisco. Ginsberg was introduced to Buddhism by Kerouac, but only became a serious Buddhist practitioner around 1970, when he met the brilliant and charismatic Tibetan lama Chögyam Trungpa Rinpoche (1939-1987); much of his later poetry utilizes Buddhist themes and imagery. Snyder studied Chinese Buddhism in college and graduate school, and lived in a Zen monastery in Japan for a number of years, before returning to the United States to establish a homestead in the Sierra Nevada mountains of California and write widely celebrated poems and essays on religious, social, and environmental themes. Di Prima practiced Zen for many years, but later in life turned increasingly toward Tibetan traditions; Buddhist influences are evident throughout her poetic corpus. Obviously, such figures—and others categorized as "Beat"—had no single perspective on Buddhism or its ideas and practices, but it is safe to say that, in a style typical of Zen, most of their work stresses the present-day, this-worldly implications of the tradition, and leaves traditional cosmology and metaphysics well to the side, if not in complete abeyance. The same may be said of the lectures and writings of more "traditional" Zen teachers of the later twentieth century, such as Philip Kapleau (1912-2004) and Robert Aitken (1917-2010), who encountered Buddhism in Japan just after World War II and returned to the United States to found influential centers and produce pioneering writings; and roshis from Japan such as Shunryu Suzuki (1904-1971), whose *Zen Mind, Beginner's Mind* has become a modern Buddhist classic.[455] In short, while D. T. Suzuki and his heirs did much to advance knowledge of Buddhism in the West, they tended to downplay many of the tradition's more "difficult" ideas, including rebirth.

If the Beats and their contemporaries, with their proclivity toward Zen, did much to shape Euro-American understandings of Buddhism from the end of World War II until the late 1960s, in the 1970s and beyond, new forces and new voices added to the articulation of a Buddhism appropriate to the modern age. A combination of unparalleled prosperity in the Western world, youthful disillusionment with the persistence of war, poverty, and racism in supposedly enlightened societies, a "romantic Orientalist" view of the East as a source of wisdom and healing, and the ready availability of ever-swifter ways of traversing continents led an unprecedented number of young people to travel to the East, just as relaxed immigration laws (and fallout from Asian wars) led thousands upon thousands of Asians—including Buddhist masters—to settle in Europe and America. Although Zen continued to develop in the West in its own distinctive ways (especially in North America), two other traditions began to attract large followings: Theravāda Buddhism and Tibetan Buddhism.

Theravāda Buddhism, as we know, has been a dominant religious form in Sri Lanka and Southeast Asia for much of the past millennium. Particularly in the wake of the United States' involvement in the Vietnam War (1961-1975), many Southeast Asian refugees made their way to America and Europe, settling in various towns and cities, often making Buddhist temples (and monks) a crucial marker of continued cultural identity. These "immigrant" Buddhists recreated their institutions and rituals as best they could on foreign soil. They form an important component of modern Western Buddhism—we will say more about them and their fellow Buddhists from other Asian cultures shortly—but their influence on contemporary culture writ large is usually overshadowed by that of Westerners, especially Americans, who traveled to Southeast Asia in the 1960s and 1970s to study with Burmese and Thai Theravāda masters, then returned to the United States to promote the practice of the mindfulness (*satipaṭṭhāna*) or insight (*vipassanā*) meditation they had learned there, declaring it to be the key practice taught by the Buddha and the essence of Buddhism in all its different forms.

At centers like the Insight Meditation Society in Massachusetts and Spirit Rock in Northern California, teachers such as Joseph Goldstein (1944-), Sharon Salzberg (1952-), and Jack Kornfield (1945-) promulgated a version of Buddhism that focused almost entirely on meditative awareness of the present moment, and minimized ritual, devotion, and the cosmology and metaphysics of traditional Theravāda. Rebirth was acknowledged as a possibility, but largely left aside: the key was to meditate on the rise and fall of present-moment mental and physical events while also cultivating universal loving kindness. Even less traditionally Buddhist was Mindfulness-Based Stress Reduction (MBSR), a program developed by Jon Kabat-Zinn (1944-) that used Buddhist meditative techniques to help anxious modern Westerners bring a measure of tranquility to their overscheduled and often unhealthy lives. MBSR has received considerable attention—and funding—and has found its way into hospitals, psychology clinics, schools, prisons, and other secular settings. Although MBSR trainers largely eschew Buddhist terminology—not to mention Buddhist cosmology and metaphysics—the program is firmly rooted in Theravāda tradition, and it has been seen by critics—particularly among Christians—as a way of stealthily indoctrinating Westerners in Buddhism.[456] Conversely, tradition-minded critics have lamented what they consider MBSR's evisceration of indispensable Buddhist ideas and practices. It is worth noting that the presentation of Theravāda by Western teachers as minimally religious often reflected what they had heard from Buddhist modernist teachers in Asia, such as the Thai monks Buddhadasa Bhikkhu (1906-1993) and Ajahn Chah (1918-1992), and the Indian-Burmese lay teacher S. N. Goenka (1924-2013).[457] Indeed, perhaps the most influential single presentation of Theravāda Buddhism in the late twentieth century—one that still is read in the twenty-first—was that of a Buddhist bhikkhu and scholar from Sri Lanka, Walpola Rahula (1907-1997), whose book *What the Buddha Taught* is a clear and compelling presentation of Buddhist ideas and practices, but almost entirely omits discussion of traditional cosmology and metaphysics, including the idea of rebirth.[458]

Before 1959, Tibetan Buddhism was little known in the Euro-American world, and when it was, it was largely through the works of such intrepid travelers as Alexandra David-Neel, W. Y. Evans-Wentz, or Lama Anagarika Govinda (1898-1985), not to mention charlatans like T. Lobsang Rampa (1910-1981).[459] However, with the Chinese invasion of Tibet in 1950 and, especially, the diaspora incited by the suppression of a widespread rebellion on the plateau in 1959, Tibetans were brought out of their relative isolation and thrust into the outside world, first in South Asia, and later in the West. Westerners traveling east encountered refugee lamas in their newly established settlements in India and Nepal, and returned to Europe, America, and elsewhere to found Buddhist centers, and sometimes to study at universities. At the same time, lamas began traveling to the West, sometimes on teaching tours, sometimes to reside permanently. Ordinary refugee Tibetans also began to settle in the West, bringing their own distinctive ideas and practices to the modern Western stage. Through all this, Tibetan Buddhism became a third significant Buddhist voice in Euro-American culture.

Perhaps because their transition from tradition to modernity was telescoped into such a short period of time, or perhaps because of their own deep immersion in the classical Indian worldview, Tibetan lamas who taught Westerners in either South Asia or the West[460] often presented Buddhism with minimal accommodation to Western ideas. Such figures as Dudjom Rinpoche (1903-1987), Kalu Rinpoche (1905-1989), Dezhung Rinpoche (1906-1987), Geshe Lhundub Sopa (1923-2014), the Sixteenth Karmapa (1924-1981), the Forty-First Sakya Trizin (1945-), and Thubten Zopa Rinpoche (1946-) for the most part simply articulated the Dharma as they had learned it in Asia, and did not shy away from miracle stories, mind-boggling descriptions of buddhahood, or detailed analyses of the processes of karma and rebirth. In so doing, they helped counter earlier, Theosophically influenced notions of Tibetan Buddhism, and contributed greatly to Westerners' understanding of the classical tradition originating in India and consolidated in Tibet. At the same time, the lamas who tended to attract the most followers outside Asia were those who learned English and spoke to their Western students in terms they could understand, often peppering their discourses with references to modern psychology, science, and material culture. Such charismatic teachers as Tarthang Tulku (1934-) of the Nyingma Institute in Berkeley, Lama Thubten Yeshe (1935-1984) of

Kopan monastery in Nepal, and the peripatetic founder of Naropa University and the Shambhala training program, Chögyam Trungpa Rinpoche (1939-1987), evinced an extraordinary ability to present the Dharma in a manner appealing to Euro-Americans.

These teachers did not entirely ignore traditional cosmology and metaphysics but tended more strongly to emphasize other messages, which responded to their students' intellectual need to see Buddhism as "modern" and "scientific" and their psychological need to feel their own self-worth—or, as Trungpa Rinpoche put it, their "basic goodness." With this in mind, they often emphasized the importance of the Great Seal or Great Perfection practices, which, as we know, center on direct meditative realization of the empty, luminous, and blissful nature of the mind, and sometimes seem to shunt karmic eschatology to the periphery. It was Trungpa Rinpoche, as well, who provided his Western students with an alternative way to understand rebirth, as "psychological states of being... different kinds of projections, the dream worlds that we create for ourselves," and gave his discussion of the postmortem experiences described in the *Tibetan Book of the Dead* a strongly psychological hue.[461] Trungpa Rinpoche's most influential disciple, Pema Chödrön, has followed his lead in presenting Tibetan Buddhist ideas and practices primarily in psychological terms—and in language that many in the modern world find resonates deeply with their own anxieties and experiences.[462] In more recent times, other Tibetan lamas have effectively hewed to an approach intermediate between conservative traditionalism and radical modernism. Thus, popular figures such as Gelek Rinpoche (1939-2017), Sogyal Rinpoche (1947-2019), Dzongsar Khyentse Rinpoche (1961-), Tsoknyi Rinpoche (1966-), Mindroling Jetsun Khandro Rinpoche (1967-), Yongey Mingyur Rinpoche (1975-), and, most especially, the Fourteenth Dalai Lama (1935-), have upheld many of the tenets of classical Tibetan Buddhism, including rebirth, while remaining open to modern ways of investigating, conceptualizing, and expressing various aspects of the tradition. The same may be said of Tibetan lamas' more philosophically inclined Western disciples, such as

Jeffrey Hopkins (1940–), Robert Thurman (1941–), Matthieu Ricard (1946–), Anne Klein (1947–), and B. Alan Wallace (1950–). In short, of the three forms of Buddhism most influential on post-World War II Western culture—Zen, Theravāda, and Tibetan—it is the Tibetan tradition that arguably displays the greatest variety, and while any number of Tibetan lamas have been willing to downplay rebirth or give symbolic explanations for it, it is among the Tibetans and their Western followers that the most detailed presentations and defenses of the classical notion of the idea tend to be found.

Two other elements of modern Buddhism in the West, and especially North America, deserve at least brief mention. The first element is "Engaged Buddhism," which, like liberation theology within Christianity, uses traditional religious ideas and attitudes (such as universal compassion or the bodhisattva ideal) as a basis for serious engagement in contemporary social, political, economic, and environmental causes. Many of the earliest and most earnest Engaged Buddhist voices were those of Asians, including Anagarika Dharmapala of Sri Lanka and, after World War II, the Indian Dalit (untouchable) leader B. R. Ambedkar (1891–1956), the Vietnamese Thien (Zen) monk Thich Nhat Hanh (1926–), and the Thai lay social reformer Sulak Sivaraksa (1933–). Westerners who have followed their example include Beat writer-activists Allen Ginsberg, Gary Snyder, and Diane di Prima, Zen teachers Robert Aitken, Issan Dorsey (1933–1990), Bernie Glassman (1939–2018), and David Loy (1947–), and feminist scholar-activists Rita Gross (1943–2015), Karma Lekshe Tsomo (1944–), Anne Klein, and Jan Willis (1948–). Whatever their individual beliefs or Buddhist affiliations, these teachers tended in their social writings to focus above all on the overcoming of "defilement" (*kleśa*) in social and political institutions, and often, though not always, leave matters of metaphysics and cosmology well to the side. In this sense, they can seem, like so many of the modern Buddhists we have surveyed, as intent on avoiding *discussion* of rebirth as they are of avoiding actually being reborn.

The second element, already alluded to in passing, is the communities of "immigrant" or "ethnic" Buddhists that have lived in

America since the arrival of Chinese in the United States in the mid-nineteenth century, followed by settlers from Japan in the early twentieth century, and refugees from Southeast Asia and Tibet in the late twentieth century. As suggested, these communities tended—at least in the first and second generations—to hew closely to the language, customs, ideas, and practices that they brought with them from their native lands. As a result, Buddhist temples that were established in the West often doubled as cultural centers, where the traditions of the old country could be preserved and transmitted. Thus, although non-Asians in America who learned of East Asian culture typically were drawn above all to Zen and to the idea that meditation was the essential Buddhist practice, Chinese and Japanese settlers more often focused on Pure Land traditions, with their distinctive focus on devotional recitation as the surest path to rebirth in the western paradise of Amitābha Buddha. Given the number of people of Chinese and Japanese descent in the United States, Pure Land may actually be the most popular of all Buddhist forms there, even today. Another East Asian devotional tradition that has taken root is Nichiren, in which recitation of an homage to the *Lotus Sūtra* often is used as a means of attaining worldly goals, though the ideal of liberation is not ignored. Nichiren, which is less eschatological in orientation than Pure Land, has followers among Japanese Americans, and also has attracted support from non-Asians, including significant numbers of non-White Americans.

A final historical note is in order. As in every culture to which Buddhism has been exported, so in the West over the course of time the pioneering teachers raised in traditional Buddhist settings are increasingly being replaced by teachers from the recipient culture. Indeed, Buddhism never has succeeded in a culture where it did not raise up "native" masters, whether Sri Lankan, Thai, Chinese, Japanese, Tibetan, or Mongolian. We already see this process at work: where thirty or forty years ago the most significant teachers in the West were mostly Asian, today there are a large number of qualified Western teachers expounding the Dharma, and their numbers are certain to increase in the years ahead. Since these teachers are products of Western culture, it would not be surprising to see them push rebirth even closer to the margins of contemporary Buddhist concerns. At the same time, however, Asian teachers continue to travel to the West and oversee centers there, and to the degree that they have received sound traditional training in Asia, they—and their Western disciples—may serve as something of a counterforce to the modernizing tendencies so powerfully at work in the West and elsewhere in the world.

CHAPTER 15

Contemporary Debates and Future Prospects

When we turn to the writings of philosophically inclined scholars of Buddhism published in the past several decades, we find a remarkable variety of positions on rebirth, ranging from deliberate silence, to outright rejection, to the doctrine's acceptance on metaphysical, empirical, or other grounds.

Some Recent Analyses

A number of writers who wish to place Buddhism in dialogue with contemporary philosophy and science are content to leave traditional cosmology and metaphysics—especially the notion of rebirth—in abeyance. Thus, philosopher and neuroscientist Owen Flanagan writes, in *The Bodhisattva's Brain*, of his desire to "naturalize" Buddhism within modern philosophical discourse, in part by bracketing out such unproven and likely unprovable notions as rebirth, karmic causation, nirvāṇa, magical powers, heavens and hells, and nonphysical states of mind.[463] Similarly, in his best-selling *Why Buddhism Is True*, journalist Robert Wright specifies that the Buddhism he claims is "true" is *not* "the 'supernatural' or more exotically metaphysical parts of Buddhism—reincarnation, for example—but rather... the naturalistic parts: ideas that fall squarely within modern psychology and philosophy."[464] Even philosopher and Buddhism scholar Jay Garfield specifies at the outset of his

Engaging Buddhism: Why It Matters to Philosophers that he will "not discuss Buddhist theories of rebirth, of karma, or approaches to meditation... not because I take these to be unimportant.... [but] because I do not see them as principal sites of engagement with Western philosophy."[465] The underlying assumption here, obviously, is that most contemporary philosophers and scientists simply will not consider nonphysicalist accounts of the operations of mind, let alone belief in life after death. Similar attitudes are evinced by Western Buddhist scholar-practitioners intent on aligning the tradition with modern culture. Stephen Batchelor, for instance, surveys a range of Buddhist rational, empirical, and ethical justifications for rebirth, finds them inconclusive at best, and concludes that

> all the pictures I entertain of heaven and hell, or cycles of rebirth, merely serve to replace the overwhelming reality of the unknown with what is known and acceptable.... To cling to the idea of rebirth, rather than treating it as a useful symbol or hypothesis, can be spiritually suffocating. If we are able to take Buddhism as an ongoing existential encounter with our life here and now, then we will only gain by releasing our grip on such notions.[466]

Similarly, and even more pointedly, Richard Hayes asserts that the potential of Buddhism in the West "will never be realized... [until it] is purged of some of the Asian habits it has acquired down through the millennia," and goes on to specify that the first of the teachings that should be discarded "are the obstructive doctrines... of rebirth and karma... [reflection on which] dulls the mind and impairs the faculty of reasoning"—although he does also concede that it may be a useful fiction for Buddhists as they seek to find their way in the modern world,[467] a perspective to which we will return later. Batchelor and Hayes know Buddhism well enough to recognize the importance of rebirth for traditional Buddhists, but both are convinced that it is possible to be Buddhist without taking the doctrine literally, and go on to imagine what a nonmetaphysical Buddhism might be like.

As we saw earlier, the standard argument for rebirth in the Indian and Tibetan Buddhist philosophical circles was that of Dharmakīrti, and while notoriously complex, it has not gone unremarked upon by modern scholars. While Dharmakīrti's arguments generally have sufficed for traditionally trained Tibetan Buddhists and their Western disciples, philosophically trained Western scholars who have studied them usually find them less persuasive. I cannot lay out their critiques in detail, but want at least to mention some of the approaches they have taken. The first such scholar to express a view on the arguments, Martin Willson, adduced a number of criticisms, which may be reduced to two: (1) the nonmaterialist explanations of sentient beings' birth processes proffered by Dharmakīrti and his followers are based on outdated science and insufficient evidence, and (2) Dharmakīrti's attempts to argue against materialist presentations of the mind-body problem do not decisively refute the possibility that mind is actually an emergent property of the body (or, in modern terms, the brain).[468] I raised similar points in my own 1993 translation and analysis of Gyaltsab Darma Rinchen's fifteenth-century Tibetan commentary on Dharmakīrti, and further observed that the supposedly clinching argument—that mind cannot arise from body because the former is coarse, insentient, and physical, while the latter is clear, knowing, and immaterial—appears to beg the question, by defining terms in such a way that the desired conclusion is unavoidable.[469]

Around the same time, Richard Hayes summarized and partially translated a number of Dharmakīrti's arguments against materialism and in favor of rebirth, commenting along the way that, ingenious as they are, they do not fully succeed in dismantling materialist claims about the physical basis of mind or in establishing mind as ultimately independent of physical causes.[470] In his 2012 study of the problem of intentionality in Buddhist and contemporary philosophies of mind, Dan Arnold faulted Dharmakīrti for discussing mental causation in terms that actually are based on the model of *physical* causation that we observe in the world, pointing out that modern cognitive philosophers frequently eschew such classic causal language when attempting to make sense of how the mind works—and that doing so would have made a case like Dharmakīrti's easier rather than more difficult to argue.[471] Finally, in his 2015 magnum opus, *Waking, Dreaming, Being*, Evan Thompson observed that Dharmakīrti's arguments would fail to convince a modern philosopher of mind, for they are based on definitions of matter and consciousness that set them apart as mutually exclusive and foreclose the possibility that matter could ever be the basis of what we call "the mental." For his part, Thompson suggests that we need "to work our way to a new understanding of what it means for something to be physical, in which 'physical' no longer means essentially nonmental or nonexperiential."[472]

Thompson, like Flanagan, Arnold, and a number of other recent writers concerned with the mind-body problem in Buddhism and contemporary philosophy, is prompted to reflection in part by the outlook of the Fourteenth Dalai Lama, who has repeatedly reframed Dharmakīrti's arguments for rebirth in his discourses and published writings, most notably, perhaps, his discussion of Buddhism vis à vis science, *The Universe in a Single Atom*. The Dalai Lama has famously declared that if a Buddhist doctrine is contradicted by irrefutable scientific evidence, then the doctrine ought to be discarded, and in the case of the traditional flat-earth theory, he has proposed just that. When it comes to rebirth, however, he argues, although not in so many words, that because absence of evidence does not constitute evidence of absence, he cannot accept that the doctrine has been refuted. He continues to present Dharmakīrti's arguments, at least in a general way, and to insist that although there may be a stronger connection between neurological events and *ordinary* mental states than traditional Buddhists believe, there remains the possibility that there are *extraordinary* mental states that do not depend on the neurological system, namely, the meditative experiences of advanced tantric yogīs, especially those who have entered the postmortem concentration on the clear-light nature of the mind known as *thukdam* (discussed above, in chapter 13).[473] Along roughly similar lines, Robert Thurman has asserted that Dharmakīrti's arguments simply do not work with respect to ordinary states of mind, but that proof of the existence of mental states independent of physical functions is provided by the theory and practice of the completion stage of Unexcelled Yoga Tantra, with *thukdam* as a striking case in point.[474] The Dalai Lama has encouraged neuroscientific studies of meditators in *thukdam*, although whether these will provide evidence for either the materialist or Buddhist position on mind and body remains to be seen: the *presence* of subtle neural activity in such contemplatives might prompt revisions of current notions of death, but would not prove that the yogī who has passed out of *thukdam* moves on to another realm; while the *absence* of neural activity would not assure that the meditative state assumed by tradition is *not* occurring, only that it is clinically undetectable—and if it is real but undetectable, then our current definitions of death—and consciousness—certainly will require rethinking.

Other contemporary thinkers seek to justify rebirth, and Buddhist mind-body metaphysics, not by reframing Dharmakīrti's arguments but by embracing alternative scientific cosmologies that make the mind or consciousness, rather than matter, the driving force in the universe, hence its passage from one life to the next relatively unproblematic. B. Alan Wallace has argued long and passionately that science's prejudice against "first-person" subjective experiences as a source of knowledge both overestimates the reliability of science's "third-person," measurable methods and underestimates the role and reliability of what is often dismissed as "mere subjectivity." This is especially true at the quantum level, where it appears that mind plays an active role in shaping so-called external reality. Indeed, says Wallace, an important implication of cutting-edge research in quantum mechanics is that the universe is properly conceived not—as classical physics insisted—as a physical system but as "fundamentally an information-processing system, from which the appearance of matter emerges at a higher level of reality."[475] He adds,

> On the macroscopic scale this implies a shift from a materiocentric view of the universe to an empiricocentric view of the

> universe, and on a microcosmic scale, this requires a shift from a neurocentric to an empiricocentric view of human existence... [in which] meaning is fundamental.[476]

On such a view, the independence of mind from body is easier to maintain, and rebirth easier to defend. In a somewhat similar fashion, David Loy proposes a "new evolutionary myth," inspired by the work of cultural historian Thomas Berry (1914-2009), which sees the universe as an organism and "evolution as the creative groping of a self-organizing cosmos that is becoming more self-aware."[477] If, as suggested by such a scenario, "consciousness is basic—if there might be rudimentary awareness even at the quantum level, as some physicists now believe—then there may be some plausibility to the notion of sanhkara [karmic formations] persisting after death."[478] This might not end up entailing individual survival in the manner usually described by traditional Buddhists, for in the absence of a self that is reborn, there is simply the emptiness/infinity that is the nature of the cosmos, which endlessly seeks and assumes form after form; in this sense, concludes Loy, "there is *only* rebirth," but nothing resembling individual immortality.[479] It is worth remarking briefly that the stances taken by Wallace and Loy, while influenced by radical interpretations of contemporary physics and cosmology, are also redolent of Yogācāra "idealism," and compatible in a number of ways with such Mahāyāna contemplative traditions as Zen, Tantra, and the Great Perfection.

Descending from the world of metaphysics, we find that a number of contemporary Buddhist thinkers are intent on demonstrating rebirth by appealing to empirical evidence, whether that evidence be the result of scientific investigation or meditative experience. Thus, the French-born Tibetan Buddhist monk Matthieu Ricard finds that "the certainty arising from a life of contemplative practice, or a life lived with a spiritual teacher, is just as powerful as that arising from the demonstration of a theorem," hence must be granted some epistemic value.[480] B. Alan Wallace, with his insistence on the importance of "first-person" evidence for knowledge about the world and his confidence in the deliverances of profound meditative concentration, argues that the experiences of advanced contemplatives give us real information about the world, and that the memories of past lives often unearthed by such yogīs may therefore be reliable—hence evidence of the possibility of rebirth.[481] In support of his claim, Wallace cites not just the experiences of yogīs but also the work of Ian Stevenson (1918-2007), who researched a large number of cases "suggestive of reincarnation."[482] Indeed, for modern Buddhists intent on providing empirical arguments for rebirth, Stevenson's case histories are a gold mine and commonly cited. Thus, Martin Willson, despite his dismissal of Dharmakīrti's rational arguments for rebirth, seems quite receptive to the evidentiary value of spontaneous recollections like those reported by Stevenson, and also is willing to entertain the reliability of other ways people remember past lives, such as deliberate training, hypnotic regression, and psychic readings.[483]

More recently, Bhikkhu Anālayo has examined a number of modern grounds for accepting rebirth. He delves deeply into Stevenson's research—agreeing that there are a small number of cases that truly seem inexplicable without the notion of rebirth—and investigating in particular detail a case with which he is personally familiar, that of a Sri Lankan boy whose style of reciting Pāli texts was completely unknown early in his life, but turns out, on the basis of more recent research, to have been prevalent in an earlier era, of which the boy claims to have memories.[484] These cases are, as Stevenson says, *suggestive* of rebirth, but hardly conclusive. As Evan Thompson notes, Stevenson's studies may be faulted on a number of methodological grounds, particularly as relates to the time lag between a child's first report of a past-life memory and the time they were interviewed by researchers, leaving "a large amount of room for false memory and after-the-fact reconstruction."[485] And, Stephen Batchelor observes that even if some such reports are reliable, and certain people *have* undergone rebirth, "this in itself would not furnish any proof whatsoever either that they themselves would experience rebirth again or that anyone else was reborn in the past or will be in the future."[486] In other words, even an "empirical" proof of rebirth—were there one—would not necessarily confirm the *Buddhist* theory of rebirth, either in its broad strokes or its fine details.

Along with children's alleged past-life memories, Bhikkhu Anālayo also examines two other "empirical" arguments for rebirth. One is near-death experiences (NDEs), in which persons who have undergone clinical death and then were revived frequently report a powerful sense of moving toward a brilliant light and feeling themselves in the presence of deceased relatives and/or divine beings—experiences that often are taken as conclusive evidence that there is an afterlife. A second kind of empirical argument examined by Anālayo is based on experiences evoked through past-life regression analysis, which often evokes in patients lucid memories of experiences they supposedly had during previous existences. Anālayo finds each of these types of experience suggestive of the complexity of the brain-mind relation, and perhaps even as pointing to the mind's independence of the brain—but he does not see them as conclusive proof of the reality of rebirth.[487] NDEs, we might note, may be quite subjectively powerful and metaphysically persuasive, but they are *near*-death experiences, not death itself, hence still experiences had by a living being, which may tell us nothing about what, if anything, lies across the border in that "undiscovered country from whose bourn no traveler returns" (*Hamlet*, Act 3, scene 1). Another empirical claim, not discussed by Anālayo but related to that based on NDEs, looks to out-of-body experiences (OBEs), which involve a sense of complete separation of mind from body. Sometimes these occur during surgeries or medical emergencies but they also may occur, apparently quite spontaneously, in everyday life. In either case, after the experience, memories often remain of facts about the external world that the mind seems to have witnessed, including people, places, and conversations—and independent confirmation of these may provide a powerful sense of "objectivity" to the experience. Like NDEs, OBEs often are taken by those who undergo them as evidence that mind is independent of the brain, hence capable of surviving death. But, also like NDEs, OBEs may be subject to naturalistic explanation—and even if they do suggest mind's independence, and possible survival, of the death of the brain, they do not establish any particular version of the afterlife, let alone Buddhist karmic eschatology.[488]

It should be added that any Buddhist claims about metaphysical truths, such as rebirth, that are based solely on extrasensory or other special, "mystical" perceptions must inevitably face comparison with special-experience-based claims in other religious traditions, which may point to a very different way of "seeing" the cosmos—and in the absence of "third-person," publicly available evidence, there is no way to give priority to one claim or the other, except on purely dogmatic grounds. As William James puts it,

> Mystics have no right to claim that we ought to accept the deliverance of their peculiar experiences....The utmost that they can ask of us in this life is to admit that they establish a presumption...for they form a consensus and have an unequivocal outcome.[489]

"But," adds James, "even this presumption from the unanimity of mystics is far from being strong," for their unanimity dissolves upon closer inspection, since the philosophical positions and ways of life developed by mystics are quite various, admitting, for instance, of pantheism, monism, dualism, or theism; asceticism, celebration, or self-indulgence; and images of darkness or of light.[490] James is discussing mysticism in general, but even if we were to push the dubious claim that all accomplished Buddhist "mystics," wherever they have been, have enjoyed the same vision of the cosmos and its nature, those mystical claims—including claims to have seen the reality of karma and rebirth—cannot stand on their own as evidence, for they invite inevitable comparison with conclusions drawn by mystics in other traditions, which point in very different metaphysical and cosmological directions. The only way, then, to establish that a Buddhist vision is more "correct" than that of, say, a

Christian or a Hindu would be to return to "common" philosophizing like that of Dharmakīrti—and that, as we have seen, is unlikely to prove conclusive.

A Debate: Batchelor vs. Thurman, 1997

If there is a crystallizing example of the nature of the discourse on rebirth intrinsic to modern Buddhism, it is a debate between two figures we have encountered before, Stephen Batchelor and Robert Thurman. The debate was arranged under the auspices of *Tricycle: The Buddhist Review*, a bellwether journal of modern Western Buddhism, which published a transcript of the conversation in 1997.[491] The debate was staged on the occasion of the publication of Batchelor's *Buddhism Without Beliefs: A Contemporary Guide to Awakening*.[492] Batchelor is a British-born, French-based independent scholar and teacher. In his twenties he was a Buddhist monk in the Tibetan tradition; he also has delved deeply into Korean Son (Zen) traditions and taken up the study of early Buddhism. *Buddhism Without Beliefs* is, in effect, a Buddhist modernist manifesto, which has served since its appearance as both a touchstone and a lightning rod, laying out a vision of the Buddha, and of Buddhism, in which the key tenets of the Dharma are regarded not as cosmological or metaphysical claims but, rather, as ontological, existential, psychological, and ethical guidelines for living. Batchelor does not dispute that the Buddha propounded a cosmology involving six realms of saṃsāric existence or a metaphysics entailing the precise operations of karma through a series of rebirths undergone by each sentient being, but (as we saw in chapter 3) he argues that these ideas were incidental to Śākyamuni's true purpose: to help us transcend anxiety and attain an authentic way of being that is informed by both a deep understanding of reality and compassion broad enough to encompass all beings.[493]

Batchelor's chapter on "Rebirth" in *Buddhism Without Beliefs* is brief,[494] but crucial to understanding his argument and his debate with Thurman. He acknowledges that rebirth is difficult to accept for those, like him, who have been shaped by the scientific worldview, and argues that the Buddha used the concept simply as an easily understandable scaffolding for his more important psychological and ethical teachings. He further argues that—the claims of later Asian Buddhists notwithstanding—acceptance of rebirth is by no means crucial to those teachings' truth and effectiveness. Invoking the critical spirit that he sees the Buddha encouraging in his followers, Batchelor says that we moderns need not accept the reality of rebirth simply on the tradition's say-so or because we fear that we will not be able to live ethically in the absence of an elaborate but unproven metaphysic. He himself does not reject rebirth—he declares himself agnostic on the matter—but he clearly thinks that the question is largely irrelevant to the practice of Dharma, and ought to be left in abeyance.

Unsurprisingly, Batchelor's views on rebirth were, and are, anathema to many traditionalists—whose stated aim, after all, is to avoid *taking* rebirth rather than to avoid *discussing* it—but he also was criticized by many thoroughly modern Buddhists, among them Robert Thurman, a professor at Columbia University, translator and publisher of many Buddhist works, and, like Batchelor, a former monk in the Tibetan tradition. Thurman, who once was named by *Time* magazine as one of the twenty-five most influential people in America, also is a proponent of his own distinctive vision of modern Dharma, on which he has written widely.[495] Decades later, the *Tricycle* exchange between him and Batchelor still crackles with intelligence, as two scholar-practitioners grapple honestly—and often quite subtly—with difficult questions of history, culture, and philosophy. The lively back-and-forth of the conversation only can be appreciated by reading the transcript, but it is worthwhile to identify the key questions debated by the two men (and the stances taken by each), because, arguably, they remain questions that sooner or later all modern Buddhists must face.

The central question animating the debate is, quite simply, can we be Buddhist without believing in rebirth? Batchelor argues that we can—that the Buddha's teachings on ethics, meditation, emptiness, and the nature and workings of the mind all can "work" perfectly well even in the absence of a metaphysics of karma-influenced personal spiritual continuity, i.e., rebirth. For Thurman, the abandonment of such a metaphysics, with its implication that we only live once, undercuts our motivation to behave ethically—let alone to try to attain buddhahood in order to free all sentient beings from suffering, the stated goal of most Mahāyāna Buddhists. What's more, Thurman argues, there is ample empirical evidence for rebirth, both in the experiences of the Buddha and his awakened followers and in more recent scientific investigations of past-life reports, most notably those of Ian Stevenson. Batchelor is skeptical about the evidentiary power of claims based on the alleged superknowledges attributed to or even claimed by long-dead humans, and, as noted, finds the cases studied by Stevenson intriguing but far from fully probative of the universality and operations of the Buddhist system of rebirth.

Batchelor and Thurman do agree on the definitive truth—and centrality—of the Buddhist doctrine of emptiness, but for Thurman this serves as a basis for confidence in the Buddha's key conventional teachings, including those of karma and rebirth, while according to Batchelor taking emptiness literally does *not* vouchsafe other Buddhist teachings, least of all those on karma and rebirth. Such ideas, he believes, must be either eschewed entirely or, if retained, they must be read existentially, psychologically, and/or metaphorically: in effect, as myths that inspire us to live authentically within a cosmos of which we know precious little. For his part, Thurman finds it hard to take inspiration from a vision we don't take more or less literally; a corollary is that it is impossible to take our bodhisattva vows seriously without believing in a multiplicity of lives in which we might work for others. Batchelor brings the discussion to a close by admitting that, for his part, the best he could do would be to "try to behave as if there were infinite lifetimes in which I would be committed to saving beings."[496] In short, for Batchelor, it doesn't matter in the end whether there is rebirth or not, while for Thurman, it matters a great deal.

Final Thoughts

Although most Buddhists in premodern Buddhist cultures accepted, and sometimes defended, the traditional Buddhist karmic eschatology, it is evident from the analysis in this and the previous chapter that since Asian Buddhists began to take account of modernity and Western Buddhists to take account of Asian traditions, those Buddhists that have bothered to talk about rebirth at all (and many have not), have typically done so by adopting one or the other of the four possible approaches to rebirth outlined in chapter 14.

(1) Among literalists—who accept traditional descriptions of the karma-rebirth cosmology and arguments for it either unquestioningly or on the basis of their own analysis—the most common constituency is Asian Buddhists, whether in Asia or the West. These would include many traditionally trained Theravāda monks and Tibetan lamas, with the latter category including such abovementioned figures above as Sakya Trizin, Dudjom Rinpoche, Lama Zopa Rinpoche, and Kalu Rinpoche. Many of these teachers' Western disciples have adopted a literalist idea of rebirth, as well, though they do not often write about their views, and what they do write is sometimes difficult to find outside of small Buddhist tracts and magazines.

(2) Neo-traditionalists—who seek to justify traditional cosmology and metaphysics in more "up-to-date" terms—comprise a large and diverse group. Among them, we might count Robert Thurman, who has argued for the truth and importance of the classical notion of rebirth but reframed it in evolutionary terms; B. Alan Wallace, who has argued on the basis of quantum physics that the mind is a more prominent factor in the cosmos than materialist science will allow, and, in the spirit of William James, that first-person experience is more reliable as a source of knowledge than philosophers will admit; Martin Willson, who finds rational arguments for rebirth unpersuasive but regards several types of empirical or experiential evidence as very promising; and the Fourteenth Dalai Lama, who accepts many of the premises and conclusions of Dharmakīrti's

arguments, but limits their true applicability to the very subtlest level of the operations of mind and body, conceding that ordinary consciousness may indeed be impossible without neural activity.

(3) Modernists, who are uncertain about the literal truth of the traditional cosmology and metaphysics and generally unpersuaded by arguments for it, seek in various ways to maintain the language and imagery of karma, rebirth, and the realms of saṃsāra—but recast in symbolic, psychological, or existential terms that are more amenable to modern sensibilities. Stephen Batchelor, with his "existential" interpretation of Buddhism, is the most prominent Western exponent of such an approach, but there are many others, as well. Alan Watts, for example, understood claims about past and future lives as a way of describing the multiple social roles we adopt in our present life. Trungpa Rinpoche seems (at times, at least) to have favored a largely psychological explanation of the six realms of rebirth and traditional ideas about death. David Loy recasts notions of rebirth within a new cosmological myth that effectively removes them from the traditional individual-survival framework. Richard Hayes regards rebirth as, at best, a useful fiction.

(4) Like those in the other groups, secularists vary in their motives and arguments, but are in accord that rebirth just doesn't matter very much. Even if it was taught by the Buddha and his followers over the past two millennia, it is actually superfluous to the real meaning of the Dharma, today as in pre-B.C.E. India: as a way to understand reality and live wisely, compassionately, and meaningfully within our present lives and in the common world we share. Thus, writers like Owen Flanagan, Robert Wright, and Jay Garfield deliberately put rebirth in abeyance when attempting to engage Buddhism with modern philosophy or psychology. Engaged Buddhists either reject the idea outright, as B. R. Ambedkar did, or largely ignore it, like Thich Nhat Hanh and many others. And, for the many modern people who do not identify as Buddhist but wish to draw on Buddhist insights and meditation techniques for specific purposes in their daily lives, rebirth is irrelevant at best, a distraction at worst, and in any case hardly worth worrying about.

These categories must be taken with many grains of salt: the lines between one and the other are not always sharp, such that, for instance, the difference between literalism and neo-traditionalism is not always clear, nor that between modernism and secularism. By the same token, many of the thinkers discussed here are too complex to assign solely to one category. Thus, in various contexts, the Fourteenth Dalai Lama may be read as a literalist, a neo-traditionalist, or a modernist—and he even has propounded a secular ethics that might align him with the fourth camp. Batchelor and Hayes may be classified as modernists but show strong secularist tendencies; indeed Batchelor, for his part, has most recently described his as a secular Buddhism, even though he presents Buddhist doctrines, including rebirth, symbolically and existentially, as a modernist would. And a figure like Thich Nhat Hanh, who largely eschews discussion of rebirth, hence appears "secularist," clearly has both traditional and modern elements at work in his public ministry—and perhaps in his private convictions as well.

It might be argued that the very effort to think about Buddhism vis à vis modernity that generates these four categories is itself open to criticism. Most of the thinkers we have surveyed attempt in one way or another to align traditional Buddhist cosmology and metaphysics with modern Western ideas and practices, whether simply to make it comprehensible, to defend it, to reject it, or to reinterpret it along less traditionally "religious" lines. One might suggest, though, that such efforts stem from a failure to recognize that traditional Buddhism is in fact almost entirely incommensurable with modern science, psychology, and aesthetics. This is the stance taken by Donald Lopez in his analysis of "the Scientific Buddha"—the Buddha imagined by moderns as perfectly consonant in his life and teachings with the scientific perspective and procedures developed in the past several centuries in the West. Lopez finds that such a Buddha never existed, and to posit him is to do serious violence to the way Buddhists have traditionally understood and lived in the world. According to Lopez, the Buddha and the tradition he founded are in most ways incompatible with modern, Western ideas and values, and must be acknowledged as such. Indeed, says Lopez,

> The Old Buddha, not the Scientific Buddha, presented a radical challenge to the way we see the world, both the world that was seen two millennia ago and the world that is seen today. What he taught is not different, it is not an alternative, it is the opposite. That the path we think will lead us to happiness instead leads to sorrow. That what we believe is true is instead false. That what we imagine to be real is unreal. A certain value lies in remembering that challenge from time to time.[497]

Lopez says, in effect: don't try to align Buddhism with science, psychology, or contemporary philosophy, don't try to justify it, don't try to reimagine it; rather, understand it as a radical critique of modernity and its complacencies. Perhaps, then, this is a fifth approach: literalism as radical cultural critique.[498]

Lopez's approach is a demanding one, for it forces modern Buddhists to hold in mind opposing ways of understanding the world, an exercise in "negative capability"[499] only sustainable by a few. The vast majority, I expect, will opt for one of the four approaches to rebirth outlined above, or some combination of them. Each of them, I believe, has a role to play in the ongoing colloquy among Buddhists as to how the tradition ought to be imagined and enacted in the modern world: literalists remind us of the classical Buddhist outlook, so different from our own; neo-traditionalists provide ways to argue for the traditional cosmology and metaphysics, or something akin to it; modernists either suspend or reject the classical paradigm, but find new, nonmetaphysical ways of making it meaningful; while secularists raise vital questions about just how much of tradition can be jettisoned in the process of finding a place for Buddhism in our disenchanted world.

My own view—certainly debatable—is that one or another form of modernism best points the way forward. I am particularly drawn to the various forms of "Buddhist agnosticism" that have been articulated in recent decades. The term was coined by Stephen Batchelor, but may appropriately be applied to any thinker who finds traditional rational, empirical, or faith-based arguments in favor of rebirth problematic but does not reject the idea outright, admitting that—with our present limitations—we simply do not know whether past and future lives are real. One interesting agnostic argument comes from an unexpected source, the late Tibetan lama Lati Rimpoche, who in a 1986 conversation with Richard Hayes suggested that Westerners uncertain about karma and rebirth (which Rimpoche concedes are "beyond absolute proof") should remain open to the possibility that the traditional cosmology and metaphysics are true, and in any case *behave* as if they were true by living ethically and compassionately. In that way, they will generate happiness for themselves and others in this life, and if there are future lives, they will be happy ones; conversely, if they behave negatively, they will bring misery to themselves and others in this life, and face a sorrowful rebirth, if rebirths there are.[500] As Hayes rightly notes, this argument (which we encountered in Indian form in chapter 10) is akin to Pascal's famous "wager" regarding the existence of God and the reality of final judgment. Leaving aside the question whether so tentative an acceptance of religious claims might itself be problematic in the eyes of God or amidst the subtleties of karma, we may agree with Hayes that Rimpoche

> seems to place these doctrines in a mythical space, as opposed to a historical or scientific framework. Access to this mythical space can be gained, not by logical proof or through a methodical empirical investigation of the sensible world, but by exercising one's imagination and then having the courage of one's imaginings.[501]

For Hayes, reading traditional cosmology and metaphysics as myth—as "fictional"—allows modern people to imagine ways of living quite different from their own, not unlike a good novel; to the degree that a novel or other work of art may widen our perspective and ennoble our lives, to the same degree engaging with the traditional Buddhist imaginary allows modern Buddhists to enter more meaningfully into the streams of Buddhist life and provide meaning within their own.[502]

Along similar lines, Batchelor opts for a "middle way" agnosticism in which one "does not have either to assert [rebirth] dogmatically or deny it; one neither has to adopt the literal versions presented by tradition nor fall into the other extreme of believing that death is the final annihilation."[503] This, he asserts, does not mire us in indecision. Rather, it allows us, as in Zen, to confront with ruthless honesty "the Great Matter of Life and Death," and "is a powerful catalyst for action, since in shifting concern away from a hypothetical future life, to the dilemmas of the present, it demands . . . a compassion-centered ethic" that will bring joy to our lives and the lives of others.[504] In his writings, Batchelor seems ambivalent about entertaining traditional cosmology and metaphysics even at the symbolic level; he often implies that we simply ought to get beyond these outmoded conceptions. Recall, however, that at the conclusion of his debate with Thurman, he says that *if* he were to utilize the traditional Buddhist vision, "I would try to behave as if there were infinite lifetimes in which I would be committed to saving beings."[505]

I myself would argue without ambivalence for what I call "As-If Agnosticism." My stance is agnostic because, like Hayes and Batchelor (and many others), I do not find traditional descriptions of karma and rebirth literally credible, nor am I fully persuaded by arguments in their favor, whether rational, empirical, or faith-based; on the other hand, I cannot rule out the possibility that such descriptions (or something akin to them) may in fact be true. The universe, after all, is surpassingly strange. In the spirit of Wallace Stevens's famous statement that "we believe without belief, beyond belief,"[506] I propose that we live *as if* such descriptions were true. I am not suggesting we simply take up wishful thinking: *if only* there were past and future lives, *if only* karma works the ways tradition says it does, *if only* glorious and perfect buddhahood awaited us all at the end of the rainbow. Maybe they do, maybe they don't. But as Buddhists have argued for millennia, Western humanists have claimed for centuries, and scientists have recently begun to recognize, the world is actually built far more on our ideas, aspirations, and speculations—the As-If—than we suppose, and the solid foundations we presume to lie beneath us—the "As-Is"—are much more difficult to find than we assume. It's not, therefore, that by living *as if* certain doctrines were true we really are in flight from some bedrock, objective reality, because that reality—though it certainly imposes limitations on us, most notably at the time of death—turns out to be far more a matter of convention and far less "just the way things are" than we had thought. Freed from the illusion of perfect objectivity, therefore, why *not* think and live as if Buddhism were true? In doing so, we empower ourselves to enter, as fully as is possible in a skeptical age, into the ongoing, ever-changing life of the Dharma, adopting Buddhist ideals, telling Buddhist stories, articulating Buddhist doctrines, performing Buddhist rituals, and embodying Buddhist ethics in ways that make meaning for ourselves, provide a measure of comfort to others, and perhaps contribute in some small way to the betterment of the imperfect and imperiled world in which we all live.[507]

Let the final word belong not to me, however, but to the Buddha, who in the *Rohitassa Sutta* (*Discourse about Rohitassa*) recounts a previous life as a seer named Rohatissa, "possessing magical potency, able to travel through the sky... [with] speed like that of a light arrow easily shot by a firm-bowed archer." Conceiving the wish to find the ends of the earth, he traveled for a hundred years as fast as the wind, yet "died along the way without having reached the end of the world." There is no "end" to the geographic world, explains the Buddha, but that is not, in any case, the end-of-the-world we should be seeking. Rather, we must seek the place "where one is not born, does not grow old and die, does not pass away and get reborn." And where is the end of the world in this deeper sense—nirvāṇa—to be found? "It is," he says, "in this fathom-long body endowed with perception and mind that I proclaim (1) the world,

(2) the origin of the world, (3) the cessation of the world, and (4) the way leading to the cessation of the world." As a result,

> "...the wise one, the world-knower,
> who has reached the world's end and lived the spiritual life,
> having known the world's end, at peace,
> does not desire this world or another."[508]

Notes

1. Becker 1973.
2. Buddhists also frequently employ the general term "arising" (*upapatti*).
3. See, for example, G. Obeyesekere 2002, 127; Brons 2014.
4. See G. Obeyeskere 2002. For a historical and philosophical analysis by a modern philosopher, see Ducasse 1961.
5. See G. Obeyesekere 2002, 72–76, 90.
6. G. Obeyeskere 2002, 78–84.
7. For more detailed treatment, see G. Obeyesekere 2002 (including the excellent bibliography).
8. G. Obeyesekere 2002, 22–28. They also are referred to as the Ibo.
9. G. Obeyesekere 2002, 28.
10. G. Obeyesekere 2002, 28–37.
11. G. Obeyeskere 2002, 33.
12. G. Obeyesekere 2002, 37. He adds, however, that "[rebirth's] centrality in the overall cosmology of each group is difficult to ascertain," in part because contact with Western cultures over the past several centuries has in many cases altered long-standing beliefs—a problem that arises in almost any present-day encounter with small-scale societies.
13. G. Obeyesekere 2002, 43–44.
14. G. Obeyesekere 2002, 58–70, 92.
15. G. Obeyeskere 2002, 59.
16. G. Obeyesekere 2002, 59.
17. G. Obeyesekere 2002, 59–60.
18. G. Obyesekere 2002, 90.
19. Herodotus, *The History,* 2.123 (David Grene translation), cited in G. Obeyesekere 2002, 193–94.
20. G. Obeyesekere 2002, 317.
21. See, for example, G. Obeyesekere 2002, chaps. 5–6. Besides those I will survey, notable figures discussed by Obeyesekere include the poet Pindar

(232-236), the later Pythagorean Empedocles (214-232), and the Neo-Platonist Plotinus (290-308); Orphic ideas are discussed on pp. 236-40.

22. G. Obeyesekere 2002, 193-214; note especially the chart on p. 198.
23. G. Obeyesekere 2002, 240-87; note especially the chart on p. 273.
24. Plato, *Republic*, 614b-622d; G. Obeyesekere 2002, 240-48.
25. G. Obeyesekere 2002, 271.
26. Platonism also informed Manicheism, a Persian-based religious movement that exercised considerable influence in Europe and the Mideast in the early centuries of the Common Era—but also shows evidence of Zoroastrian, Christian, Indic, and even Daoist influences. Rebirth has a significant place in Manichean cosmology, as does the idea that for a gnostic elite, liberation is possible. There are strong resonances between Manicheism and Christian Gnosticism.
27. Friedrich Nietzsche, *Beyond Good and Evil*, preface: www.marxists.org/reference/archive/nietzsche/1886/beyond-good-evil/preface.htm.
28. Indeed, a 2018 Pew Research Center survey showed that fully a third of all Americans believe in reincarnation; see Gecewicz 2018.
29. G. Obeyesekere 2002, 313-18.
30. For good overviews of early and classical Indian views on rebirth (and karma), see the essays in O'Flaherty 1983; as well as Collins 1982, chap. 1; and Phillips 2009, chap. 4.
31. The other great influence on South Asian culture prior to the late first millennium C.E. came from those speaking Dravidian languages (the most prominent being Tamil, Telugu, Kannada, and Malayalam), which still predominate in south India, and whose interactions with Indo-Aryan culture over the millennia have been complex and sometimes contentious.
32. In terms of a Hindu "canon," *śruti* is defined in contrast to the "remembered" (*smṛti*) tradition enshrined in later (and often more popular) texts such as the great epics (the *Mahābhārata* and *Rāmāyaṇa*, the former including the *Bhagavad Gītā*), various treatises (*sūtras* or *śāstras*) on society, religion, and philosophy, and devotional "histories" known as Purāṇas.
33. For a complete translation, see Jamison and Brereton 2017; for a well-selected anthology, see Doniger 1981.
34. *Ṛgveda* 10.16.6, trans. O'Flaherty 1981, 49-50.
35. In the *Chāndogya Upaniṣad* 6.8.7-15; see, for example, Radhakrishnan 1968, 458-65.
36. For a good, concise summary of this, see, for example, Collins 1982, 29-30.
37. Campbell 1962, 139, 211-18.
38. See, for example, the discussion in G. Obeyesekere 2002, 3-4, 13-14.
39. *Śatapatha Brāḥmaṇa* 10.4.3(9), 10.4.5.1(4), trans. Eggeling 1897, 357, 365, respectively.

40. *Bṛhadāraṇyaka Upaniṣad* 4.4.3–4, trans. Radhakrishnan 1968, 271; cf. G. Obeyesekere 2002, 5.
41. *Bṛhadāraṇyaka Upaniṣad* 6.2.16, trans. Radhakrishnan 1968, 314–15; cf. G. Obeyesekere 2002, 8.
42. *Bṛhadāraṇyaka Upaniṣad* 3.2.13, trans. Radhakrishnan 1968, 217; cf. G. Obeyesekere 2002, 4.
43 See G. Obeyesekere 2002, 10–13. The *Chāndogya* (5.10.9; see trans. Radhakrishnan 1968, 434) does list four cardinal sins that will result in a "fall": stealing gold, drinking liquor, killing a brahmin, or cuckolding one's guru. The *Kauṣītaki* (1.1–7, trans. Radhakrishnan 1968, 753–60) outlines a rebirth process a bit like that of the *Bṛhadāraṇyaka*. The idea is not, on the other hand, very evident in the other two Upaniṣads accepted as "early": the *Aitereya* and the *Taittirīya*.
44. The brāḥmaṇa-śramaṇa distinction already is evident in the inscriptions of Aśoka, which date from the mid-to-late third century B.C.E. (see, e.g., Nikam and McKeown 1959, 27), not to mention in Buddhist texts that must pre-date Aśoka because he recommends them; see Thanissaro 1993.
45. Among other places, these teachers are detailed in D 2.16–33 (*Samaññaphala Sutta*), trans. Walshe 1987, 93–97; a range of brāḥmaṇa and śramaṇa views on various matters—including past-life memories and our postmortem condition—are laid out, and rejected, in the *Brahmajāla Sutta* (D sutta 1), trans. Walshe 1987, 67–90; see, for example, 1.29–37, 2.38–39, trans. Walshe 1987, 73–74, 82, respectively.
46. D 2.23 (*Samaññaphala Sutta*), trans. Walshe 1987, 95–96.
47. See Chattopadyaya 1992, 1994.
48. *Dīgha Nikāya* 2.17 (*Samaññaphala Sutta*), trans. Walshe 1987, 94. See also G. Obeyesekere 2002, 102–3.
49. See, for example, Basham 1951; G. Obeyesekere 2002, 104–7.
50. D 2.20 (*Samaññaphala Sutta*), trans. Walshe 1987, 94–95.
51. G. Obeyesekere 2002, 107.
52. D 2.29 (*Samaññaphala Sutta*), trans. Walshe 1987, 97. The term for "restraint" (*vāri*) also means "water," and there has been considerable discussion as to how this passage ought to be read, both as to its literal meaning and to its tone, which may be satirical. Neither the fourfold restraint (nor a notion of four waters) is known to classical Jainism. See Walshe 1987, 545n115.
53. M 14.15, trans. Ñāṇamoli and Bodhi 1995, 187.
54. M 14.17 (*Cūḷadukkhakkhandha Sutta*), trans. Ñāṇamoli and Bodhi 1995, 188.
55. M 14.20–22 (*Cūḷadukkhakkhandha Sutta*), trans. Ñāṇamoli and Bodhi 1995, 188–89.

56. This is a very general outline; for more detail and nuance, see, for example, Campbell 1962, 218–40, Jaini 1983.
57. This term is often employed nowadays in preference to "Hīnayāna," or "Lesser Vehicle," a pejorative term coined by Indian Mahāyāna writers to distinguish their texts and perspectives from those of the earlier schools. Other terms that have been used include "Foundational" Buddhism and "Nikāya" Buddhism.
58. It is important to recognize that the textual tradition is not our only source for understanding early Buddhist ideas and practices; inscriptions, images, and other archeological evidence must be considered as well. See, for example, Schopen 1997, 2005. Here, however, I will focus primarily on canonical texts.
59. See, respectively, Ashva-ghosha 2008, Jones 1949–56, Bays 1983, Jayawikrama 1990.
60. *Dhammapada* 153–54, trans. Buddharakkhita 1966, 73. I have slightly altered the translation and rearranged it into poetic lines that reflect the original verse structure.
61. S 56.11, trans. Bodhi 2005, 77.
62. M 12.44–59, trans. Ñāṇamoli and Bodhi 1995, 173–76.
63. M 12.57–59, trans. Ñāṇamoli and Bodhi 1995, 176.
64. M 26.17–18 (*Ariyapariyesanā Sutta*), trans. Ñāṇamoli and Bodhi 1995, 259–60.
65. M 26.27ff. (*Ariyapariyesanā Sutta*), trans. Ñāṇamoli and Bodhi 1995, 264ff.
66. S 12:65, trans. Bodhi 2000, 601–4.
67. M 4.27, trans. Ñāṇamoli and Bodhi 1995, 105.
68. M 4.27, trans. Ñāṇamoli and Bodhi 1995, 105–6.
69. M 4.32, trans. Ñāṇamoli and Bodhi 1995, 106.
70. D sutta 17, trans. Walshe 1987, 279–90.
71. D sutta 19, trans. Walshe 1987, 301–13.
72. See, for example, Shaw 2007.
73. D 18.1, trans. Walshe 1987, 291.
74. M 12.36–41 (*Mahāsīhanāda Sutta*), trans. Ñāṇamoli and Bodhi 1995, 169–72.
75. See Masefield 1989.
76. See *Petavatthu (Ghost Stories)*.
77. M 130.29 (*Devadūta Sutta*), trans. Ñāṇamoli and Bodhi 1995, 1036.
78. As in the Pāli canon and its Sanskrit equivalents, and such texts as Vasubandhu's *Abhidharmakośa* (AK 3.1ff., trans. La Vallée Poussin 1988, II, 365) and Asaṅga's *Abhidharmasamuccaya* (ASm, 81).
79. See, for example, Bodhi 1993, 190, as well as the later Mahāyāna traditions of India and Tibet.

80. See S 56.102–130, trans. Bodhi 2000, 1885–88.
81. Deities who have attained the formless attainments during their previous lifetime lack the aggregate of matter.
82. *Dīgha Nikāya* sutta 1, trans. Walshe 1998, 67–90.
83. See, for example, *Dīgha Nikāya* sutta 63 (*Cūḷamālunkya Sutta; Shorter Discourse to Mālunkya*), trans. Ñāṇamoli and Bodhi 1995, 533–36.
84. See, for example, *Majjhima Nikāya* 44.2–8 (*Cūḷavedalla Sutta; Shorter Discourse on Questions and Answers*), trans. Ñāṇamoli and Bodhi 1995, 396–98. See also *Majjhima Nikāya* 22.15–16 (*Alaggadūpama Sutta; Discourse on the Simile of the Snake*), trans. Ñāṇamoli and Bodhi 1995, 229–30.
85. See, for example, M 117. 5 (*Mahācattārīsaka Sutta; Discourse on the Great Forty*), trans. Ñāṇamoli and Bodhi 1995, 934. Cf. above, p. 22.
86. M 114.10 (*Sevitabbāsevitabba Sutta; Discourse on What Is to Be Cultivated and Not Cultivated*), trans. Ñāṇamoli and Bodhi 1995, 919.
87. D sutta 23 (*Pāyāsi Sutta; Discourse on Pāyāsi*), trans Walshe 1987, 351–68. See also Duncan 2015; Anālayo 2017, 45–48.
88. D 12. 10 (*Lohicca Sutta; Discourse to Lohicca*), trans. Walshe 1987, 182.
89. M 9.28, trans. Ñāṇamoli and Bodhi 1995, 132–44.
90. D 28.28, trans. Ñāṇamoli and Bodhi 1995, 283.
91. S 12.15, trans. Bodhi 2005, 356–57.
92. See, for example, S 22:59 (*Anattalakkhaṇa Sutta; Discourse on the Mark of No-Self*), trans. Bodhi 2005, 341–42. In the Pāli commentarial tradition, Buddhaghosa devotes all of chapter 18 of his *Visuddhimagga* (*Path of Purification*) to the "purification of view"; see Ñāṇamoli n.d., 679–92.
93. M 117.7, trans. Ñāṇamoli and Bodhi 1995, 935.
94. M 114.10, trans. Ñāṇamoli and Bodhi 1995, 919.
95. See, for example, Saddhatissa 1985, 91–113. The succeeding chapter, the *Pārāyanavagga* (*Chapter of the Way to the Beyond*), is regarded by many scholars as equally ancient; see, for example, Saddhatissa 1985, 114–33.
96. Collins 1982, 129.
97. Saddhatissa 1985, ix.
98. Fronsdal 2016, 3–4.
99. See, respectively, SN 9:5 (839), and 5:8 (803), trans. Saddhatissa 1985, 99, 95, respectively.
100. SN 2:5 (776), trans. Saddhatissa 1985, 92. Emphasis mine.
101. SN 5:5 (800), trans. Saddhatissa 1985, 95.
102. SN 9:5 (839), trans. Saddhatissa 1985, 99. For discussion, see Collins 1982, 129–31; Fuller 2005, 148–50.
103. See, for example, Saddhatissa 1985, Batchelor 2015, Fronsdal 2016.
104. See M 22.13 (*Alaggadūpama Sutta; Discourse on the Smile of the Snake*), trans. Ñāṇamoli and Bodhi 1995, 228–29.

105. See Gómez 1976.
106. Fuller 2005, 157–59; see also Collins 1982, 120–23.
107. Fronsdal 2016, 137–47.
108. Batchelor 2015, 26.
109. See, for example, Thuken 2009, 47, which cites Vinītadeva's analysis of the four major schools and their sub-schools.
110. See *Saṃyutta Nikāya* 56.102–130, trans. Bodhi 2000, 1885–88, which excludes the asuras and only implies the population distribution. See also Dharmachakra Translation Committee 2021.
111. D 130.29 (*Devadūta Sutta*), trans. Ñāṇamoli and Bodhi 1995, 1032–36.
112. The three "lotus" hells are so named because in the first, the body turns blue like an utpala flower, in the second it splits open like separating lotus petals, and in the third it cracks open completely.
113. See, for example, Vasubandhu, AkBh on AK 3.59a–b, trans. La Vallée Poussin 1988, II, 457–59; Anuruddha, AS 5.4, trans. Bodhi 1993, 189–90.
114. For one detailed list, centered on the ten nonvirtues listed earlier, see A 3.163–82, trans. Bodhi 2012, 374–76.
115. S 56.102–130, trans. Bodhi 2000, 1885–88.
116. A 3.100, trans. Bodhi 2012, 958.
117. M 129. 18–22 (*Balapaṇḍita Sutta*), trans. Ñāṇamoli and Bodhi 1995, 1019–20.
118. AK 4.97a, trans. La Vallée Poussin 1988, II, 680. The view is not universally accepted by Buddhists.
119. See, for example, D 129.24–26 (*Balapaṇḍita Sutta*), trans. Ñāṇamoli and Bodhi 1995, 1020–21.
120. For discussion of this and other issues connected to animals in early Buddhism, see Ohnuma 2017.
121. Rhys Davids 1963, II, 262. I have altered the pronouns to reflect the fact that ghosts may be either male or female.
122. Rhys Davids 1963, II, 151. For a recent study, see Rotman 2021.
123. D 32: 5 (*Aṭānāṭiyā Sutta*), trans. Walshe 1987, 473.
124. AkBh on AK 3.83b–d, trans. La Valle Poussin 1988, II, 473.
125. See, for example, Bodhi 1993, 190.
126. See, for example, D 20.12 (*Mahāsamaya Sutta; Discourse on the Mighty Gathering*), trans. Walshe 1987, 318. See also A 4.19, trans. Bodhi 2012, 1143.
127. See D 20:12 (*Mahāsamaya Sutta*), trans. Walshe 1987, 318. For another way of classifying asuras, see A 4.91, trans. Bodhi 2012, 473. Elsewhere, they are said to live *on* Mount Meru, not far from the gods who continually best them—this is how they are typically depicted in paintings of the "wheel of life" (on which, see chapter 7).

128. D 24.1.7 (*Pāṭikaputta Sutta*), trans. Walshe 1987, 373.
129. See, for example, Nāgārjuna 1979, 119–20.
130. See, for example, D 130.24 (*Balapaṇḍita Sutta*), trans. Ñāṇamoli and Bodhi 1995, 1020–21.
131. A 7.73, trans. Bodhi 2012, 1095–98.
132. See, for example, A 7.73, trans. Bodhi 2012, 1095–98.
133. See, for example, A 8.36, trans. Bodhi 2012, 1170.
134. See, for example, A 8.36, trans. Bodhi 2012, 1170–72.
135. See, respectively, A 8.46, trans. Bodhi 2012, 1183–84; S 37.24, trans. Bodhi 2000, 1289; S 1.77, trans. Bodhi 2000, 136; S 3.15, trans. Bodhi 2000, 179.
136. A 4.80, trans. Bodhi 2012, 465.
137. S 37.32, trans. Bodhi 2000, 1292.
138. S 37.2, trans. Bodhi 2000, 1287.
139. M 115.15, trans. Ñāṇamoli and Bodhi 1995, 929.
140. S 1.58, trans. Bodhi 2000, 129.
141. A 5.55, trans. Bodhi 2012, 683.
142. M 67.19, trans. Ñāṇamoli and Bodhi 1995, 565.
143. A 2.61, trans. Bodhi 2012, 168.
144. See, for example, A 1.1–10, trans. Bodhi 2012, 89–90.
145. D 16.5.9, trans. Walshe 1987, 264. I have changed the formatting for ease of reading.
146. See, for example, A 8.51, trans. Bodhi 2012, 1188–92; for the Mūlasarvāstivāda account see, Paul 1985, 83–85.
147. See, for example, for receiving teachings, M 146 (*Nandakovāda Sutta; Advice from Nandaka*), trans. Ñāṇamoli and Bodhi 1995, 1120–25; M 142.7 (*Dakkhināvibhaṅga Sutta; Discourse on the Exposition of Offerings*), trans. Ñāṇamoli and Bodhi 1995, 1104–5; for advice giving, A 10.28, trans. Bodhi 2012, 1378–79; for teaching the deathless, S 10.9, trans. Bodhi 2000, 313; for receiving offerings, M 142.7 (*Dakkhināvibhaṅga Sutta; Discourse on the Exposition of Offerings*), trans. Ñāṇamoli and Bodhi 1995, 1104–5; for gaining higher rebirths, A 5.116, trans. Bodhi 2012, 738; for attaining stream-entry, S 55.39, trans. Bodhi 2000, 1826; for final deliverance, M 68.569 (*Naḷakapāna Sutta; Discourse at Naḷakapāna*), trans. Ñāṇamoli and Bodhi 1995, 569.
148. D 16.3.7–8, trans. Walshe 1987, 247.
149. M 73.8, trans. Ñāṇamoli and Bodhi 1995, 596.
150. See, respectively, S 5, trans. Bodhi 2000, 221–30; Hallisey 2015.
151. S 5.2, trans. Bodhi 2000, 222–23.
152. Hallisey 2015, 15.
153. Hallisey 2015, 53.
154. Hallisey 2015, 35.

155. Indeed, in the earliest datable Buddhist literature we possess, the edicts of Aśoka (mid-late third century B.C.E.), the only postmortem destination extolled is heaven (see, e.g., Nikam and McKeown 1959, 47)—although Aśoka does, in one of his inscriptions—recommend specific Buddhist texts, which themselves describe nirvāṇa as the ultimate goal of all striving (Nikam and McKeown 1959, 47; for a translation of these texts, see Thanissaro 1993).
156. S 55.1, trans. Bodhi 2000, 1788.
157. See, for example, D 41.18-42 (*Sāleyyaka Sutta; Discourse to the Sāleyyakas*), trans. Ñāṇamoli and Bodhi 1995, 384.
158. See AkBh on AK 3.65-68, trans. Pruden 1988, II, 463-64.
159. On this "cosmological anomaly," see, for example, Sharf 2014, 151-57.
160. For mockery of Brahmā, see, for example, D 2.1-6 (*Brahmajāla Sutta*), trans. Walshe 1987, 75-77; D 11.80-83 (*Kevaddha Sutta; Discourse about Kevaddha*), trans. Walshe 1987, 178-79.
161. See, for example, A 3:178, trans. Bodhi 2012, 374-76.
162. This is made explicit at *Aṅguttara Nikāya* 4.85, trans. Bodhi 2012, 467.
163. There is, nevertheless, a monastic prohibition against injuring seeds and plants, which is variously attributed to the need to respect popular "animist" ideas, or the fact that plants, especially shrubs and trees, may harbor deities or animals that will be harmed if their habitat is destroyed, or the possibility that destroying plants may be harmful to human life. See Schmithausen 1991, especially 105-6.
164. *Manopubbaṅgamā dhammā / mano seṭṭhā mano mayā / manasā ce paduṭṭhenā*. My translation. See, for example, Buddharakkhita 1966, 2.
165. S 12:65, trans. Bodhi 2000, 601-4; see above, p. 31.
166. M 28.28 (*Mahāhatthipadopama Sutta*), trans. Ñāṇamoli and Bodhi 1995, 283.
167. *Mahāvagga* 1.23.1-10, trans. Thanissaro 1996.
168. See, for example, S 12:41, trans. Bodhi 2000, 579.
169. The most concentrated treatment of them in the Sutta collection is found in the *Nidānasaṃyutta* (*Connected Texts on the Links*), which is part 12 of the *Saṃyutta Nikāya,* analyzed and translated in Bodhi 2000, 516-26 and 533-620, respectively. See also the expansive discussion of them in the *Mahānidāna Sutta* (*Great Discourse on Origination*), D 15, trans. Walshe 1987, 215-30. In later literature, see, for example, AkBh on AK 3.21-24, trans. La Vallée Poussin 1988, II, 402-4; VM chapter XVII, trans. Ñāṇamoli n.d., 592-678; and Anuruddha, AS 8.3-10, trans. Bodhi 1993, 294-303.
170. M 38.17, trans. Ñāṇamoli and Bodhi 1995, 353-54. I have added the numbers, and have changed the translation of the ninth link (*upadāna*) from "clinging" to "grasping" and the tenth (*bhāva*) from "being" to "becoming."

171. M 38.18–22, trans. Ñāṇamoli and Bodhi 1995, 354–57.
172. In the case of being in the formless sphere, there is no form aggregate per se, though the seeds for future bodies continue in the aggregate of mental formations.
173. For a description of the links coordinated in a single moment—an act of murder—see AkBh on AK 3.24d, trans. La Vallée Poussin 1988, II, 404.
174. As Asaṅga notes (ASm, chap. I), formations "distribute beings in the different destinies of existence." See Asaṅga 2001, 57.
175. For more detailed accounts of these processes, see, for example, AkBh on AK 3.21–24, trans. La Vallée Poussin 1988, II, 402–4; VM chap. 17, trans. Ñāṇamoli n.d., 592–692; and AS 8.3–10, trans. Bodhi 1993, 294–303.
176. Becoming is listed as both an action and a result because it incites birth and is itself a result of clinging. For elaboration of these modes of analysis, see, for example, AkBh on AK 3.26a–b, trans. La Vallée Poussin 1998, II, 406–7; and AS 8.7–9, trans. Bodhi 1993, 299–302.
177. ASm, chap. I, trans. Asaṅga 2001, 56.
178. Bodhi 2000, 522–23.
179. S 12:20, trans. Bodhi 2000, 552.
180. AkBh on AK 3.28a–b, trans. La Vallée Poussin 1988, II, 413.
181. For a discussion, see, for example, AS 8.11–28, trans. Bodhi 1993, 303–24.
182. Sujato n.d.
183. AS 8.25, trans. Bodhi 1993, 321. For further discussion of the twenty-four conditions, see VM XVII.66–100, trans. Ñāṇamoli n.d., 611–22.
184. AkBh on AK 2.54c–d, trans. La Vallée Poussin 1988, I, 274.
185. AkBh on AK 2.61c–62, trans. La Vallée Poussin 1988, I, 296–304.
186. See, for example, PV 2.189a–190b, and the commentary by Gyaltsab Jé (Rgyal tshab rje), trans. Jackson 1993, 385–86; cf. Nagatomi 1957, 185.
187. M 141.13, trans. Ñāṇamoli and Bodhi 1995, 1098.
188. Bodhi 1993, 220, commenting on AS 5.34.
189. Bodhi 1993, 220, commenting on AS 5.34.
190. A 6.19, trans. Bodhi 2012, 877.
191. See, for example, A 4.184, 6.15, trans. Bodhi 2012, 550–52, 870–71, respectively.
192. S 55.21, trans. Bodhi 2000, 1808.
193. AkBh on AK 2.15a–16b, trans. La Vallée Poussin 1988, I, 176–77.
194. AkBh on AK 43c–44a, trans. La Vallée Poussin 1988, II, 449.
195. AkBh on AK 44b, trans. La Vallée Poussin 1988, II, 449.
196. AkBh on AK 3.37d–38b, trans. La Vallée Poussin 1988, II, 439; cf. VM 14.111, trans. Ñāṇamoli n.d., 514.
197. Bodhi 1993, 204, commenting on AS 5.19.
198. MP II.2.6, trans. Rhys Davids 1963, 71.

199. The last two concepts will be addressed briefly in chapter 10.
200. A notable exception to this consensus, the Yogācāra school of Mahāyāna philosophy, will be addressed in chapter 8.
201. S 44.9, trans. Bodhi 2000, 1393.
202. See, for example, Collins 1982, 238–47.
203. See. for example, VM 14.111–16, trans. Ñāṇamoli n.d., 514–15; and the discussion in Bodhi 1993, 122ff.
204. AkBh on AK 3.10, trans. La Vallée Poussin 1988, II, 383. Translation slightly modified.
205. AK 3.13a–b, trans. La Vallée Poussin 1988, II, 390.
206. AkBh on AK 3.13–14, trans. La Vallée Poussin 1988, II, 390–93.
207. AkBh on AK 3.14d, trans. La Vallée Poussin 1988, II, 393.
208. AkBh on AK 3.14d, trans. La Vallée Poussin 1988, II, 394.
209. M 93:18, trans. Ñāṇamoli and Bodhi 1995, 769–70.
210. AkBh on AK 3.15a–b, trans. La Vallée Poussin 1988, II, 395.
211. See, for example, AkBh on AK 3.15–16, trans. La Vallée Poussin 1988, II, 395–98; VM 8.30, trans. Ñāṇamoli n.d., 254; Kritzer 2014.
212. For a study, a critical edition of the Tibetan version, and an English translation based on Chinese and Tibetan sources, see Kritzer 2014.
213. On the vexed question of Buddhist "theodicy," see, for example, Herman 1976; Kaufman 2005; and Chadha and Trakakis 2007. For a more general critique of Buddhist karma theory, see Griffiths 1982.
214. AK 4.1a, trans. La Vallée Poussin 1988, II, 551.
215. See, for example, AkBh on AK 2.64d, trans. La Vallée Poussin 1988, I, 306–8; PV 2.8–28, trans. Nagatomi 1957, 17–37.
216. Such inactivity, in the Buddhist view, is characteristic of the Jain approach to metaphysics and soteriology.
217. A 6.63, trans. Bodhi 2012, 963.
218. AK 4.1b, trans. La Vallée Poussin 1988, II, 551.
219. My translation. See, for example, Buddharakkhita 1966, 2.
220. A 4.77, trans. Bodhi 2012, 463.
221. D 33.29, trans. Walshe, 1987, 492.
222. The fourth type of karma described by the Buddha—neither-good-nor-bad karma that has neither good nor bad results—is the "action" of an awakened being, who by virtue of their insight into the nature of things and their destruction of the defilements, does not project further karma, hence will not experience the results of action in the interim between their awakening and their passage to final nirvāṇa.
223. A 4.233, trans. Bodhi 2012, 602.
224. S 3.20, trans. Bodhi 2000, 183–84.
225. M 135.5–18, trans. Ñāṇamoli and Bodhi 1995, 1053–57.

226. Bodhi 1993, 201–2, commenting on AS 5.18.
227. Bodhi 1993, 203–4, commenting on AS 5.19.
228. Bodhi 1993, 205–4, commenting on AS 5.20. I have slightly altered the punctuation for the sake of consistency.
229. Bodhi 1993, 206–10, commenting on AS 5.21–26.
230. See, for example, AkBh on AK 59 c–d, trans. La Vallée Poussin 1988, II, 635; ASm 2.2, trans. Asaṅga 2001, 126.
231. AkBh on AK 50a–51b, trans. La Vallée Poussin 1988, II, 625–27.
232. ASm 2.2, trans. Asaṅga 2001, 116.
233. ASm 2.2, trans. Asaṅga 2001, 116.
234. ASm 2.2, trans. Asaṅga 2001, 125–26.
235. ASm 2.2, trans. Asaṅga 2001, 114.
236. AkBh on AK 3.61–62, trans. La Vallée Poussin 1988, II, 636–37.
237. AkBh on AK 4.81a–c, trans. La Vallée Poussin 1988, II, 664.
238. AkBh on AK 3.41, trans. La Vallée Poussin 1988, II, 444.
239. AkBh on AK 4.119, trans. La Vallée Poussin 1988, II, 700.
240. ASm 2.2, trans. Asaṅga 2001, 120.
241. AkBh on AK 4.54, trans. La Vallée Poussin 1988, II, 629–30.
242. See Vasubandhu's discussion of this issue at AkBh on AK 4.55a–c, trans. La Vallée Poussin 1988, II, 630.
243. See AkBh on AK 4.54, trans. La Vallée Poussin 1988, II, 630.
244. ASm 2.2, trans. Asaṅga 2001, 128–29.
245. Vasubandhu, for instance, devotes an entire work, the *Karmasiddhiprakaraṇa* (*Explanation of the Establishment of Action*), to an exposition of the "hard problems" entailed by the karma theories of the different Buddhist schools; see, for example, Lamotte 1988.
246. See AkBh on AK 4.51c–d, trans. La Vallée Poussin 1988, II, 627.
247. See AkBh on AK 4.53, trans. La Vallée Poussin 1988, II, 629.
248. M 135.20, trans. Ñāṇamoli and Bodhi 1995, 1057.
249. ASm 2.2, trans. Asaṅga 2001, 130–31.
250. S 14.16, trans. Bodhi 2000, 640.
251. Malalasekera 1967, 87.
252. S 4.21, trans. Bodhi 2000, 1278–79.
253. AkBh on AK 4.1a, trans. La Vallée Poussin 1988, II, 551.
254. For Western-trained readers, this claim sometimes raises the specter of determinism, for it seems to imply that we are thoroughly conditioned, hence have no "free will." It is quite clear that for the Buddha and his successors, this is a pseudo-problem, for however thoroughly we may be conditioned, in the present moment we as humans are free in the significant sense that we can choose to alter our attitudes and actions from a more negative to a more positive direction, hence progress toward liberation.

255. *Cetanā Sūtra* (*Discourse on Intention*), Madhyama Āgama sūtra 15, ed. Bingenheimer et al. 2013, 85; cf. A 10.217, trans. Bodhi 2012, 1535.
256. Bodhi 2012, 1857n2181, on A 10.217.
257. See, for example, Strong 2001, 32–34.
258. See, respectively, Spiro 1982; Samuel 1993.
259. Tharchin 1984, 13.
260. For the relevant *Mūlasarvāstivāda Vinaya* passage, see Tharchin 1984, 9–23; for the *Divyāvadāna* passage (in which the king's name is Rudrāyaṇa), see Rotman 2017, 289–93.
261. VM 7.7–8, trans. Ñāṇamoli n.d., 207. I have cited the simpler of two ways of imagining the wheel, found in verse 8.
262. See, for example, Talim 2006–07. There has been much debate as to how many realms and how many links actually were depicted.
263. See, respectively, *Petavatthu* n.d.; Masefield 1989; Shaw 2007; Rotman 2008, 2017, 2021.
264. See, respectively, Ashva-ghosha 2008; Jones 1949–56; Bays 1983; Jayawickrama 1990.
265. D 1.1.21–27, trans. Walshe 1987, 71–73. See also van Schaik 2020, 45–46.
266. Van Schaik 2020, 44.
267. See, for example, *Kevaddha Sutta* (*Discourse about Kevaddha*), D sutta 11, trans. Walshe 1987, 175–80.
268. See, for example, Fiordalis 2008.
269. See, for example, Sayers 2013.
270. On the former, see, for example, Sayers 2013, chap. 5; on the latter, see for example, Schopen 1997, 114–47.
271. The "impossible ethical ideal" is a term coined by Reinhold Niebuhr to describe the teachings of Jesus, especially his Sermon on the Mount; see Niebuhr 1935, chapters II, IV.
272. Indeed, it may be that it was only when tantra entered Buddhism as a distinctive ritual system that the Mahāyāna began to gain real traction in India.
273. I-tsing 1982, 14–15.
274. For discussion, see, for example, Walser 2005, chap. 1; Boucher 2008, 11–16, 40–43; Williams 2009, 21–44.
275. These claims are not, of course, accepted by all Mahāyāna texts, teachers, and traditions, but are propounded commonly enough to warrant inclusion here.
276. On the "wisdom traditions" represented by these views, see, for example, Williams 2009, chaps. 2–4.
277. On the multiplicity of buddhas and the idea of pure lands, see, for example, Williams 2009, 132–38, 149–61, 214–18, 238–54; on Amitābha's pure land, see Gómez, 1996.

278. On the bodies of a buddha, see, for example, Williams 2009, chap. 8.
279. On the buddhanature doctrine, see, for example, Williams 2009, chap 5, and 152-54; Jones 2020.
280. On the bodhisattva, the bodhisattva stages, and the bodhisattva perfections, see, for example, Dayal 1978, chaps. I-II, V; Wangchuk 2007; Williams 2009, 187-94, 200-8.
281. On the bodhisattva's compassion and awakening mind, see, for example, Dayal 1978, chap. III; Williams 2009, 194-200.
282. On "savior" bodhisattvas, see, for example, Williams 2009, 218-31.
283. On pedagogical skillful means, see, for example, Williams 2009, 150-57; Powers 1995, chap. 7.
284. On the ethical corollary of skillful means, see for example, Pye 2003.
285. For buddhahood and awakening, see Conze 1973b, 197, 229; for pure lands, see Conze 1973b, 269, 279; for bodhisattva practices, including wisdom and means, see, Conze 1973b, 19, 52, 38, 161; for the superiority of the perfection of wisdom, see Conze 1973b, 15, 17, 105.
286. Conze 1973b, 150.
287. Conze 1973b, 10.
288. On defilement, see Conze 1973b, 173; on merit, see Conze 1973b, 41.
289. Conze 1973b, 197.
290. Conze 1973a, 132-35.
291. Conze 1973a, 140.
292. Conze 1973a, 140-41.
293. Conze 1975, 629.
294. These passages are found, respectively, in Chang 1991, 20; and Chang 1991, 31.
295. Thurman 1976, 90-91.
296. Thurman 1976, 54.
297. The specific arguments are found, respectively, in chapters 1, 11, 17, and 25 (verse 19) of the *Madhyamakakārikā*; see, respectively, Siderits and Katsura 2013, 17-30, 121-28, 171-92, 302.
298. The discussion covers verses 30-51; see Westerhoff 2010, 30-51, 65-94.
299. Powers 1995, 93-146.
300. Powers 1995, 81-91.
301. Powers 1995, 71-81.
302. Powers 1995, 155.
303. Cleary 1993, 751.
304. *Laṅkāvatāra*, chap. 2, section IX, trans. Suzuki 1978, 38.
305. *Laṅkāvatāra*, chap. 2, section XXVIII, trans. Suzuki 1978, 68.
306. *Laṅkāvatāra*, chap. 7, section LXXXIX, trans. Suzuki 1978, 209.
307. Brunnhölzl 2018, 181-83.
308. See Anacker 1984, 161-75.

309. See Williams 2009, chap. 5; Jones 2020.
310. Also known as the *Ratnagotravibhāga* (*Distinguishing the Precious Lineage*).
311. Wayman and Wayman 1974, 106.
312. Verse 2.29 (196), trans. Ārya Maitreya 2000, 47.
313. Grosnick 1995, 96.
314. See Griffiths 1994, chap. 6.
315. Cleary 1993.
316. Williams 2009, 132.
317. Cleary 1993, 925.
318. Cleary 1993, 1453.
319. Cleary 1993, 65 and 147, respectively.
320. Cleary 1993, 85, 373, and 452, respectively. Cf. the statement in the *Laṅkāvatāra Sūtra* to the effect that "Suchness, emptiness, the limit, Nirvana, and the Dharmadhatu . . . these I point out as synonymous" (Suzuki 1978, 241).
321. Cleary 1993, 377.
322. MK 24.8-10; Siderits and Katsura 2013, 272-73.
323. MK 24.11; Siderits and Katsura 2013, 274.
324. MK 24.14; Siderits and Katsura 2013, 276.
325. MK 24.18-20; Siderits and Katsura 2013, 277-79.
326. Westerhoff 2010, 41.
327. It is equivalent to the *Kaccānagotta Sutta* of the *Saṃyutta Nikāya*, cited above on p. 41.
328. Respectively, these are found at Conze 1973a, 197; Powers 1995, 107; and Cleary 1993, 745. An early Mahāyāna text that focuses exclusively on dependent origination, while relating the process to Buddhist ideas of ultimacy, is the *Śālistambha Sūtra* (*Discourse on the Rice Seedling*), for which see Reat 1993.
329. See, respectively, Dharmachakra Translation Committee 2020; Mus 1939. The *Ṣaḍgatikārikā* is sometimes attributed to Aśvaghoṣa.
330. For good accounts of Indian Buddhist tantra, see, for example, Snellgrove 1987, vol. 1; Williams 2000, 192-244; Davidson 2002.
331. Wayman 1985, 97. The translation is mine.
332. GT 2.8; Fremantle 1971, 194-95; cf. her translation, 36. See also GT 7.34; Fremantle 1971, 49.
333. HT I.viii.40-41; Snellgrove 2010, 77.
334. HT II.ix.10; Snellgrove 2010, 117.
335. HT II.iv.69, 73-74; Snellgrove 2010, 107.
336. Jackson 2004, 135.
337. *Dohākoṣagīti* 23, trans. Jackson 2004, 65 (adapted).

338. See, for example, GT 7.15–27, 17.17–35; Fremantle 1971, 47–48, 124–27, respectively.
339. *Dohākoṣopadeśanāma* 50, trans. Jackson 2012, 180.
340. See, for example, Guenther 1963.
341. This is the view of Christian Wedemeyer (2013), who sees "tantric conduct" as simply one phase in a monastic career. He is critical of the stance taken by Ronald Davidson (2002), who tends to see the great adepts as genuinely countercultural rebels.
342. For a fine selection of texts along these lines, see Paul 1985.
343. Thurman 1974, 61–62.
344. Cleary 1993, 1599.
345. Chang 1991, 91.
346. Watson 1993, 187–88.
347. Paul 1985, 41–42.
348. *Bodhicaryāvatāra* 8. 41–69, trans. Śāntideva 1996, 91–94.
349. Beyer 1973, 64–65. I have been unable to trace this story to the Indian tradition, but it is recounted and recorded by numerous Tibetan scholars.
350. Willson 1996, 101.
351. Willson 1996, 243, 244, and 245, respectively.
352. GT 14.38–47; Fremantle 1971, 93–94.
353. GT 17.71–75; Fremantle 1971, 137–38; for a chart, see 24–25.
354. GT 15.1–18; Fremantle 1971, 95–96. Cf. HT II.8.1–9; Snellgrove 2010, 116.
355. HT II.iv.41, 45–47; Snellgrove 2010, 104–105.
356. See English 2002.
357. Shaw 1995, especially chaps. 4–5.
358. Cited in Gray 2011, 471.
359. Cited in Willson 1996, 24.
360. That this was so is argued by Shaw 1995, chap. 6.
361. For examples of such interpretations, see, for example, Gross 1992, Klein 2008.
362. M 4.27, trans. Ñāṇamoli and Bodhi 1995, 105–106.
363. M 130.29 (*Devadūta Sutta*), trans. Ñāṇamoli and Bodhi 1995, 1036.
364. This common formula is found in, for example, the *Mahātaṇhasankhaya Sutta*: M 38.25, trans. Ñāṇamoli and Bodhi 1995, 358.
365. A 3.65, trans. Bodhi 2012, 281.
366. D sutta 23, trans. Walshe 1987, 351–68, which is discussed above, p. 40.
367. Contrast, for instance, the views of Jayatilleke (1980, 416–76), often seen as the originator of the "Buddhist empiricism thesis," and Hoffman (1982), who systematically dismantles the idea.
368. M 60.9, trans. Ñāṇamoli and Bodhi 1995, 508.
369. A 3.65, trans. Bodhi 2012, 283.

370. Jayatilleke 1980, 410–11.
371. *Karmasiddhiprakaraṇa* XVII.1, trans. Lamotte 1988, 78.
372. MP III.6.9, trans. Rhys Davids 1963, I, 120.
373. MP III.5.9, trans. Rhys Davids 1963, I, 113.
374. MP II.2.2, trans. Rhys Davids 1963, I, 65–66.
375. Chang 1983, 224–25.
376. Chang 1983, 225–32.
377. For a discussion of this, see Jackson 1985.
378. See, for example, Steinkellner 2005, 11.
379. Translation mine. See, for example, Nagatomi 1957, 41; Franco 1997, 159. Note that not all numbering systems for the chapter are consistent with one another.
380. For more extensive discussions, as well as translation, see Nagatomi 1957 (from Sanskrit); Jackson 1993 (from Tibetan); Franco 1997 (from Sanskrit).
381. *Tattvasaṃgraha* verses 1939–41, trans. Jha 1986, II, 930.
382. MP II.2.1, trans. Rhys Davids 1963, I, 63–65.
383. MP II.2.6, trans. Rhys Davids 1963, I, 71–75. See the discussion in Collins 1982, 185–88.
384. See AkBh on AK 2.45c–46b, trans. La Vallée Poussin 1988, I, 238–47.
385. See, for example, Collins 1982, 238–47.
386. AK 2.36b–40, trans. La Vallée Poussin 1988, I, 206–19.
387. See, for example, the discussion in chapter 9 of the AkBh, trans. La Vallée Poussin 1988, IV, 1313–42.
388. See, for example, Waldron 2003.
389. That tradition only has been designated as "Theravāda" in recent times. Typically, its adherents simply referred to it as the Sāsana, the Teaching.
390. On Buddhist imaginaries, see, for example, Collins 1982, 2006.
391. See, for example, Geiger 1986.
392. See, for example, Holt 2017, 67–130.
393. On these developments, see Gombrich and Obeyesekere 1988.
394. See Gombrich 1991, 254–63.
395. See, for example, Gombrich and Obeyesekere 1988, 384–410.
396. See, for example, Gombrich 1991, 265–84; Kariyawasam 1995, 42–45.
397. Kariyawasam 1995, 43–44.
398. Kariyawasam 1995, 44–45.
399. For the Indian women's stories, see R. Obeyesekere 2001; for the Yaśodharā poems, see R. Obeyesekere 2009.
400. For a good overview, see Swearer 2010.
401. See, for example, Spiro 1982, 453–68.
402. On these developments, see, for example, Ch'en 1964.
403. Teiser 1994, 4.

404. Teiser 1994, 14.
405. Teiser 1994, 4.
406. Teiser 1994, 14.
407. Teiser 1994, 14–15.
408. Teiser 2014, 6.
409. See, for example, Teiser 1988; Orzech 1996.
410. See, for example, Kieschnick 2005.
411. On this question, see, for example, Schmithausen 2009.
412. See, for example, Foard, Solomon, and Payne 2006.
413. For a more traditional view of the tradition, see, for example, Dumoulin 2005; for a more critical take, see, for example, McRae 2004.
414. See, for example, Yü n.d., 244–76.
415. See, for example, Aitken 1990, 19–27.
416. See Grant 2003.
417. See, for example, Yu 2001.
418. For more detailed discussions of these matters, see, for example, Snellgrove and Richardson 1967, Samuel 1993, and Kapstein 2006.
419. See Tatz and Kent 1977.
420. See, for example, Gampopa 2017; Tsong-kha-pa 2000–2002.
421. There is a large literature on these matters, but see, especially, Lati and Hopkins 1979; Mullin 1986; Sogyal 1993; Lopez 1997, 421–510; Dorje 2005.
422. See, for example, Mullin 1986, 149–72
423. See, for example, Mullin 1986, 126–48.
424. See, for example, Lati and Hopkins 1979, 32–48; Mullin 1986, 71–72; Sogyal 1993, 244–56.
425. See, for example, Lati and Hopkins 1979, 49–57; Dorje 2005, 224–303.
426. See, for example, Mullin 1986, 61, 173–91; Dorje 2005, 200–216.
427. See, for example, Gamble 2018.
428. See, for example, Michael 1982.
429. See, for example, Bärlocher 1982.
430. See Pommaret 1997; Cuevas 2008.
431. Pommaret 1997, 499.
432. See, for example, Karmay 1988; Tulku Thondup 2014.
433. See, for example, Roberts 2014; Jackson 2019.
434. This felicitous term was first utilized in Faure 1994.
435. See, for example, Willis 1987; Gyatso and Havnevik 2005.
436. Geertz 1968, 16.
437. For an interesting survey of the range of views to be found in a single Buddhist organization, the Triratna Buddhist Community, see Liebenrood 2015.
438. See Batchelor 1994.

439. See Gopnik 2009.
440. D'Amato and Moore 2011, 37.
441. Abelsen 1993, 259-60; Batchelor 1994, 250-71.
442. See, for example, Panaïotti 2013.
443. See, for example, Fields 1992, 54-69.
444. Carreira 2010.
445. Querido 1997, xxxiii-xxxiv.
446. Whitman 1892, sections 27, 49, 43.
447. See, for example, Fields 1992, 83-118; Theosophy 2019.
448. See McMahan 2008, 94-113; Lopez 2002, 15-23.
449. See, for example, Lopez 2002, 78-84.
450. See, for example, Fields 1992, 130-45; and the chapters on each author in Lopez 2002. I will say more about Suzuki momentarily.
451. See, for example, Suzuki 1996; McMahan 2008, 122-34.
452. Watts 1961, 67, 76; see also Lopez 2002, 159-71.
453. See, for example, Fields 1992, 195-225; Tonkinson 1995; Lopez 2002, 172-81, 194-200, 207-10.
454. Kerouac 1959, 211.
455. See, for example, Fields 1992, chaps. 11-12.
456. See, for example, Wilson 2014.
457. On the rise of the "mindfulness movement" in Asia, see Braun 2016.
458. See Rahula 1974.
459. On Govinda, see, for example, Lopez 2002, 98-105; on Rampa, see Lopez 1998, 86-113.
460. See, for example, Fields 1992, chaps. 13-14; Paine 2004.
461. Trungpa 1973, 131.
462. See, for example, Chödrön 2016.
463. Flanagan 2011, 3; see also his discussion of matter and consciousness, 70-90.
464. Wright 2017, xi.
465. Garfield 2015, 4.
466. Batchelor 2017, 125.
467. Hayes 1998, 59, 61, 62, 80.
468. Willson 1987, 39-46. Willson is actually commenting on a text by a modern Geluk lama, the late Losang Gyatso, but the arguments Gyatso cites are mostly Dharmakīrti's.
469. Jackson 1993, 128-39, 366n36. I now would modify my position somewhat, conceding that Dharmakīrti has, in his own way, raised what contemporary philosophers of mind call the "hard problem": how the *experiences* the mind undergoes can possibly be reduced to brain states or neurological processes. This does not guarantee that an interactionist dualism of the

sort espoused by Dhamakīrti is true, but it does complicate attempts to argue for a reductive materialism.

470. Hayes 1993.
471. Arnold 2012, 40–47.
472. Thompson 2015, 82, 105. Although he explicitly rejects the label, Thompson's position is suggestive of panpsychism; for a recent presentation of this venerable "third way" between dualism and monism, see Goff 2019.
473. See Dalai Lama 2005, 117–61.
474. Thurman, in conversation, 2014; see Thompson 2015, 293–99; Burke 2021.
475. See Wallace 2012, 84.
476. Wallace 2012, 85.
477. Loy 2015, 85.
478. Loy 2015, 139.
479. Loy 2015, 142.
480. Revel and Ricard 1998, 78.
481. Wallace 2012, 149.
482. See, for example, Stevenson 1977. A number of Stevenson's Buddhist cases are also discussed in Story 1975, part 2.
483. Willson 1987, 17–32.
484. Anālayo 2017, part III.3–4, and part IV.
485. Thompson 2015, 290.
486. Batchelor 2017, 121.
487. Anālayo 2017, 66–89. For the classic modern presentation of near-death experiences, see Moody 1975; for a more nuanced, history-of-religion-based analysis, which includes medieval Christian examples, see Zaleski 1987. For a naturalistic explanation of NDEs, see, for example, Nuland 1995, 137–39. See also Thompson 2015, 299–314.
488. For an influential modern account of OBEs, see Monroe 1992. For a phenomenological, psychological, physiological, and/or philosophical analysis see, e.g., Metzinger 2009, 75–114; Thompson 2015, 309–10.
489. James 1961, 332.
490. James 1961, 333.
491. Tricycle 1997.
492. Batchelor 1997. An even earlier foray into the topic, first published in 1992, is reprinted in Batchelor 2017, 111–25.
493. Batchelor first makes the case for an "existential approach to Buddhism" in *Alone with Others* (1984), but it was *Buddhism Without Beliefs*, more than a decade later, that captured the attention of a broader public.
494. Batchelor 1997, 34–38.
495. See, for example, Thurman 1999.
496. Tricycle 1997, 18.

497. Lopez 2012, 131–32.
498. For another take on this question, see Cho and Squier 2016, especially 140–58.
499. The term was coined by the English poet John Keats, and revived in the twentieth century by Jack Kerouac and other Beat writers as an aesthetic ideal.
500. Hayes 1998, 78–79.
501. Hayes 1998, 79–80.
502. Hayes 1998, 80–81.
503. Batchelor 2017, 123.
504. Batchelor 2017, 125.
505. Tricycle 1997, 18.
506. Stevens 1971, 336.
507. I gestured at such an approach to Buddhism—terming it "aesthetic"—in Jackson 2000 (223–27). For a preliminary presentation of my As-If/As-Is analysis (which I hope to expand to book length in the future), see Jackson 2016.
508. A 4.45, trans. Bodhi 2012, 434–36.

Bibliography

Abelsen, Peter. 1993. "Schopenhauer and Buddhism." *Philosophy East and West* 43.2: 255–78.

Anacker, Stephan. 1984. *Seven Works by Vasubandhu: The Buddhist Psychological Doctor*. Delhi: Motilal Banarsidass.

Anālayo, Bhikkhu. 2017. *Rebirth in Early Buddhism and Current Research*. Boston: Wisdom Publications.

Arnold, Dan. 2012. *Brains, Buddhas, and Believing: The Problem of Intentionality in Classical Buddhist and Cognitive-Scientific Philosophy of Mind*. New York: Columbia University Press.

Ārya Maitreya. 2000. *Buddha Nature: The* Mahayana Uttara Tantra Shastra *with Commentary*. Translated by Rosemarie Fuchs. Ithaca: Snow Lion Publications.

Asaṅga. 2001. Abhidharmasamuccaya: *The Compendium of the Higher Teaching (Philosophy) by Asaṅga*. French translation by Walpola Rahula; English translation of the French by Sara Boin-Webb. Berkeley: Asian Humanities Press.

Ashva-ghosha. 2008. *Life of the Buddha*. Translated by Patrick Olivelle. Clay Sanskrit Library. New York: New York University Press/JJC Foundation.

Bärlocher, Daniel. 1982. *Testimonies of Tibetan Tulkus: A Research among Reincarnate Buddhist Masters in Exile*. 2 vols. Rikon, Switzerland: Tibet-Institut.

Basham, A. L. 1951. *History and Doctrines of the Ājīvikas*. London: Luzac.

Batchelor, Stephen. 1984. *Alone with Others: An Existential Approach to Buddhism*. New York: Grove Press.

Batchelor, Stephen. 1994. *The Awakening of the West: The Encounter of Buddhism and Western Culture*. London: Aquarian.

Batchelor, Stephen. 1997. *Buddhism Without Beliefs: A Contemporary Guide to Awakening*. New York: Riverhead Books.

Batchelor, Stephen. 2015. *After Buddhism: Rethinking the Dharma for a Secular Age*. New Haven: Yale University Press.

Batchelor, Stephen. 2017. *Secular Buddhism: Imagining the Dharma in an Uncertain World*. New Haven: Yale University Press.

Bays, Gwendolyn, trans. 1983. *The Voice of the Buddha: The Beauty of Compassion*. Emeryville, CA: Dharma Publishing.

Becker, Ernest. 1973. *The Denial of Death*. New York: Free Press.

Beyer, Stephan. 1973. *The Cult of Tārā: Magic and Ritual in Tibet*. Berkeley, Los Angeles, and London: University of California Press.

Bingenheimer, Marcus, with Bhikkhu Anālayo and Roderick S. Bucknell, eds. and trans. 2013. *The Madhyama Āgama (Middle-Length Discourses)*. Vol. I. BDK English Tripiṭaka Series. Berkeley: Bukkyo Dendo Kyokai America.

Bodhi, Bhikkhu, ed. and trans. 1993. *A Comprehensive Manual of Abhidhamma: The* Abhidhammatha Sangaha*; Pali Text, Translation and Explanatory Guide*. Kandy: Buddhist Publication Society.

Bodhi, Bhikkhu, trans. 2000. *The Connected Discourses of the Buddha: A Translation of the Saṃyutta Nikāya*. Boston: Wisdom Publications.

Bodhi, Bhikkhu, trans. 2005. *In the Buddha's Words: An Anthology from the Pāli Canon*. Boston: Wisdom Publications.

Bodhi, Bhikkhu, trans. 2012. *The Numerical Discourses of the Buddha: A Translation of the Aṅguttara Nikāya*. Boston: Wisdom Publications.

Boucher, Daniel. 2008. *Bodhisattvas of the Forest and the Formation of the Mahāyāna: A Study and Translation of the* Raṣṭrapālaparipṛcchā-sūtra. Honolulu: University of Hawai'i Press.

Braun, Erik. 2016. *The Birth of Insight: Meditation, Modern Buddhism, and the Burmese Monk Ledi Sayadaw*. Chicago: University of Chicago Press.

Brons, Lajos L. 2014. "The Incoherence of Denying My Own Death." *Journal of Philosophy of Life* 4.2 (May 2014): 68–89.

Brunnhölzl, Karl, trans. 2018. *A Compendium of the Mahāyāna: Asaṅga's* Mahāyānasaṃgraha *and Its Indian and Tibetan Commentaries*. Boulder: Shambhala Publications.

Buddharakkhita Thera, Venerable Ācharya, ed. and trans. 1966. *Dhammapada: A Practical Guide to Right Living*. Bangalore: Buddha Vacana Trust, Maha Bodhi Society.

Burke, Daniel. 2021. "The Thukdam Project: Inside the First-Ever Scientific Study of Post-Mortem Meditation." *Trike Daily. Tricycle*, July 28, 2021. https://tricycle.org/trikedaily/thukdam-project. Accessed August 14, 2021.

Campbell, Joseph. 1962. *The Masks of God: Oriental Mythology*. New York: The Viking Press.

Carreira, Jeffrey. 2010. "Evolution, Enlightenment, and Reincarnation (Part 2)." *Philosophy is Not a Luxury*. https://philosophyisnotaluxury.com/2010/07/05/evolution-enlightenment-and-reincarnation-part-2/. Accessed October 23, 2019.

Chadha, Monima, and Nick Trakakis. 2007. "Karma and the Problem of Evil: A Response to Kaufman." *Philosophy East and West* 54.4: 533–56.

Chang, Garma C. C., trans. 1991 [1983]. *A Treasury of Mahāyāna Sūtras: Selections from the Mahāratnakūṭa Sūtra*. Delhi: Motilal Banarsidass.

Chattopadhyaya, Debiprasad. 1992 [1959]. *Lokāyata: A Study in Ancient Indian Materialism*. 7th ed. New Delhi: People's Publishing House.

Chattopadhyaya, Debiprasad. 1994. *Cārvāka/Lokāyata: An Anthology of Source Materials and Some Recent Studies*. New Delhi: People's Publishing House.

Ch'en, Kenneth. 1964. *Buddhism in China: A Historical Survey*. Princeton: Princeton University Press.

Cho, Francesca, and Richard K. Squier. 2016. *Religion and Science in the Mirror of Buddhism*. New York and London: Routledge.

Chödrön, Pema. 2016 [2000]. *When Things Fall Apart: Heart Advice for Difficult Times*. Boulder: Shambhala Publications.

Cleary, Thomas, trans. 1993. *The Flower Ornament Scripture: A Translation of the* Avataṃsaka Sūtra. Boston and London: Shambhala Publications.

Collins, Steven. 1982. *Selfless Persons: Imagery and Thought in* Theravāda *Buddhism*. Cambridge: Cambridge University Press.

Collins, Steven. 2006. *Nirvāṇa and Other Buddhist Felicities*. Cambridge: Cambridge University Press.

Conze, Edward, trans. 1973a. *Perfect Wisdom: The Short Prajñāpāramitā Texts*. London: Luzac & Co.

Conze, Edward, trans. 1973b. *The Perfection of Wisdom in Eight Thousand Lines and Its Verse Summary*. Bolinas, CA: Four Seasons Foundation.

Conze, Edward, trans. 1975. *The Large Sūtra on Perfect Wisdom, with the Divisions of the Abhisamyālaṃkāra*. Berkeley: University of California Press.

Cuevas, Brian J. 2008. *Travels in the Netherworld: Buddhist Popular Narratives of Death and the Afterlife in Tibet*. New York: Oxford University Press, 2008.

Dalai Lama [XIV]. 2005. *The Universe in a Single Atom: The Convergence of Science and Spirituality*. New York: Morgan Road Books.

D'Amato, Mario, and Robert T. Moore. 2011. "The Specter of Nihilism: On Hegel on Buddhism." *Indian International Journal of Buddhist Studies* 12: 23–49.

Davidson, Ronald M. 2002. *Indian Esoteric Buddhism: A Social History of the Tantric Movement*. New York: Columbia University Press.

Dayal, Har. 1978 [1931]. *The Bodhisattva Doctrine in Buddhist Sanskrit Literature*. New York: Samuel Weiser.

Dharmachakra Translation Committee, trans. 2020. *The Questions of Pratibhānamati. Pratibhānamatiparipṛchhā Sūtra*. 84000: Translating the Words of the Buddha. https://read.84000.co/translation/toh151.html. Accessed October 9, 2020.

Dharmachakra Translation Committee. 2021. *The Noble Application of Mindfulness of the Sacred Dharma. Āryasaddharmasmṛtyupasthāna*. 84000. Translating the Words of the Buddha. https://read.84000.co/translation/toh287.html. Accessed July 12, 2021.

Doniger, Wendy, trans. 2001. *The Rig Veda: An Anthology*. London: Penguin.

Dorje, Gyurme, trans. 2005. Padmasambhava. *The Tibetan Book of the Dead. First Complete Translation*. Edited by Graham Coleman and Thupten Jinpa. New York: Penguin Books.

Ducasse, C. J. 1961. *A Critical examination of the Belief in Life after Death*. Springfield, IL: Charles C. Thomas.

Dumoulin, Heinrich. 2005 [1988]. *Zen Buddhism: A History. Volume I: India and China*. Translated by James W. Heisig and Paul Knitter. Bloomington, IN: World Wisdom.

Duncan, Alexander. 2015. "Payasi the Prince." Paliesque. https://palisuttas.wordpress.com/2015/03/29/payasi-sutta/#:~:text=The%20description%20is%20nearly%20that,they%20wisely%20await%20its%20ripening. Accessed June 15, 2020.

Eggeling, Julius, trans. 1897. *Śatapatha Brāḥmaṇa*, part IV. Sacred Books of the East, 43. Internet Sacred Text Archive. www.sacred-texts.com/hin/sbr/sbe43/index.htm. Accessed June 3, 2020.

English, Elizabeth. 2002. *Vajrayoginī: Her Visualizations, Rituals, and Forms*. Boston: Wisdom Publications.

Faure, Bernard. 1994. *The Rhetoric of Immediacy: A Cultural Critique of Chan/Zen Buddhism*. Princeton: Princeton University Press.

Fields, Rick. 1992. *How the Swans Came to the Lake: A Narrative History of Buddhism in America*. 3rd ed. Boston and London: Shambhala Publications.

Fiordalis, David. 2008. "Miracles and Superhuman Powers in South Asian Buddhist Literature." PhD diss., University of Michigan. http://hdl.handle.net/2027.42/61721.

Flanagan, Owen. 2011. *The Bodhisattva's Brain: Buddhism Naturalized*. Cambridge, MA: MIT Press.

Foard, James Harlan, Michael Solomon, and Richard K. Payne, eds. 2006. *The Pure Land Tradition: History and Development*. Fremont, CA: Jain Publishing.

Franco, Eli. 1997. *Dharmakīrti on Compassion and Rebirth*. Wiener Studien zur Tibetologie und Buddhismuskunde, heft 38. Wien: Arbeitskreis für Tibetische und Buddhistische Studien Universität Wien.

Fremantle, Francesca. 1971. "A Critical Study of the Guhyasamāja Tantra." PhD diss., University of London.

Fronsdal, Gil. 2016. *The Buddha Before Buddhism: Wisdom from the Early Teachings*. Boulder: Shambhala Publications.

Fuller, Paul. 2005. *The Notion of Diṭṭhi in Theravāda Buddhism: The Point of View*. London: Routledge.

Holt, John Clifford. 2017. *Theravada Traditions: Buddhist Ritual Cultures in Contemporary Southeast Asia and Sri Lanka*. Honolulu: University of Hawai'i Press.

Gamble, Ruth. 2018. *Reincarnation in Tibetan Buddhism: The Third Karmapa and the Invention of a Tradition.* New York: Oxford University Press.

Gampopa. 2017. *Ornament of Precious Liberation.* Translated by Ken Holmes. Boston: Wisdom Publications.

Garfield, Jay. 2015. *Engaging Buddhism: Why It Matters to Philosophy.* New York: Oxford University Press.

Gecewicz, Claire. 2018. "'New Age' beliefs common among both religious and nonreligious Americans." Pew Research Center. www.pewresearch.org/fact-tank/2018/10/01/new-age-beliefs-common-among-both-religious-and-nonreligious-americans/#:~:text=Overall%2C%20roughly%20six%2Din%2D,%25)%20and%20astrology%20(29%25). Accessed October 23, 2020.

Geertz, Clifford. 1968. *Islam Observed: Religious Development in Morocco and Indonesia.* Chicago: University of Chicago Press.

Geiger, Wilhelm, trans., assisted by Mabel Haynes Bode. 1986 [1912]. *The Mahāvaṃsa or the Great Chronicle of Ceylon.* New Delhi: Asian Educational Services.

Goff, Philip. 2019. *Galileo's Error: Foundations for a New Science of Consciousness.* New York: Pantheon Books.

Gombrich, Richard. 1991 [1971]. *Buddhist Precept and Practice: Traditional Buddhism in the Rural Highlands of Ceylon.* Delhi: Motilal Banarsidass.

Gombrich, Richard, and Gananath Obeyesekere. 1988. *Buddhism Transformed: Religious Change in Sri Lanka.* Princeton: Princeton University Press.

Gómez, Luís O. 1976. "Proto-Madhyamaka in the Pāli Canon." *Philosophy East and West* 26.2: 137–65.

Gómez, Luís O., trans. 1996. *The Land of Bliss: The Paradise of the Buddha of Measureless Light. Sanskrit and Chinese Versions of the Sukhāvatīvyūha Sūtras.* Honolulu: University of Hawai'i Press.

Gopnik, Alison. 2009. "Could David Hume Have Known about Buddhism? Charles Francois Dolu, the Royal College of La Flèche, and the Global Jesuit Intellectual Network." *Hume Studies* 35.1–2: 5–28.

Grant, Beata, trans. 2003. *Daughters of Emptiness: Poems of Chinese Buddhist Nuns.* Boston: Wisdom Publications.

Gray, David B. 2011. "Imprints of the Great Seal: On the Expanding Semantic Range of the Term *Mudrā* in Eighth through Eleventh Century Indian Buddhist Literature." *Journal of the International Association of Buddhist Studies* 34.1–2: 421–81.

Griffiths, Paul J. 1982. "Notes Towards a Critique of Buddhist Karmic Theory." *Religious Studies* 18.3: 277–91.

Griffiths, Paul J. 1994. *On Being Buddha: The Classical Doctrine of Buddhahood.* Albany: State University of New York Press.

Grosnick, William H. 1995. "The *Tathāgatagarbha Sūtra.*" In *Buddhism in Prac-*

tice. Edited by Donald S. Lopez, Jr., 92–106. Princeton Readings in Religions. Princeton: Princeton University Press.

Gyatso, Janet, and Hanna Havnevik, eds. 2005. *Women in Tibet*. New York: Columbia University Press.

Hallisey, Charles, ed. and trans. 2015. *Therīgāthā: Poems of the First Buddhist Women*. Murty Classical Library of India. Cambridge, MA: Harvard University Press.

Hayes, Richard P. 1993. "Dharmakītri on *punarbhava*." In *Studies in Original Buddhism and Mahāyāna Buddhism*. Edited by Egaku Maeda, I, 330. Kyōto: Nagata Bunshodo.

Hayes, Richard P. 1998. *Land of No Buddha: Reflections of a Sceptical Buddhist*. Birmingham, UK: Windhorse Publications.

Herman, A. L. 1976. *The Problem of Evil in Indian Thought*. Delhi: Motilal Banarsidass.

Hoffman, Frank J. 1982. "The Buddhist Empiricism Thesis." *Religious Studies* 18.2 (June 1982): 151–58.

I-tsing. 1982 [1896]. *A Record of the Buddhist Religion as Practised in India and the Malay Archipelago*. Translated by J. Takakusu. New Delhi: Munshiram Manoharlal.

Jackson, Roger R. 1985. "For Whom Emptiness Prevails: An Analysis of the Religious Implications of Nāgārjuna's *Vigrahavyāvartanī* 70." *Religious Studies* 21: 407–14.

Jackson, Roger R. 1993. *Is Enlightenment Possible? Dharmakīrti and rGyal tshab rje on Knowledge, Rebirth, No-Self and Liberation*. Ithaca: Snow Lion Publications.

Jackson, Roger R. 2000. "In Search of a Postmodern Middle." In *Buddhist Theology: Critical Reflections by Contemporary Buddhist Scholars*. Edited by Roger R. Jackson and John Makransky, 215–46. Richmond, Surrey, UK: Curzon Press.

Jackson, Roger R. 2004. *Tantric Treasures: Three Collections of Mystical Verse from Buddhist India*. Oxford and New York: Oxford University Press.

Jackson, Roger R. 2012. "Saraha's *Queen Dohās*." In *Yoga in Practice*. Edited by David Gordon White, 162–84. Princeton Readings in Religions. Princeton: Princeton University Press.

Jackson, Roger R. 2016. "As Is/As If: The Anxious First-Year's Guide to Argument and Inquiry." Unpublished lecture, Carleton College Argument and Inquiry convocation, September 23, 2016.

Jackson, Roger R. 2019. *Mind Seeing Mind: Mahāmudrā and the Geluk Tradition of Tibetan Buddhism*. Studies in Indian and Tibetan Buddhism. Boston: Wisdom Publications.

Jackson, Roger R. 2021. "Avoiding Rebirth: Modern Buddhist Views on Past and

Future Lives." In *Secularizing Buddhism: New Perspectives on a Dynamic Tradition*. Edited by Richard K. Payne, 239–63. Boulder: Shambhala Publications.

Jaini, Padmanabh. 1983. "Karma and the Problem of Rebirth in Jainism." In *Karma and Rebirth in Classical Indian Traditions*. Edited by Wendy Doniger O'Flaherty, 217–38. Delhi: Motilal Banarsidass.

James, William. 1961 [1902]. *The Varieties of Religious Experience*. London: Collier-Macmillan.

Jamison, Stephanie, and Joel Brereton, trans. 2017. *The Rigveda: The Earliest Religious Poetry of India*. Oxford: Oxford University Press.

Jayatilleke, K. N. 1980 [1963]. *Early Buddhist Theory of Knowledge*. Delhi, Varanasi, and Patna: Motilal Banarsidass.

Jayawickrama, N. A., trans. 1990. *The Story of Gotama Buddha (Jātaka-Nidāna)*. Oxford: Pali Text Society.

Jha, Ganganatha, trans. 1986 [1931]. *The Tattvasaṅgraha of Shāntarakṣita, with the Commentary of Kamalashīla*. 2 vols. Delhi: Motilal Banarsidass.

Jones, C. V. *The Buddhist Self: On Tathagatagarbha and* Ātman. Honolulu: University of Hawai'i Press, 2020.

Jones. J. J., trans. 1949–56. *The Mahāvastu*. 3 vols. Sacred Books of the Buddhists. London: Luzac & Co.

Kapstein, Matthew T. 2006. *The Tibetans*. Malden, MA: Wiley and Blackwell.

Kariyawasam, A. G. S. 1995. *Buddhist Ceremonies and Rituals of Sri Lanka. The Wheel* Publication No. 402/404. Kandy: Buddhist Publication Society.

Karmay, Samten Gyaltsen. 1988. *The Great Perfection: A Philosophical and Meditative Teaching of Tibetan Buddhism*. Leiden: E. J. Brill.

Kaufman, Whitney R. P. 2005. "Karma, Rebirth, and the Problem of Evil." *Philosophy East and West* 55.1: 15–32.

Kerouac, Jack. 1959. *Mexico City Blues [242 Choruses]*. New York: Grove Press.

Kieschnick, John. 2005. "Buddhist Vegetarianism in China." In *Of Tripod and Palate: Food, Politics, and Religion in Traditional China*. Edited by Roel Sterckx, 186–212. New York: Palgrave Macmillan.

Kritzer, Robert, trans. 2014. *Garbāvakrantusūtra: The* Sūtra on Entry into the Womb. Studia Philological Buddhica Monograph Series XXXI. Tokyo: International Institute for Buddhist Studies.

La Vallée Poussin, Louis de, trans. 1988. *Abhidharmakośabhāṣyam*. Translated by Leo M. Pruden. 4 vols. Berkeley: Asian Humanities Press.

Lamotte, Étienne, trans. 1988. *Karmasiddhiprakaraṇa: The Treatise on Action by Vasubandhu*. Translated by Leo M. Pruden. Berkeley: Asian Humanities Press.

Lati Rinbochay and Jeffrey Hopkins. 1979. *Death, Intermediate State and Rebirth in Tibetan Buddhism*. Valois, NY: Gabriel/Snow Lion.

Liebenrood, Mark. 2015 "Do Buddhists Believe in Rebirth?" *Windhorse*, March

5, 2015. www.windhorsepublications.com/do-buddhists-believe-in-rebirth/. Accessed October 16, 2019.

Lopez, Jr., Donald S., ed. 1997. *Religions of Tibet in Practice*. Princeton Readings in Religion. Princeton: Princeton University Press.

Lopez, Jr., Donald S. 1998. *Prisoners of Shangri-La: Tibetan Buddhism and the West*. Chicago: University of Chicago Press.

Lopez, Jr., Donald S., ed. 2002. *A Modern Buddhist Bible: Essential Readings from East and West*. Boston: Beacon Press.

Lopez, Jr., Donald S. 2012. *The Scientific Buddha: His Short and Happy Life*. New Haven: Yale University Press.

Loy, David R. 2015. *A New Buddhist Path: Enlightenment, Evolution, and Ethics in the Modern World*. Boston: Wisdom Publications.

Malalasekera, G. P. 1967. "'Transference of Merit' in Sinhalese Buddhism." *Philosophy East and West* 17: 85-90.

Masefield, Peter, trans. 1989. *Vimana Stories*. Bristol, UK: Pali Text Society.

McMahan, David L. 2008. *The Making of Buddhist Modernism*. Oxford and New York: Oxford University Press.

McRae, John R. 2004. *Seeing through Zen: Encounter, Transformation, and Genealogy in Chinese Chan Buddhism*. Berkeley: University of California Press.

Metzinger, Thomas. 2009. *The Ego Tunnel: The Science of the Mind and the Myth of the Self*. New York: Basic Books.

Michael, Franz. 1982. *Rule by Incarnation: Tibetan Buddhism and Its Role in Society and State*. Boulder: Westview Press.

Monroe, Robert A. 1992. *Journeys Out of the Body*. New York: Broadway Books.

Moody, Raymond. 1975. *Life after Life*. Tracy, CA: Mockingbird Books.

Mullin, Glenn H. 1986. *Death and Dying: The Tibetan Tradition*. Boston, London, and Henley: Arkana.

Mus, Paul. 1939. *La Lumière sur les Six Voies: Tableau de la Transmigration Bouddhique*. 2 vols. Paris: Institut d'Ethnologie.

Nāgārjuna. 1979. *Nāgārjuna's Letter: Nāgārjuna's "Letter to a Friend," with a Commentary by the Venerable Rendawa Zhon-nu Lo-Dro*. Translated by Geshe Lobsang Tharchin and Artemus B. Engle. Dharmamsala: Library of Tibetan Works and Archives.

Nagatomi, Masatoshi. 1957. "A Study of Dharmakīrti's *Pramāṇavārttika*: An English Translation and Annotation of the *Pramāṇavārttika*, Book I." PhD diss., Harvard University.

Ñāṇamoli, Bhikkhu, trans. n.d. [1956]. *The Path of Purification, by Bhadantācariya Buddhaghosa*. Taipei: Corporate Body of the Buddha Educational Foundation.

Ñāṇamoli, Bhikkhu, and Bhikkhu Bodhi, trans. 1995. *The Middle Length Dis-*

courses of the Buddha: A New Translation of the Majjhima Nikāya. Boston: Wisdom Publications.

Niebuhr, Reinhold. 1935. *Interpretation of Christian Ethics*. New York: Harper & Brothers.

Nietzsche, Friedrich. *Beyond Good and Evil*. Translated by Helen Zimmern. Project Gutenberg. www.marxists.org/reference/archive/nietzsche/1886/beyond-good-evil/index.htm. Accessed May 28, 2020.

Nikam, N. A., and Richard McKeown, ed. and trans. 1959. *The Edicts of Asoka*. Chicago and London: University of Chicago Press.

Nuland, Sherwin B. 1995. *How We Die: Reflections on Life's Final Chapter*. New York: Vintage Books.

Obeyesekere, Gananath. 2002. *Imagining Karma: Ethical Transformation in Amerindian, Buddhist, and Greek Rebirth*. Berkeley, Los Angeles, and London: University of California Press.

Obeyesekere, Ranjini, trans. 2001. *Portraits of Buddhist Women: Stories from the* Saddharmaratnāvaliya. Albany: State University of New York Press.

Obeyeskere, Ranjini, trans. 2009. *Yasodharā, the Wife of the Bōdhisattva: The Sinhala* Yasodharāvata (The Story of Yasodharā) *and the Sinhala* Yasodharāpanāya (The Sacred Biography of Yasodharā). Albany: State University of New York Press.

O'Flaherty, Wendy Doniger, ed. 1983. *Karma and Rebirth in Classical Indian Traditions*. Delhi: Motilal Banarsidass.

Ohnuma, Reiko. 2017. *Unfortunate Destiny: Animals in the Indian Buddhist Imagination*. New York: Oxford University Press.

Orzech, Charles. 1996. "Saving the Burning-Mouth Hungry Ghost." In *Religions of China in Practice*. Edited by Donald S. Lopez, Jr., 278–83. Princeton Readings in Religions. Princeton: Princeton University Press.

Paine, Jeffrey. 2004. *Re-Enchantment: Tibetan Buddhism Comes to the West*. New York and London: W. W. Norton and Company.

Panaïotti, Antoine. 2013. *Nietzsche and Buddhist Philosophy*. Cambridge, UK: Cambridge University Press.

Paul, Diana Y. 1985. *Women in Buddhism: Images of the Feminine in the Mahāyāna Tradition*. 2nd ed. Berkeley: University of California Press.

Petavatthu (Ghost Stories). n.d. Wikipitaka—The Completing Tipitaka. https://tipitaka.fandom.com/wiki/Petavatthu. Accessed July 15, 2020.

Phillips, Stephen. 2009. *Yoga, Karma, and Rebirth: A Brief History and Philosophy*. New York: Columbia University Press.

Plato. *Republic*. Perseus Library, Tufts University. Greek and Roman Materials. [English Translation.] www.perseus.tufts.edu/hopper/text?doc=Perseus%3atext%3a1999.01.0168. Accessed May 28, 2020.

Pommaret, Françoise. 1997. "Returning from Hell." In *Religions of Tibet in Prac-*

tice. Edited by Donald S. Lopez, Jr., 499–510. Princeton: Princeton University Press.

Powers, John, trans. 1995. *Wisdom of Buddha: The Saṁdhinirmocana Mahāyāna Sūtra*. Berkeley: Dharma Publishing.

Pye, Michael. 2003. *Skilful Means: A Concept in Mahāyāna Buddhism*. 2nd ed. London and New York: Routledge.

Querido, René, ed. 1997. *A Western Approach to Karma and Reincarnation: Selected Lectures and Writings by Rudolph Steiner*. Hudson, NY: Anthroposophic Press.

Rahula, Walpola. 1974. *What the Buddha Taught*. Revised ed. New York: Grove Press.

Reat, N. Ross, ed. and trans. 1993. *The Śālistambha Sūtra: Tibetan Original, Sanskrit Reconstruction, English Translation, Critical Notes (including Pāli parallels, Chinese version and ancient Tibetan Fragments)*. Delhi: Motilal Banarsidass.

Revel, Jean-François, and Matthieu Ricard. 1998. *The Monk and the Philosopher: A Father and Son Discuss the Meaning of Life*. New York: Schocken Books.

Rhys Davids, T. W., trans. 1963 [1890–94]. *The Questions of King Milinda*. 2 vols. New York: Dover Publications.

Roberts, Peter Alan, trans. 2014. *The Mind of Mahāmudrā*. Boston: Wisdom Publications.

Rotman, Andy, trans. 2008. *Divine Stories (*Divyāvadāna*), Part 1*. Classics of Indian Buddhism. Boston: Wisdom Publications.

Rotman, Andy, trans. 2017. *Divine Stories (*Divyāvadāna*), Part 2*. Classics of Indian Buddhism. Boston: Wisdom Publications.

Rotman, Andy, 2021. *Hungry Ghosts*. Boston: Wisdom Publications.

Saddhatissa, H., trans. 1985. *The Sutta-Nipāta*. London: Curzon Press.

Samuel, Geoffrey. 1993. *Civilized Shamans: Buddhism in Tibetan Societies*. Washington and London: Smithsonian Institution Press.

Śāntideva. 1996. *The Bodhicaryāvatāra*. Translated by Kate Crosby and Andrew Skilton. Oxford and New York: Oxford University Press.

Sayers, Matthew. 2013. *Feeding the Dead: Ancestor Worship in Ancient India*. New York: Oxford University Press.

Schmithausen, Lambert. 1991. *The Problem of the Sentience of Plants in Earliest Buddhism*. Studia Philologica Buddhica Monograph Series VI. Tokyo: The International Institute for Buddhist Studies.

Schmithausen, Lambert. 2009. *Plants in Early Buddhism and the Far Eastern Idea of the Buddha-Nature of Grasses and Trees*. Lumbini: Lumbini International Research Institute.

Schopen, Gregory. 1997. *Bones, Stones, and Buddhist Monks: Collected Papers on the Archaeology, Epigraphy, and Texts of Monastic Buddhism in India*. Honolulu: University of Hawai'i Press.

Schopen, Gregory. 2005. *Figments and Fragments of Mahāyāna Buddhism in India: More Collected Papers*. Honolulu: University of Hawai'i Press.

Sharf, Robert H. 2014. "Is Nirvāṇa the Same as Insentience? Chinese Struggles with an Indian Buddhist Ideal." In *India in the Chinese Imagination: Myth, Ritual, Thought*. Edited by John Kieschnick and Meir Shahar, 141–70. Philadelphia, University of Pennsylvania Press.

Shaw, Miranda. 1995. *Passionate Enlightenment: Women in Tantric Buddhism*. Princeton: Princeton University Press.

Shaw, Sarah. 2007. *The Jataka: Birth Stories of the Bodhisatta*. Baltimore: Penguin Books.

Snellgrove, David. 1987. *Indo-Tibetan Buddhism: Indian Buddhists and Their Tibetan Successors*. 2 vols. Boston: Shambhala Publications.

Snellgrove, David. 2010 [1959]. *The Hevajra Tantra: A Critical Study*. Bangkok: Orchid Press.

Snellgrove, David, and Hugh Richardson. 1967. *A Cultural History of Tibet*. New York: Praeger.

Sogyal Rinpoche. 1993. *The Tibetan Book of Living and Dying*. San Francisco: HarperCollins.

Spiro, Melford. 1982. *Buddhism and Society: A Great Tradition and Its Burmese Vicissitudes*. 2nd ed. Berkeley, Los Angeles, and London: University of California Press.

Steinkellner, Ernst. 2005. *Dignāga's Pramāṇasamuccaya, Chapter 1: A Hypothetical Reconstruction of the Sanskrit Text with the Help of the Two Tibetan Translations on the Basis of the Hitherto Known Sanskrit Fragments and the Linguistic Materials Gained from Jinendrabuddhi's Ṭīkā*. www.ikga.oeaw.ac.at/Mat/dignaga_PS_1.pdf. Accessed October 27, 2020.

Stevens, Wallace. 1971 [1954]. *Collected Poems*. New York: Alfred A. Knopf.

Stevenson, Ian. 1977. *Cases of the Reincarnation Type: Vol. II: Ten Cases in Sri Lanka*. Charlottesville: University of Virginia Press.

Story, Francis. 1975. *Rebirth as Doctrine and Experience: Essays and Case Studies*. Kandy: Buddhist Publication Society.

Strong, John S. 2001. *The Buddha: A Brief Biography*. Oxford: Oneworld Publications.

Sujato, Bhikkhu. n.d. "Abhidhamma." SuttaCentral. https://suttacentral.net/abhidhamma. Accessed 19 July 2020.

Suzuki, Daisetz Teitaro, trans. 1978 [1932]. *The Laṅkāvatāra Sūtra*. Boulder: Prajñā Press.

Suzuki, Daisetz Teitaro. 1996 [1956]. *Zen Buddhism: Selected Writings of D. T. Suzuki*. Edited by William Barrett. New York: Harmony Books.

Swearer, Donald K. 2010. *The Buddhist World of Southeast Asia*. 2nd ed. Albany: State University of New York Press.

Talim, Meena. 2006–07. "The Wheel of 'Law of Causation' in Ajanta Paintings."

Bulletin of the Deccan College Post-Graduate and Research Institute 66/67: 245–58.

Tatz, Mark, and Jody Kent. 1977. *Rebirth: The Tibetan Game of Liberation*. Garden City, NY: Anchor Press/Doubleday.

Teiser, Stephen F. 1988. *The Ghost Festival in Medieval China*. Princeton: Princeton University Press.

Teiser, Stephen F. 1994. *The Scripture on the Ten Kings and the Making of Purgatory in Medieval Chinese Buddhism*. Honolulu: University of Hawai'i Press.

Thanissaro, Bhikkhu, trans. 1993. "That the True Dhamma May Last a Long Time: Readings Selected by King Asoka." Access to Insight. www.accesstoinsight.org/lib/authors/thanissaro/asoka.html. Accessed July 13, 2020.

Thanissaro, Bhikkhu, trans. 1996. "Upatissa-pasine: Upatissa's (Sariputta's) Question." Access to Insight. www.accesstoinsight.org/tipitaka/vin/mv/mv.01.23.01-10.than.html. Accessed July 18, 2020.

Tharchin, Sermey Geshe Lobsang. 1984. *King Udrayana and the Wheel Life: The History and Meaning of the Buddhist Teaching on Dependent Origination*. Howell, NJ: Mahayana Sutra and Tantra Press.

Theosophy. 2019. "Theosophy." Wikipedia. https://en.wikipedia.org/wiki/Theosophy_(Blavatskian). Accessed October 23, 2019.

Thompson, Evan. 2015. *Waking, Dreaming, Being: Self and Consciousness in Neuroscience, Meditation, and Philosophy*. New York: Columbia University Press.

Thuken Losang Chökyi Nyima. 2009. *The Crystal Mirror of Philosophical Systems: A Tibetan Study of Asian Religious Thought*. Translated by Geshé Lhundub Sopa et al. Edited by Roger R. Jackson. Library of Tibetan Classics, 25. Boston: Wisdom Publications.

Thurman, Robert A. F., trans. 1976. *The Holy Teaching of Vimalakīrti*. University Park, PA: The Pennsylvania State University Press.

Thurman, Robert A. F. 1999. *Inner Revolution: Life, Liberty, and the Pursuit of Real Happiness*. New York: Riverhead Books.

Tonkinson, Carole, ed. 1995. *Big Sky Mind: Buddhism and the Beat Generation*. New York: Riverhead Books.

Tricycle. 1997. "Reincarnation: A Debate: Batchelor v. Thurman." *Tricycle* (Summer 1997). https://tricycle.org/magazine/reincarnation-debate/. Accessed November 17, 2019.

Trungpa, Chögyam. 1973. *Cutting Through Spiritual Materialism*. Berkeley: Shambhala Publications.

Tsong-kha-pa. 2000–2002. *The Great Treatise of the Stages of the Path to Enlightenment. Lam rim chen mo*. Translated by the Lamrim Chenmo Translation Committee. Edited by Joshua W. Cutler. 3 vols. Ithaca, NY: Snow Lion Publications.

Tulku Thondup, trans. 2014. *The Practice of Dzogchen: Longchen Rabjam's Writ-*

ings on the Great Perfection. Edited by Harold Talbott. Ithaca, NY: Snow Lion Publications.

van Schaik, Sam. 2020. *Buddhist Magic: Divination, Healing, and Enchantment through the Ages*. Boulder: Shambhala Publications.

Waldron, William. 2003. *The Buddhist Unconscious: The Ālaya-Vijñāna in the Context of Indian Buddhist Thought*. London and New York: Routledge.

Wallace, B. Alan. 2012. *Meditations of a Buddhist Skeptic: A Manifesto for the Mind Sciences and Contemplative Practice*. New York: Columbia University Press.

Walser, Joseph. 2005. *Nāgārjuna in Context: Mahāyāna, Buddhism, and Early Indian Culture*. New York: Columbia University Press.

Walshe, Maurice, trans. 1987. *Thus I Have Heard: The Long Discourses of the Buddha. A New Translation of the* Dīgha Nikāya. London: Wisdom Publications.

Wangchuk, Dorji. 2007. *The Resolve to Become a Buddha. A Study of the Bodhicitta Concept in Indo-Tibetan Buddhism*. Studia Philologica Buddhica Monograph Series XXIII. Tokyo: The International Institute for Buddhist Studies.

Watson, Burton, trans. 1993. *The Lotus Sutra*. New York: Columbia University Press.

Watts, Alan. 1961. *Psychoanalysis East and West*. New York: Ballantine Books.

Wayman, Alex. 1985, trans. and annot. *Chanting the Names of Mañjuśrī: The Mañjuśrī Nāma-saṃgīti, Sanskrit and Tibetan Texts*. Boston and London: Shambhala Publications.

Wayman, Alex, and Hideko Wayman, trans. 1974. *The Lion's Roar of Queen Śrāmālā: A Buddhist Scripture on the Tathāgatagarbha Theory*. New York: Columbia University Press.

Wedemeyer, Christian K. 2013. *Making Sense of Tantric Buddhism: History, Semiology, and Transgression in the Indian Traditions*. South Asia Across the Disciplines. New York: Columbia University Press.

Whitman, Walt. 1892. "Song of Myself (1892 version)." *The Poetry Foundation*. www.poetryfoundation.org/poems/45477/song-of-myself-1892-version. Accessed October 23, 2019.

Williams, Paul. 2009. *Mahāyāna Buddhism: The Doctrinal Foundations*. 2nd ed. London and New York: Routledge.

Williams, Paul, with Anthony Tribe. 2000. *Buddhist Thought: A Complete Introduction to the Indian Tradition*. London and New York: Routledge.

Willis, Janice D., ed. 1987. *Feminine Ground: Essays on Women and Tibet*. Ithaca: Snow Lion Publications.

Willson, Martin. 1987. *Rebirth and the Western Buddhist*. London: Wisdom Publications.

Willson, Martin, trans. 1996. *In Praise of Tārā: Songs to the Savioress*. Boston: Wisdom Publications.

Wilson, Jeff. 2014. *Mindful America: The Mutual Transformation of Buddhist Meditation and American Culture*. New York: Oxford University Press.

Wright, Robert. 2017. *Why Buddhism Is True: The Science and Philosophy of Meditation and Enlightenment*. New York: Simon and Schuster.

Yu Chun-fang. 2001. *Kuan-yin: The Chinese Transformation of Avalokiteśvara*. New York: Columbia University Press.

Yü, Lu K'uan (Charles Luk), trans. n.d. *The Śūraṅgama Sūtra (Len yeng Ching)*. [Battaramulla,] Sri Lanka: Bright Hill Buddhist Centre.

Zaleski, Carol. 1987. *Otherworld Journeys: Accounts of Near-Death Experience in Medieval and Modern Times*. New York: Oxford University Press.

Index

Buddhist cosmologies (*continued*)
spread of, 181
story-traditions of, 103
tantric, 139
in Tibet, 212-15
Burma. *See* Myanmar (formerly Burma)
Burnouf, Eugéne, 237

Cakrasaṃvara, 149
Cakrasaṃvara Tantra, 136
Cambodia, 179, 180, 182, 190
Campbell, Joseph, 17
Candrakīrti, 175
Carus, Paul, 240
Cārvāka, 22
caste, 15, 18, 20-21, 58
Cātumā Sutta, 60
causation, 124, 157. *See also* dependent origination
causes and conditions, 69, 94, 172, 281n254
cooperative conditions, 76-77, 164
homogeneous causes, 164
six causes and four conditions, 76
substantial causes, 76-77, 164, 166
celibacy, 25
Central Asia, 178, 179, 193, 194, 196, 202, 210
Chah, Ajahn, 244
Chan Buddhism, 179, 197, 202, 203-5, 227, 228
Chāndogya Upaniṣad, 19, 20, 273n43
chaos theory, 158
China, 210
as adaptation culture, 193-94
Mahāyāna canon in, 110
nuns' ordination in, 206
revenants in, 225
Tibetan Buddhism in, 232
women in, 205-6
Chinese Buddhism
expansion of, 179-80, 194-96
influence of, 193, 207
persecution of, 202
variant views in, 201-2
yoga tantras in, 136
See also Chan Buddhism; Huayan school (China); Pure Land school (China); Tiantai school (China); Zhenyan school (China)
Chöd tradition, 230
Chödrön, Pema, 246
Christianity, 28, 236, 247
eschatology of, 2, 9-10
influences on, 10-11, 272n26
mindfulness and, 244
morality in, 159
in Sri Lanka, 183
women in, 151
clear light, 141, 221. *See also* luminosity
Collins, Steven, 42
communities of practitioners (*saṅghas*)
in China, 195
collective karma of, 93
fourfold division of, 61
skepticism in, 107
śramaṇa, 21, 26
subdivisions of, 58
women in, 151-52
compassion
objectless, 116
as proof of Buddha's authority, 163, 164
of tantric gurus, 145
transgressive practices and, 144
universal, 247
completion stage, 140-41, 144, 150, 219, 221, 222, 255
concentration, higher training in, 37-39
conception, 73, 80, 81, 140, 166
conduct, tantric, 143-44, 228, 285n341
confession, 119
Confucianism, 194, 195-96, 199, 206, 207

distinguishing features of, 113-20, 282n275
in India, 110-13, 282n272
in Japan, 109, 129, 197
karmic eschatology in, 13
origins of, 111-12
in Southeast Asia, 190
spread of, 109
in Sri Lanka, 183
and tantra, relationship between, 135-36, 143, 145, 229
in Tibet, 212
Mahāyāna texts
appearance of, 49, 50
as Buddha's word, views on, 109-10
as definitive, 117
dependent origination in, 132-33
female rebirth in, 145-48
negation and paradox in, 123
scope of, 111
Mahāyānamahāparinirvāṇa Sūtra, 201
Mahāyānasaṃgraha (Asaṅga), 126-27
Mahāyoga tantras, 136-37, 138, 140, 142, 143, 149, 227
Mainstream Buddhism, 274n57
buddhas and bodhisattvas, 115
canon of, 27, 28
early schools of, 49
as first turning, 121
heaven in, 63, 278n155
human realm in, 56-57
impermanence in, 172-73
in India, status of, 135
intermediate state in, 80
Jambudvīpa in, 58
Mahāyāna implications for, 118-20
Mahāyāna practitioners and, 111
miracles in, 105
as provisional, 117
realms of existence in, 36-37, 55
rebirth's centrality in, 38-42
sentience in, 66
story-traditions in, 103-4
textual tradition of, 97, 109, 110
in Tibet, 212
transcending views in, 44-45
twelve links in, 71
Western philosophy and, 237
women in, 145, 146, 148
Maitreya, 127, 128, 129, 213, 222, 284n310
Makkhali Gosāla, 22, 23-24
Malinowski, Bronislaw, 5
maṇḍalas, 136, 140, 149, 218
Manicheism, 272n26
maṇipa (wandering preacher), 225
Mañjuśrī, 116, 117, 147, 212
Mañjuśrīnāmasaṃgīti, 138
mantras
deity, 141
hundred-syllable, 217
six-syllable, 212, 218, 225
Māra, 59, 62, 101
materialism, 235
Buddhist engagement with, 162
Dharmakīrti's response to, 164-66, 167, 253
Indian, 22-23, 26, 39-40, 41-42, 153, 158
modern, 235
Mathura, 100
Maudgalyāyana (P. Mogallana), 70, 146, 200
meditation, 58, 167, 248
of advanced yogis, 254-55
in attaining buddhafields, 114
of bodhisattvas, 116
in Chinese Buddhism, 205
on death, 220
on emptiness, 121
in Jainism, 25
Mahāyāna experimentation in, 112, 125
mental formations aggregate, 79, 85

Tibetan Buddhism
  awakening mind practices, 217-18
  death, technologies surrounding, 219-33
  earlier spread, 180, 210-11, 226
  in Euro-America, 244-47
  influence of, 182, 210, 231, 232
  on karma, 85
  later spread, 211-12, 215-16
  Mahāyāna canon in, 110
  stages of the path (*lam rim*) in, 216, 219
  styles of Buddhism in, 98
  suppression of, 211
  tantra in, 137
  tulku system in, 224-25, 230-31
  Vajrayoginī in, 150
  wheel of life in, 100, 101-2
  See also Great Perfection (Tib. *rdzogs chen*); Great Seal (Skt. *mahāmudrā*)
Tilopa, 138, 144
Tlingit, 6
transference practice, 141-42, 222-23
treasure (*gter ma*) tradition, 226
Trisong Detsen, 210
Trobriand islanders (Melanesia), 5
Trungpa Rinpoche, Chögyam, 242, 246, 264
Tsoknyi Rinpoche, 246
Tsomo, Karma Lekshe, 247
Tsongkhapa, 213
tulkus, 223-25, 230-31
Tuṣita heaven, 64, 222
twelve links of dependent origination, 41, 69, 104, 188
  emptiness of, 122
  enumeration of, 71-72
  karma and, 84
  modes of analysis of, 73-74
  Nāgārjuna's views on, 132
  purpose of understanding, 74-75
  symbols of, 102
  three-life version, 72-73
two truths, 130-31, 132, 139
  conventional, 133, 175
  ultimate, 229

Udayanavatsarājaparivarta Sūtra, 147
Udrāyaṇa, 100-101, 103
Ullambana Sūtra, 200
Unexcelled Yoga Tantra, 255. *See also* Mahāyoga tantras; Yoginī tantras
Upaniṣads, 15, 17, 26, 64
  rebirth in, 18-20, 106, 273n43
  sources of, 18
  as wrong view, 39
Uttamā, *Therīgāthā* verse of, 63
Uttarā, 190
Uttaratantra (Maitreya), 127, 128, 284n310

Vajracheddikā Sūtra, 122, 204
Vajrasattva, 217
Vajravarāhī (aka Vajrayoginī), 149-50, 213, 218, 231
Vajrayāna. *See* tantric Buddhism
Vajrayoginī. *See* Vajravarāhī (aka Vajrayoginī)
valid cognition, 124
van Schaik, Sam, 105
Vasubandhu, 127, 158, 162, 174
  and Chan, 203
  on death, 78
  on dependent origination, 75
  on determinate action, 91
  on intermediate state, 80
  on intermediate-state beings, 81, 92-93
  on karma, 83-84, 85, 87, 89, 281n245
  on moral transgression, 53, 276n118
  on volitions, 90
  Yogācāra works of, 125, 126
  See also *Abhidharmakośa*
Vasumitrā, 146